CHRISTIAN ETHICS

Wesleyan Theological Perspectives

Series Editors
John E. Hartley
R. Larry Shelton

VOLUME III

Contributors
Victor P. Hamilton
Robert W. Wall
Jerry L. Mercer
W. Stanley Johnson
Harold B. Kuhn
William S. Sailer
Lane A. Scott
Howard A. Snyder
Barry L. Callen
Leon O. Hynson
R. Duane Thompson

CHRISTIAN ETHICS

An Inquiry into Christian Ethics
from a
Biblical Theological Perspective

Edited by
Leon O. Hynson
Lane A. Scott

Published by
Warner Press, Inc.
Anderson, Indiana

Scripture passages are taken from Revised Standard Version © 1972 by Thomas Nelson Inc. unless otherwise indicated. Other translations used are the following: (1) Holy Bible: New International Version © 1978 by the New York International Bible Society. Used by permission of Zondervan Bible Publishers. (2) Today's English Version © 1976 by American Bible Society. Used by permission of American Bible Society.

Arlo F. Newell, editor in chief

ISBN: 0-87162-267-X
Printed in the United States of America

Contents

Abbreviations

BTB	Biblical Theology Bulletin
Gor R	Gordon Review
HNTC	Harper New Testament Commentary
Hor BT	Horizons in Biblical Theology
Interp	Interpretation
JBL	Journal of Biblical Literature
SBLDS	Society of Biblical Literature Dissertations Series
SNTS	Society for New Testament Studies
SVT	*Vetus testamentum,* supplement
ZNW	Zeitschrift für die neutestamentliche Wissenschaft

Introduction

Christian ethics may be defined as that branch of theology that deals with Christian living. Its field of study includes the Christian life itself, principles of Christian morality, moral decision making, and methods of implementing Christian principles in the lives of individuals, the Church, the society.[1] The central task of Christian ethics is to provide believers with instruction on living as biblical Christians in the modern world. Extremely significant economic, technological, and ideological forces have converged in recent history to produce a complex society that challenges the Christian ethic as never before. The purpose of the present volume is to provide clarity on the biblical foundations of the Christian life and on selected issues confronting God's people today.

The theological standpoint of this book is evangelicalism. A fundamental assumption held by each of the contributors is that God has revealed himself in human history and especially in the person of his Son, Jesus Christ. It is assumed, too, that Scripture presents God's word, his will, and actions—all of which inform Christians on how they should live. Hence, Scripture is viewed as the primary source of Christian faith and practice.

God's will for modern life, however, must be understood *from* Scripture. The Bible is in no sense a systematic statement on Christian ethics for twentieth-century believers! Only incidental references are made in the Bible to such great issues as citizenship, and equally significant issues such as abortion are not addressed at all. Hence, the primary task of Christian ethics is the interpretation of Scripture, that is, the understanding of the *meaning* of the Word of God for all of life.[2] The first two chapters in Part I are studies in Old Testament (Professor Victor Hamilton) and New Testament (Professor Robert Wall) ethics. In these essays the authors describe the understanding of morality in the Bible. Interpretation begins with the understanding of those aspects of morality to which Scripture does speak. Biblical ethics is foundational to modern Christian ethics, for in the former we are given the pattern for the latter.

Biblical ethics and Christian ethics must be distinguished, however. Biblical ethics describes the moral directives provided God's people in biblical times; Christian ethics is the understanding of God's will for contemporary believers. That the content of the two is not the same is clear when one considers, for example, that the Jews were forbidden the eating of pork (Lev. 11:7) while Christians are granted freedom to eat all foods (Mark 7:19).

In an attempt to interpret the biblical word and apply it today, the Christian ethicist draws on the long history of Christian doctrine. Especially helpful are the works of the great theologians: Augustine, Aquinas, Luther, Calvin, and Wesley. As a theologian the latter may not equal the others, but John Wesley's practical bent makes his extensive writings especially helpful as a source for understanding the Christian life.

It is surprising to discover that those whose theological heritage is Wesleyan (a movement that accentuates Christian living far more than scholastic theology) should nonetheless have given relatively minor attention to the understanding and clarification of its ethic. In point of fact, the Wesleyan tradition has generally lacked the patience for developing a rationale for its moral expectations and the criteria for critiquing those expectations. Profoundly informed by the Christological counsel of John Wesley, the tradition has moved toward a too-often unexamined ethic of the Holy Spirit. It is the accustomed pattern of those movements that give special attention to spiritual phenomena and praxis, from Montanism to Pentecostalism, to refrain from critical reflection upon the Spirit and the consequent expression of the Spirit in discipleship.

Wesleyans have not always followed their founder in a rational articulation of the Christian faith. Some even wish to push the problem back into the lap of John Wesley himself by suggesting that a "Wesleyan ethic" does not even exist.[3] The tendency to treat John Wesley as a cult hero whose symbolic worth is great but whose ideas are archaic has contributed to this misinformed stance.

"Doing" tends to be the preoccupation of many of Wesley's followers. Duty (or a deontological ethic) is the governing principle for this type of believer. Rules have often been proposed with no accompanying rationale. When a Spirit orientation is linked to a rule orientation, the necessity of developing a reasoned explanation of the moral life is rendered more urgent. It becomes all too easy to claim spiritual guidance even when moral criteria are so esoteric that no one else comprehends them! Rules are even presented and enforced by some with the implication that it is inappropriate or prideful to ask for reasons.

These weaknesses that are apparent in the Wesleyan tradition's Christian ethic are due in part to its failure to develop a reasoned statement of its faith and practice. But its shortcomings may also be traced to the limited understanding of Wesley's own ethic. Chapters 3 and 4 in Part I of this volume are presented as constructive interpretations of Wesley's thought. Professor Mercer provides an overview of Wesley's ethic while Professor Johnson interprets Wesley's concept of love for God.

Part II of the present volume considers selected issues in Christian ethics. Each of the writers looks to Scripture as the basis of a Christian understanding of the issue under consideration. Not every essay draws intentionally on the thought of Wesley (after all, Wesley had little or nothing to say on such issues as abortion, homosexuality, or ecology!) but each writes from a perspective informed by Wesley. Professor Kuhn considers the abortion issue, Professor Sailer writes on homosexuality, Professor Scott examines the questions of divorce and the remarriage of divorced persons, Professor Snyder writes on the economy of God and the ecology of the Church, Professor Hynson presents a Christian view of the state, Professor Callen looks at the Church as tomorrow's people for today's world, and Professor Thompson contributes an essay on the Christian view of the arts.

In these essays the reader will find an ordered and reasoned approach to ethical analysis. Attention is given to biblical and theological foundations and the ethical criteria are arrived at through the use of solid hermeneutical principles. Immediately apparent to the reader will be the absence of certain major issues. The editors have not overlooked these, but within the limits of time and space (and our resourcefulness!) offer these six essays as examples of ethical reflection on the part of Wesleyan scholars. Like Wesley himself, the writers draw upon both ancient and modern moralists. Giving cohesion to the volume is the Wesleyan correlation of faith and practice, Scripture and reason, preaching and teaching that are both didactic and prophetic. Wesley's ethic, like his theology, is teleological, oriented toward the goal of Christian love. Ever the restless inquirer after the truth of God, Wesley has bequeathed that spirit to successive generations. We are some of those who recognize him as a worthy mentor.

Leon O. Hynson
Lane A. Scott

Notes

1. We mean by the Christian life the relation with God based in his justifying grace and in the power and fellowship of his Spirit, and the relation with the world in which the believer has his or her existence.
2. Interpretation is used here in the broad sense. It refers to the exegesis, exposition, and application of God's Word. Volume II of this series of studies in Wesleyan theology, *Interpreting God's Word for Today* (Wayne McCown and James Earl Massey, eds. [Anderson, Ind: Warner Press, 1982]), provides excellent studies of key aspects of the work of interpretation.
3. See James Gustafson, *Christ and the Moral Life* (Chicago: University of Chicago Press, 1968), pp. 61–115. The chapter is titled "Jesus Christ, the Sanctifier" and develops the theological ethic of John Wesley in a significant way.

Part I
Biblical and Theological Foundations

Victor P. Hamilton (Ph.D., Brandeis University), professor of religion, Asbury College

The Ethics of the Old Testament

Some Problems in Discussing Old Testament Ethics

TO WRITE an essay on the ethics of the Old Testament can be either a fairly straightforward task or a challenge that can be described only as Olympian. It would be possible, for example, to confine the Old Testament's understanding of ethics to the Ten Commandments and therefore produce what is essentially a commentary on the Decalogue. Such an approach would dismiss the literature of the primeval and patriarchal periods plus the prophetic and wisdom corpus. What would emerge is a very truncated view of the Old Testament's understanding of the causal nexus between belief(s) and behavior.

Let us, however, go to the other possibility of trying to reproduce what each of the parts of the Old Testament contributes to the whole, and the issues become legion. To illustrate, when we refer to the ethics of the "Old Testament," to what Old Testament do we refer? Do we refer to the Old Testament on its own terms or as it has been reconstructed by much of critical scholarship. For instance, are the narratives in Genesis reflective of life in Canaan in the middle-bronze age, or are they reflective of life in Canaan in the Davidic-Solomonic period?

Even if we take the Old Testament as it stands, we are still faced with the task of describing a period of history that covers more than a thousand years, say, 1800 B.C. to 400 B.C. It is safe and reasonable to surmise that over that period some fundamental ethical principles would disappear and be replaced by others, or at least be revised. For an analogy one thinks of our own conservative holiness tradition in which until the last few years some ethical convictions were held to be quite fundamental to a sanctified ethos and life-style—dress codes and entertainment preferences (or avoidances), for example. But now many of these have been—for better or worse—jettisoned as anachronistic. Amazingly, all this change has occurred within a couple of decades! What about Israel and possible mutations over a millennium?

Perhaps the ultimate problem is the application of Old Testament ethics to those who live under the new covenant.[1] Not infrequently, sectors of the Church have, in the formulation of ethical principles, appealed primarily to the Old Testament and have ignored the New Testament. A parade example would be the restriction placed by the medieval church on its members charging interest on money loans. The rationale for the prohibition was to be found in passages such as Exodus 22:25; 25:35–37 and Deuteronomy 23:20. The fact that Jesus apparently countenanced the lending of money with interest (Matt. 25:27) was glossed over.[2]

These and other problems indicate the care with which the ethicist must approach the Old Testament in doing

Christian ethics. In the following pages basic ethical principles from the Old Testament are presented.

Creation Theology, And Ethics

Conservative Christians have generally not ascribed to the first two chapters of Genesis the full significance they ought to contribute to the whole of Scripture. Perhaps the reason is to be found in our unconscious view of Eden as a kind of Cinderella land, a place the reality of which we cannot know now but perhaps one day will.

As an extension of this, our preference as evangelicals is to emphasize themes such as covenant and law, that part of the Scripture that stresses covenant, law, and salvation. Redemption more than celebration is our preoccupation.

Yet we dare not sidestep the opening chapters of Genesis. For it is from these chapters that we gain our foundational view of the nature of God and persons. It is interesting to note that before sin entered the world God established two basic institutions: marriage and law. An understanding of the purpose of each of these will provide us with a glimpse of something of the direction behavioral standards will take in the Old Testament. The purpose of marriage is to teach persons how to live for something other than themselves, how to live for another. The purpose of law—"But of the tree of the knowledge of good and evil you shall not eat"—is to teach persons how to live under authority. It occurs to me that this comes quite close to Wesley's concern for holy living (i.e., living a life totally under Christ's authority and living for something other than self).

The two opening chapters of Genesis clearly picture persons as finite, not divine. They are "earthlings" as the name *Adam* can be literally translated. On the other hand, humankind is nothing less than a *cause célèbre* in God's creation. We are persons of dignity and nobility. It is not incidental that only after the sixth day does God term his act of creation "very good" and not simply "good" as before (Gen. 1:31). When God created humanity he made human beings regal creatures, creatures to rule and exercise headship (Gen. 1:28). But such a divine bequeathal does not in any way legitimate human tyranny over another human or human brutalization of nature. Even in Genesis those who would be Lord of all must be servant of all.[3]

What radically sets humanity apart from everything else in the created order is the fact that we alone are created "in God's image, after God's likeness." No small debate has centered around the meaning of "image" and the relationship of "image" to "likeness"; and I hesitate to add another suggestion to the countless ones already made as to what actually constitutes the image of God in persons.[4] I am convinced, however, that the function of "likeness" in Genesis 1 is to lend content and specificity to "image." A person is not simply an image of God but a likeness-image. He or she is more than representative of God. He or she is representational.[5]

The implication for ethics seems clear if this analysis is correct. We do not have to wait until Scripture—"Be holy for I am holy" (Lev. 19:2)—trumpets the theme of *imitatio dei*. In life and in life-style we are called to reflect the glory of God, to conduct ourselves in such a way that is consistent not only with our divine origin, but also with our divine mission. For this reason I find the catchy but basically incorrect statement of G. K. Chesterton quite untenable: "The Old Testament hero is no more supposed to be of the same nature as God than a saw or a hammer is supposed to be of the same shape as the carpenter."[6] Thus we conclude this section by observing the emphasis within the creation pericope on the essential goodness of human nature, a goodness that is a divine bestowal. Nowhere is there any indication yet that "humanness is seen as a barrier to righteousness."[7]

Of course, we need to take into consideration the warping or crippling of this goodness brought about by sin. Yet it appears to me that we also need to give full weight to the work of Christ in the full rectifying of this perversion so that once again the individual can live as a true divine image bearer. This would seem to be one of the emphases of the Wesleyan tradition.[8] Conversion and sanctification may then be viewed as a recovery of goodness.

The Patriarchal Narratives

To many Christians, chapters 12–50 of Genesis are not only familiar but very meaningful. For here are found at least three rich semibiographies of men—Abraham, Jacob, Joseph, whose lives are paragons of faith, obedience, and virtue. After all, is not Abraham the model for faith in the New Testament, a model appealed to by Paul (Rom. 4, Gal. 3), James (chap. 2), and by the writer of Hebrews (chap. 11)? Or again, is anybody in all of Scripture as flawless as Joseph? Here indeed we would expect to find public examples of ethical norms at their highest.

Such is not the case, however. A reading of the text reveals something of both confirmation and rejection of this idyllic picture. There are, of course, before us in this part of Genesis illustrations of lives lived essentially on the premise of obedience to the word of God. Abraham does go out when God tells him to, not knowing where he is going (Heb. 11:9).[9] He obeys and does proceed to place Isaac on the Moriah altar. Jacob is blessed by God, receives a new name (Gen. 32), and from that point on lives a life that is blameless. And Joseph in Egypt refutes effectively the opportunity of moral compromise. He is able to rise above the temptation to retaliate against his brothers by viewing all of his unpleasant experiences as grist for the mill in God's sovereign plan for the sparing of his convenant people (see Genesis 45:5; 50:20).

But what shall we make of Abraham's behavior in Egypt and in Philistia, two occasions on which he not only lied and engaged in deception, but also requested his spouse to make herself vulnerable for his safety (Gen. 12:10–20; 20:1–18)? The same type of ruse was later perpetuated by Isaac (Gen. 26:6–11).[10]

Well, of course, anyone can tell a lie, even the saints. I suspect that what is most perplexing here is not the act of deception *per se,* but the fact that neither Abraham nor Isaac is anywhere called to task by God for his reprehensible behavior. To add insult to injury, the innocent pharaoh is afflicted with plagues for his part in the scenario, Sarah becomes an adulteress—"she was 'taken' into pharaoh's house"—and Abraham leaves Egypt with an enormous number of gifts. Where is a fulminating Nathan and his "you are the man"?

What of Jacob? He is introduced to us as exploiter (Gen. 25:29–34) and deceiver (Gen. 27:1–45). No one will be able to stand in the way of this ruthless entrepreneur, not even a brother or a father. Through all these schemes the voice of God is not heard. But on the night of that dream God does speak for the first time. Alas, God's first word to this burglar and swindler is a word of promise and blessing (Gen. 28:13–15). Not a word is spoken about his the-end-justifies-the-means philosophy by which he victimized his family.

Finally there is Joseph. He is loyal, uncompromising, patient, forgiving, seemingly virtuous and above reproach. And perhaps if there is such a thing portrayed in Genesis as a sterling individual it is he.

What shall we do, however, with treatment of his brothers when they come to Egypt to purchase grain? His accusation that they are spies (Gen. 42:9) is clearly a trumped-up charge. He knows they are not spies. Certainly putting the brothers' grain money back into the sacks (Gen. 42:25) is a perfect frame-up for theft, as is the placing of Joseph's silver cup into Benjamin's sack (Gen. 44:2).[11] Is Joseph now throwing his brothers into a pit he has dug, as once he himself was thrown in by them? Is he able to curb completely the desire for at least some retaliation?

We can add to these examples others that describe arrangements to deal with childlessness. One thinks of this particular issue in regard to sterile Sarah providing her husband with a surrogate (Gen. 15:2), Lot's daughters' seduction of their father (Gen. 19:32), barren Rachel and Leah providing maidens to Jacob (Gen. 30:3,9), Tamar tricking her father-in-law into cohabitation, and by whom she has twins (Gen. 38:26). We observed in the preceding paragraphs, none of these actions produce a word of judgment from God. Never does the biblical narrator moralize on the behavior of his characters.

Walter Eichrodt calls such a *modus vivendi* "popular morality," for which his definition is "Those rules of conduct which proceed from the natural impulses of community and self-preservation."[12] This kind of morality is then immanental and instinctive, something that emerges out of the group. Presumably this value system would be prevalent wherever the larger unit (the tribe, the clan, the family) is more crucial than the rights of the individual. The operation of this kind of morality is illustrated by the institution of levirate marriage (Gen. 28, Deut. 25:5–10, Ruth), surely somewhat distasteful in its arrangements to contemporary readers of Scripture. In the Genesis story the second son, Onan, is killed not because God is opposed to birth control, but because the son placed his own interests ahead of his commitments to his family.[13]

Several observations may be made about the ethical behavior of the leading individuals in Genesis. Their actions, and the silence of God in response to those actions may be indicative of a growth in moral sensitivity, from the primitive to the more refined.[14] This in no way exonerates the early practitioners of deception, or lying, or adultery, or what have you. Nor does it indicate that this behavior was ever viewed as acceptable by ancient society. Notice how quickly Abraham became a *persona non grata* when the true identity of Sarah became known to the king!

We also need to remember that the recording without commentary or evaluation of an incident by a writer of Scripture does not necessarily mean approval. Silence is not necessarily an indication of approbation.[15] Although the writers in the New Testament held up Abraham as a model for justification by faith, this does not imply that they were blind to some of the shortcomings of the father of the faithful. As a matter of fact, a perusal of the list of the faithful of Hebrews 11 shows that a majority of them at some point or points in their lives were spiritual casualties.

Perhaps the biblical writer has not bothered to comment on some of these moral deviations, for such moralizing is not relevant to his main thesis. He is more a narrator, theologian, and historian than he is an ethicist. I would concur with those who see in the Abraham story the initial stages, via promise, of a divine plan for the redemption of humanity. God's first and last word to both Abraham (Gen. 12:1-3; 22:15, 18) and Jacob (28:13-15; 35:11-12; 46:3–4) are promises, and thus this theme brackets the narratives. Manipulation, rascality, and shenanigans will not thwart this plan, even when the greatest dangers to the plan are the bearers of the promises themselves.

In Jacob's case one wonders if there is not a rebuke from God, but in a subtle way. To begin with, may God's first word to Jacob—"I am the Lord, the God of Abraham your father and the God of Isaac"—be interpreted not only as a promise but as an indirect rebuke? What better and more efficient way to produce a sense of guilt than by reminding persons who they are—called children of God?[16]

We also need to remember that Jacob's life has more than its share of misfortunes. Do his sins eventually find him out? He who is "Mr. Trickster" is later tricked by Laban (Gen. 29) and by his sons (Gen. 37), a classic illustration of nemesis.[17]

To me, the most beautiful element in the Jacob story is the narration of his "conversion" (Gen. 32:22–32). Everything in Jacob's life that is morally dubious is pre-Peniel. From Genesis 33 on, his behavior is exemplary.[18] There is hardly a more dramatic narrative in Scripture of the relationship between spiritual transformation and consequential right living. One need only compare Jacob's first "swear to me" (Gen. 25:33) with his last "swear to me" (Gen. 47:31) to see how far he has come in his pilgrimage from manipulator to saint extraordinary.

Covenant And Law

Not without justification writers have appealed to the Ten Commandments as the foundational statement on Old Testament ethics. Here is the pith and marrow of both the character and the source of obedient living, encapsulated in ten brief statements.

It cannot be denied that the very introduction to Exodus 20 places the Decalogue in a category all by itself. In the rest of Exodus, God always spoke to his people through an intermediary, Moses.[19] But here, and here alone, God dictates the Decalogue to his people directly—"And God spoke all these (Exod. 20:1). In this one instance Moses joins his own people and shifts from transmitter to listener.

It is important to note, however, that the Book of Exodus does not begin with the Ten Commandments. M. Greenberg cites an ancient Jewish parable to explain why not.

> A man entered a country and said "Make me your king." The people replied, "What have you ever done for us so that we

should make you our king?" So he built them walls, made them water-works, fought wars on their behalf. Then he said to them, "Make me your king," and they replied, "Yes, indeed!"[20]

Before God asks for the allegiance of Israel, he first of all, shall we say, demonstrates his worthiness to request that allegiance. Israel is challenged to loyalty because God is good and faithful and supportive. It is not coerced into loyalty because God is omnipotent and potentially intimidating and threatening.

Not only do the *magnalia dei* (Exod. 12–17) precede the revelation of the Law (Exod. 20), but the announcement of covenant (Exod. 19) precedes the announcement of Law (Exod. 20). The positioning of Exodus 19 and 20 is important. One chapter without its companion would be like an airplane with one wing. Brevard Childs comments appropriately on the proximity of law and covenant in Exodus: "Theologically, the juxtaposition guards against a legalistic interpretation of the law apart from the covenant, on the one hand, and, on the other hand, against an alleged covenant of grace conceived of without a content."[21]

We should not ignore the fact that it is indeed a covenant of grace that supplies the incentive and the chief motive for obedience to God's commandments. The Old Testament does not engage in the old philosophical question, is an act right simply because God commands it, or does God command the act because it is right?[22] Certainly we observe in this section of the Torah no command to blind obedience: Israel is to obey simply because God had spoken.

And what is the ultimate purpose of God's law to which the people are to respond positively? Moses answers that question for us in the immediate sequel to the Decalogue (Exod. 20:18–20). He states, "Do not fear; for God has come to prove you, and that the fear of him may be before your eyes, that you may not sin" (v. 20). Here is the positive function of law. Actually Moses is doing nothing more than providing details on how Israel is indeed to become a "holy nation" (Exod. 19:6). The Law specifies the holiness expected of Israel.

It may well be that the Decalogue does not contribute any new philosophical insights into ethics or law. Certainly Israelite society was not the only one to prohibit adultery and stealing.[23] It is hard to imagine any society in which the legal codes would define such actions as virtuous and commendable. There is no "thou shalt steal" in Hammurabi's Code. Of course, one would be hard-pressed to duplicate in pagan legal literature the equivalent of the first four commandments.

What does take place at Sinai is the creation of a new unity between God and Israel. All that Israel has known before this is unsufferable treatment at the hands of the Egyptians. It is tragically easy, in the passage of time, for the oppressed to become the oppressors, to move out of the slave's seat and into the driver's seat. The function of the Law is to squelch the possibility of that development, for at Sinai there is now new grounds in the establishment of a community, "a formation based on common obligations rather than common interests—on ethic, rather than covetousness."[24]

The Decalogue is followed by a series of laws covering civil, criminal, and religious issues (Exod. 20:22–23:33). For many Christians the application of this portion of Scripture to their lives is less apparent than that of the Decalogue. I am in essential agreement with those scholars who see in these particular laws a moral loftiness, a distinctiveness, a humaneness, not found in their pagan counterparts.[25]

Nevertheless, there are some statements made here that may appear less than desirable, ethically. For example, male slaves may go free after six years of service, but that privilege is not extended to female slaves (Exod. 21:1–11); if a male slave received his wife from his master he may not take her with him if he chooses to leave (21:4); killing a free person is a capital offense (21:12, 14), killing a slave is not (21:20, 21, 32). These laws stand in dramatic contrast to other statements about mistreating the poor and the weak found in the same pericope.

I present this particular issue simply as a caution against approaching Scripture, and the Old Testament in particular, as some kind of a "flat Bible," an immutable code of social and personal ethics cast in monolithic form. Perhaps we need to see the development of ethical sensitivity "as a dynamic process, underway, pressing, but never coming to rest and fulfillment,"[26] at least until the new covenant emerges.

Imitatio Dei

In dealing with motives for moral conduct the Old Testament itself moves beyond simple submission to the will of God. Those who have addressed themselves to the issue of Old Testament ethics have drawn our attention to the motive of conforming one's actions after the pattern of God's own nature and disposition.[27] A key verse that reinforces this idea is, of course, Leviticus 19:2—"You shall be holy; for I the Lord your God am holy." And then there follows through chapter 26 a list of moral, religious, and cultic requirements, each motivated by the summons to holiness. Behavior is to be modeled on God's, for his behavior is precisely what ours should be.

It is this kind of motivation to moral accountability that is underscored by the frequent exhortations "to walk in his ways" (Deut. 8:6; 10:12; 11:22; 19:9; 26:17; 28:9; 30:16). To walk in "God's ways" is to walk as he walks. Here is one place where his "ways" are our ways (unlike Isaiah 55:8).[28] Walking in God's way is the opposite of standing "in the way of sinners" (Ps. 1:1). In such passages "way" does not mean path, but something like "life-style" or "behavioral patterns."

Along the same lines of an ethic of imitation, or perhaps as an extension of this ethic, is an ethic of remembrance. What one does with the seventh day of the week is to parallel that first seventh day (Exod. 20:8–11). On the seventh day the employer releases his employees from manual obligations, just as God once released them from manual slavery in Egypt (Deut. 6:12–15). Israel may not take advantage of a stranger, because it, too, was once a stranger who subsequently was befriended by God (Exod. 22:21).

Perhaps the real significance of this ethic of imitation becomes most forceful when we recall the proliferation of imitation as an important element in the fertility rituals of nature religions. At the heart of such rituals is the principle of sympathetic magic. The participants act out the desired results. Marduk triumphs over Tiamat annually. So do Baal and Anat over Mot and Yamm. And the recitation of such liturgy by the people is a way of expressing their hope for order to prevail over chaos. But in the Old Testament the concern is moral imitation, not cultic imitation.[29]

The Prophets And Ethics

It was fashionable in Old Testament scholarship of an earlier era to say that "ethical monotheism" appears with the eighth-century B.C. prophets. Prior to that time religion and morals in Israel were thought to be primitive, if not downright savage and superstitious. Israel came of age with the prophets. While there are few, if any, who still sing that tune, still many believe that in the prophets the ethical cream of the Old Testament rises to the surface.

It is safe to say that in any current push for justice or

social reform Amos will get better coverage than Deuteronomy. And those who push for a religion of the heart with right relationships with their fellows over a religion of ritual and ortho-praxis will find their position supported by Jeremiah. And on and on we could go.

The point is that the prophets are often pictured as radical innovators. Well, perhaps they were radicals, but they hardly can be called innovators. James Barr is quite correct when he says that "the prophets for the most part were not reformers. . . . Theirs was not a novel analysis . . . the social perspectives and perceptions of the prophets were essentially conservative. What they declared was the traditional morality exacted by the God of Israel."[30] Muilenburg attempts to isolate five areas to which the prophets addressed their ethically loaded message: (1) the political order; (2) the economic order; (3) land; (4) the administration of justice; (5) power and pride.[31] It was hard for me to detect the prophets doing much more than echoing Moses' remarks as I read Muilenburg's synopsis.

Perhaps Amos makes a novel contribution in his opening diatribes against the nations surrounding Israel (Amos 1 and 2). To speak a word of divine indictment against a nation that has abused Yahweh's people is quite normal in the prophetic corpus. In this way Amos is not unique. What is novel here is that the prophet condemns Moab for war crimes against Edom (Amos 2:1–3), and Israel/Judah is not involved! Amos appears to be saying that ethical obligations are extended to the nations, not in terms of their relationship with Yahweh's people only, but in terms of the rights of human beings as human.[32]

But this emphasis is not without precedent. This is the focus of Sodom and Gomorrah and the inferno with which they were hit. Never did these two cities figure as part of "God's territory." They were situated outside the boundaries of the Promised Land. And yet Yahweh incinerated them both for their promiscuity (Gen. 18 and 19) and for their social vices (Ezek. 16:49, 50).

One may look at least to Jeremiah 31, for here is something *de novo*: the prediction of a *new* covenant. But what is new about the new covenant? Many of its features, such as the writing of the Law on the heart, find reverberation in the Old Testament. While we do not dispute the old to new transition, to which Hebrews testifies so magnificently, still there may be a tinge of irony in Jeremiah's announcement of a *new* covenant.[33] So far are his contemporaries from a vivid walk with God that they do not recognize the new covenant to be in many ways a continuum of the old covenant.

Sapiential Ethics

The wisdom literature of the Old Testament has always been something of an enigma to the readers and scholars of Scripture. The problem centers around the uniqueness, or lack of uniqueness, of this literature. Many of its proverbial statements seem more international than distinctively Israelite. Or again, if we locate the crucible of divine revelation in the historical acts of God (the Exodus, the Passover, the migration, the covenant, the Law), what shall we do with this corpus of literature that is patently a-historical? There is no summons in Proverbs or Ecclesiastes to reflect on the great acts of God in the past. That is not their concern.

What, then, is the (ethical) purpose of wisdom literature? It is hardly blind, unreflective obedience to the revealed will of God. There is no Moses here, nor does God himself speak. Sinai's noises and scenes are not heard or observed. James Crenshaw states that wisdom is "the reasoned search for specific ways to assure well-being and the implementation of those discoveries in daily existence."[34]

Thus, in providing us with some parameters about the ethical life, the good life, wisdom literature is more likely to provide us with clues than with answers. Those who would press on for the answers must be willing to engage in that "reasoned search."

And our search will be essentially in this world. One will look in vain for any emphasis on "be good so that in the next life. . . ."[35] The Old Testament as a whole may be said to be relatively quiet—but not totally so—about blessings or curses in eternity. The blessings, or their opposite, are this-world, usually something physical and temporary.

Proverbs says we are responsible for our choices. Fearing God, we have been given rationality, common sense, discrimination. Even more, we are trusted by God. The wisdom corpus does not labor under the idea of a person who is so totally depraved and weighted down by sin that he or she is unable to make the right, ethical choice, even if he or she wants to.[36]

It is difficult to classify the information covered in a book like Proverbs. The content almost defies systematization. Thus we will of necessity have to be selective in our discussion that follows.[37]

Many of the various maxims in Proverbs cover the same area as Torah literature. All of the Ten Commandments, for example, are mentioned in Proverbs except for the graven image and Sabbath laws.[38]

But there is a difference between the formulation of the prohibition in the Pentateuch and in the wisdom literature. Let us take adultery as an illustration.[39] Proverbs concurs with the Pentateuch that adultery is a sin, but never does it appeal to the fact (a) that God through Moses outlawed it or (b) that the penalty is death via stoning. Instead Proverbs provides quite a different set of sanctions. Thus Proverbs 6:17–35 includes among its sanctions self-destruction (v. 32); wounds, loss of respect, and public disgrace (v. 33); a husband bent on revenge (v. 34); no way to buy oneself out of trouble (v. 35). Proverbs 7:1–27 also emphasizes wisdom as a safeguard against adultery. Perhaps verse 23—"He does not know that it will cost him his life"—may be at best an oblique reference to the death penalty.

Moving beyond the specific ties with Torah emphases, we may note that the motivations behind the exhortations in Proverbs refer only occasionally to the Lord. An example would be Proverbs 22:22, 23, "Do not rob the poor . . . or crush the afflicted . . . for the Lord will plead their cause." Or this one, "If your enemy is hungry, give him bread to eat . . . for you will reap coals of fire on his head, and the Lord will reward you" (Prov. 25:21, 22). But these are exceptions, certainly not the norm.[40]

What Proverbs does is to supply sanctions that are not historical but rational.[41] Confronted by a decision-making situation, the wise man will make an intelligent appropriation of the ethical. Experience will be among his greatest teachers. He will not be self-berating and self-condemning. He will not say, "I'm only human" but "Thank God, I am human." Here God will not do our work for us. For he has sanctified our reason, our insight, our integrity, our ability to question and probe. He trusts us to act responsibly.

Notes

1. The larger issue of the relationship of the Old Testament to the New Testament has been studied extensively. For an airing of the issues and positions see D. L. Baker, *Two Testaments: One Bible* (Downers Grove, Ill.: Inter-Varsity Press, 1977). Baker's book is better as a bibliographical source—over half of the book is bibliographies—than it is as a sophisticated discussion of his own thinking on the subject. For a discussion of this issue vis-à-vîs ethics see Robert Traina, "Toward a Biblically Based Ethic," *Asbury Seminarian* 25 (July 1971), pp. 3–11.
2. This is the illustration used by James Barr, *The Scope and Authority of the Bible* (Philadelphia: The Westminster Press, 1980), pp. 92ff. in his attempt to show the unjustified ways of using solely the Old Testament to legitimate social and

political institutions. My own example would be the almost exclusive use of the Old Testament by Christians to justify the execution of criminals for certain serious crimes. The appeal is partly to the Old Testament, at the point of the penalty—"He shall be put to death"—but the method of enforcement is sidestepped in that the criminal is to be stoned to death by the elders.

3. See, for example, the study of J. Limburg, "What Does It Mean—Have Dominion over the Earth?" *Dialog* 10 (1971), pp. 221–226; and James Barr, "Man and Nature—The Ecological Controversy and the Old Testament," *Bulletin of the John Rylands Library* 55 (1972), pp. 9–32.
4. I am convinced that the attempt to answer this first question ontologically (the image is the soul/rationality/conscience/ and so on) is inevitably doomed to failure. Rather, I suggest the clue is to be found in approaching the issue in a relational context.
5. I am very much in agreement with the conclusions reached by D.J.A. Clines in "The Image of God in Man," *Tyndale Bulletin* 19 (1968), pp. 53–103.
6. The quote is from Chesterton's essay on Job, "Man Is Most Comforted by Paradoxes" in *The Dimensions of Job,* N. Glatzer, ed. (New York: Schocken Books, 1969) p. 232.
7. W. Dyrness, *Themes in Old Testament Theology* (Downers Grove Ill.: Inter-Varsity Press, 1979), p. 173. Chapter 10 of this book—pp. 171–186—is devoted to a discussion of Old Testament ethics.
8. This point was made most graphically to me recently when a chapel speaker at our college was expatiating on 2 Corinthians 5:17 and the new creation. He remarked that, because of the newness Christ brings, a prostitute who gives herself to Christ becomes purer than a virgin. In fact, she becomes an arch-virgin!
9. It is important here that we make appropriate applications of Scripture such as this one (Heb. 11:9) to our own lives. Abraham is an example of how we should obey God in faith, but it does not necessarily follow that part of that obedience will include "not knowing where we are going." It may, it may not. The addition of this fact about Abraham's "ignor-

ance" is historical and nonmoral. See O.M.T. O'Donovan, "Towards An Interpretation of Biblical Ethics," *Tyndale Bulletin* 27 (1976), pp. 54–78, esp. 61ff.

10. In the period between 1930 and 1960 it was standard procedure to explain many of the social customs (or aberrations!) of the patriarchs by appealing to mid-second millennium B.C. cuneiform literature from Mesopotamia. The commentary that best illustrated this trend was E. A. Speiser, *Genesis,* in the *Anchor Bible* commentary (New York: Doubleday, 1964). An indication of a shift away from this approach may be seen in J. van Seters, *Abraham in History and Tradition* (New Haven: Yale University Press, 1975). His main thesis is that the best parallels to the patriarchal customs are in cuneiform literature from the Assyrian and neo-Babylonian period. His conclusion is, therefore, that the Abraham story emerged in Israel's exilic and postexilic community (indeed Wellhausen *redivivus!*). The reaction to van Seter's work has been either strongly critical or equally strongly supportive.
11. G. Coats, *From Canaan to Egypt: Structural and Theological Context for the Joseph Story* (Washington: The Catholic Biblical Association of America, 1976) pp. 32–38.
12. W. Eichrodt, *Theology of the Old Testament,* vol. II (Philadelphia: The Westminster Press, 1975) p. 317. All of chapter 22 of Eichrodt's theology—"The Effect of Piety of Conduct"—is germane to the thrust of this essay. Eichrodt's illustrations of popular morality come largely from Genesis, as his footnotes indicate.
13. It is not without interest that the one law in the Old Testament—Deuteronomy 25:5-10—that includes among its sanctions public disgrace and humiliation is one dealing with a shirking of obligations to the family.
14. See Eichrodt, *Theology,* II, p. 324.
15. J. Barton, "Understanding Old Testament Ethics," *Journal for the Study of the Old Testament* 9 (1978), p. 54; W. B. Greene, "The Ethics of the Old Testament," reprinted in *Classical Evangelical Essays,* W. C. Kaiser, ed. (Grand Rapids: Baker, 1972) p. 213. Green's essay on the subject deals with seven objections to Old Testament ethics as

sub-Christian and not just ante-Christian. As such his essay is completely apologetic but it abounds with sound insights.

16. I have often wondered if a similar purpose is played by Paul's opening words to the sorry church at Corinth—"Sanctified in Jesus, called to be saints" (1 Cor. 1:2). Will the saintly and the sanctified become inebriated at the Lord's table? Will the saintly and the sanctified tolerate blatant immorality?
17. N. Sarna, *Understanding Genesis* (New York: McGraw Hill, 1966), pp. 183, 184.
18. This is the reason why I have some problems with the explanation, so common in Reformed circles, of the shift back and forth from "Jacob" to "Israel" as the name of the patriarch. Thus G. Vos, *Biblical Theology: Old and New Testaments* (Grand Rapids: Wm. B. Eerdmans Publishing Co., 1948), p. 99, sees this as a reflection of the dual nature in the child of God. If that is the point in the Jacob to Israel, back to Jacob swing, then why is it that from the point of the reception of a new name, Scripture records not a blemish in his character or behavior? If the old nature is there, it certainly never surfaces post-Peniel.
19. Compare Exodus 12:2 (Passover); Exodus 14:1, 15 (the wilderness itinerary); Exodus 16:2 (the provision of manna); Exodus 19:3 (the announcement of the convenant); Exodus 19:7, 21 (preparation for receiving the covenant); Exodus 20:22; 21:1 (the giving of particular laws); Exodus 25:1; 35:4 (instructions on the tabernacle).
20. M. Greenberg, *Understanding Exodus* (New York: Behrman House Inc., 1969) p. 14, note 1.
21. B. Childs, *The Book of Exodus: A Critical, Theological Commentary* (Philadelphia: The Westminster Press, 1974), pp. 382–383. The distinctions, sociologically speaking, between law and covenant are conveniently diagramed by G. Mendenhall, *The Tenth Generation* (Baltimore: Johns Hopkins University Press, 1973) p. 200.
22. *Ius quia iustum* or *ius quia iussum?* Right because just, or right because commanded?
23. It must be observed that the side-by-side existence of a certain prohibition in both biblical and extra-biblical law codes does not necessarily mean an identical mentality is in opera-

tion. For instance, while both Israelite and Near-Eastern cultures looked with disdain at adultery, in Israel adultery is viewed as a crime, not as a civil offense. It is a sin against God, and not an offense against the husband. For that reason it demands community action rather than private action. See further, A. Phillips, "Another Look at Adultery," *Journal for the Study of the Old Testament*" 20 (1981), pp. 3–26.

24. G. Mendenhall, *The Tenth Generation,* p. 22.
25. Illustratively, S. Paul, *Studies in the Book of the Covenant in the Light of Cuneiform and Biblical Law, SVT* 18 (Leiden: E. J. Brill, 1970), and A. Phillips, *Ancient Israel's Criminal Law: A New Approach to the Decalogue* (Oxford: Oxford University Press, 1970). But compare also the rejoinder by B. Jackson, "Reflections on Biblical Criminal Law," *Journal of Jewish Studies* 24 (1973), pp. 8–38.
26. P. Hanson, "The Theological Significance of Contradiction within the Book of the Covenant," in *Canon and Authority,* G. Coats and B. Long, eds. (Philadelphia: Fortress Press, 1977) p. 127. In his probing and highly original monograph M. Weinfeld. *Deuteronomy and the Deuteronomic School* (Oxford: Oxford University Press, 1972) interprets Deuteronomy as a document illustrating this same general theme of mutation, a mutation toward "humanism" and "secularization." Needless to say, his thesis has generated a heated response.
27. For example, Eichrodt, *Theology,* II, p. 373. J. Hempel, "Ethics in the OT," *Interpreter's Dictionary of the Bible,* vol. 2, p. 158; E. Flesseman, "Old Testament 'Ethics,' " *Student World* 57 (1964), p. 221; V. Fletcher, "The Shape of Old Testament Ethics, *Scottish Journal of Theology* 24 (1971), p. 57; D. Cupitt, "God and Morality," *Theology* 76 (1973), pp. 357, 358; J. Barton, "Understanding Old Testament Ethics," *Journal for the Study of the Old Testament* 9 (1978), pp. 60, 61.
28. For the moral nuances in the Hebrew word *way,* see J. Muilenburg, *The Way of Israel: Biblical Faith and Ethics* (New York: Harper, 1961), pp. 33ff.
29. I owe this observation about the play-off between moral and cultic imitation to B. Lindars, "Imitation of God and Imita-

tion of Christ," *Theology* 76 (1973), pp. 394–402. Lindars is unhappy with the term *imitation*. That should be reserved, he says, for the New Testament and passages such as Philippians 2:5–11. He suggests that Leviticus 19:3 is not a command to imitate God's holiness, but rather a command to be holy because God is holy. The two should not be confused.

30. J. Barr, *The Scope and Authority of the Bible*, p. 100.
31. J. Muilenburg, *The Way of Israel*, pp. 77–93.
32. J. Barton, "Natural Law and Poetic Justice in the Old Testament," *Journal of Theological Studies* 30 (1979), pp. 3–4.
33. W. B. Wallis, "Irony in Jeremiah's Prophecy of New Covenant," *Journal of the Evangelical Theological Society* 12 (1969), pp. 107–110.
34. J. Crenshaw, *Old Testament Wisdom* (Atlanta: John Knox Press, 1981) p. 24.
35. As I have heard it put facetiously, "not pie in the sky, but ham where I am!"
36. We might find the title jarring and disturbing, but I recommend—with minor reservations—at this point W. Brueggemann's *In Man We Trust: The Neglected Dimension of Biblical Faith* (Atlanta: John Knox Press, 1972).
37. It is rather curious that the most recent attempt by Wesleyan authors to treat Old Testament ethics is limited almost exclusively to the wisdom texts. See W. T. Purkiser, R. S. Taylor, and W. H. Taylor, *God, Man and Salvation* (Kansas City, Mo.: Beacon Hill Press, 1977), pp. 107–119.
38. Y. Kaufmann, *The Religion of Israel* (Chicago: University of Chicago Press, 1960), p. 324, provides references.
39. H. McKeating, "Sanctions against Adultery in Ancient Israelite Society, with Some Reflections on Methodology in the Study of Old Testament Ethics," *Journal for the Study of the Old Testament* 11 (1979), pp. 57–72.
40. G. von Rad, *Wisdom in Israel* (Nashville: Abingdon Press, 1972), pp. 88–95 beautifully illustrates the dialectic between the theonomous and experiential motivations at work in the motive clauses within Proverbs. Both exist alongside of each other, and ultimately the two are not in essential conflict.
41. J. Hempel, "Ethics in the Old Testament," p. 157.

Robert W. Wall (Th.D., Dallas Theological Seminary), associate professor of biblical studies and ethics, Seattle Pacific University

New Testament Ethics

INTRODUCTION

THE NEW TESTAMENT CANON of the Church is a diverse collection of literary works, composed by different writers whose unique perceptions of God interpreted his salvation for audiences with differing needs and backgrounds. So diverse is the New Testament that there are those who find the task of writing a coherent biblical ethics difficult, if not impossible. Indeed, how can there be a single ethos[1] that ties up all the loose ends? In part, this frustration arises out of a post-Enlightenment concern that reality be configured in unified and rational schema. Diversity suggests chaos and should be eliminated at all cost—or so the modern wisdom suggests. It has been the singular occupation of biblical scholars over the last two centuries to give some unified account of the Bible's diversity, often by reducing it or adjusting it in ways that unify it.

Current efforts in organizing the diversity of the biblical ethos have proved disappointing. Some have given up and simply described the various moral programme of biblical writers without any effort to move Scripture into the life of the ongoing community of faith; Scripture remains locked into the past. On the other hand, evangelical scholarship has been content to strive for ethical uniformity through interpreting the Bible's moral diversity by a "harmonizing hermeneutics."[2] Still others tend to interpret and construe biblical ethics in ways consistent with the scholar's confessional tradition. The diverse readings of God's will contained in Scripture are collapsed into various dogmatic themes; what one ends up with is not a biblical ethic but a moral theology consistent with a particular denomination or ecclesiastical tradition.

Certainly, in each effort to take seriously what the Bible says about the moral life of the believing community, the need to authorize our moral claims by appeals to the Bible is maintained—and that is good! Yet, in disregarding the rich diversity by which Scripture describes God's will, we too often have failed to heed Scripture's own clues for recovering God's will for our own time and dilemma. If there is to be a New Testament ethic that functions in the life of the ongoing community of faith as a moral resource, we must deal with the text *as it is;* indeed, that means we must attend and even celebrate the diversity by which the biblical writers gave expression to God's will.

Canonical Criticism: Toward a New Proposal

One of the most important gains made by biblical scholarship in recent years is the work of *canonical criticism.*[3] Concerned that the guild of biblical scholars has been studying Scripture in ways that prevent the Church from using it as her "canon," certain prominent figures within that guild have called attention to the bankruptcy of critical orthodoxy, especially for the life of the believing community.[4] Scripture, they say, must be repositioned as the *normative* context for hearing and acting upon the Word of God. In fact, it is from Scripture itself that the Church recovers the normative hermeneutic by which God converses with his people. The very *interplay* between the diverse voices contained within a common book provides the Church with an apparatus to check and to correct her moral life and theology. *God speaks in many ways in order to draw his people back to the center of his will!*

Thus, the beginning point of canonical hermeneutics is the canon itself. It is the very function of the Bible to serve as the normative context of a distinctively Christian ethos. The task of writing a New Testament ethics that takes the canonical context as normative is an enormous one, and this chapter will serve only to get us under way. It intends to be more provocative than provincial, more an outline than a completed programme.

DEFINITIONS

The New Testament contains four groups of books, each positioned in a normative place with each serving a normative role as part of the Church's Bible: the *Gospels,* the *Acts of the Apostles,* the *Letters,* and the *Revelation of John.* In order to describe faithfully how the New Testament might be used to recover God's will for the ongoing community of faith, each group of New Testament books will be analyzed in three different ways: its canonical context, its ethical content, and its prophetic interplay. We now turn to a more detailed definition of these terms.

THE CANONICAL CONTEXT

B.S. Childs has argued that the theological and ethical significance of a book or of a group of books can often be determined by their "position" in the Bible.[5] This conclusion is grounded in a complex set of philosophical and practical conclusions that we must assume for the moment. Suffice it to say that the Church uses a sacred text, the Bible, to identify her beliefs (theology) and her behavior (ethics), and it is the *final shape* of that sacred text that is decisive in that conversation between community and canon; it is the *arrangement* of books and the interplay between them that is raised to a primary level for theological and ethical reflection. Thus, our first task will be to suggest what moral norms arise from an analysis of the position of each canonical group within the New Testament canon as a whole, and the importance of how the books are arranged within each group (i.e., within the Gospels and the letters) for moral reflection.

THE ETHICAL CONTENT

Our treatment of the ethical content of each group of New Testament books will follow more standard works on New Testament ethics with one possible exception: our desire will be to emphasize the *diversity* of how the biblical writers construed God's will. One must remember that an apostle's or an evangelist's perception of God's will followed logically from those personal, socio-historical, and theological factors that shaped him and that were uniquely his own.[6] Further, they were not systematic theologians writing doctrine or moral theology in a formal way. They wrote to audiences caught in certain situations at certain moments of history. The fluidity that characterizes the New Testament should check any effort simply to harmonize or uncritically collapse the distinctive features of any one book or apostle with those of another. Let us also hasten to acknowledge, so as not to become too preoccupied with New Testament diversity, the fundamental unity of the Scripture.[7] First, there is a singular commitment to the gospel of God revealed in his son, Jesus Christ, and second, there is a singular commitment to a common, sacred tradition, inspired by God to bear his redeeming and sanctifying Word to the whole world. This unity will be assumed in our study. In sum, then, by "ethical content" we intend to describe how the moral content of the New Testament is construed.

THE PROPHETIC INTERPLAY

In a series of books and articles, J.A. Sanders has articulated a profound understanding of Scripture's own hermeneutics. While accepting for the most part the contributions of historical criticism, Sanders's particular interest has been to recover the way the confessing community used the Torah (the sacred story, the Gospel) to deal effectively with its historical contingencies.[8] That is, according to Sanders, the community of faith has always conversed with its Scripture in order to find out what it means to be Israel (or the Church) and to do as she ought. To be sure, the layers of differing theological programs that form critics have found in the Old Testament are the evidence of Israel adapting its Torah to its history. With each new political or theological crisis—and there were, of course, many such crises during Israel's history—the community of faith engaged and adapted the sacred story afresh in order to hear the Word of God directing them to promise.

This interplay between community and canon offers us a pattern for using a biblical ethics today. Sanders himself appeals to the Old Testament prophet as an analogy of biblical hermeneutics.[9] Just as the prophet of Yahweh came to Israel with the Word of the Lord to bring Israel's repentance, so Scripture carries a similar freight. In the ongoing conversation between community and canon, it is the canon that bears the Word of the Lord and it is the canon that corrects and bids new Israel to repent and turn to God—a "prophetic interplay."

Our efforts will have two foci. First, we wish to describe

the conversation between biblical trajectories (e.g., Paul and James, Synoptic and Johannine gospels) as authorized patterns for the ongoing conversation between community and canon. Second, Scripture's own internal self-correcting apparatus in turn becomes the basis for informing our hermeneutics in using Scripture today as a moral resource. Two tendencies are checked by this method. The tendency to codify special interests into rigid confessions of what every Christian ought to do is checked and balanced by other interests found in Scripture. Second, the tendency to shape a simplistic moral parochialism by appeals to one biblical paradigm (e.g., Paul or the synoptic Gospels) is corrected by the diversity of New Testament options. The multivalency of the New Testament canon reminds us that God finds his people in a variety of ways even as we find him in kind.

This positive approach to biblical diversity resists the conservative tendency to rightly embrace biblical authority but only by imposing an artificial uniformity upon it. Our desire is to celebrate the Bible *as it is* as the Spirit's intended path for finding God's will and Word. Scripture enshrines, as Sanders claims, a "monotheizing pluralism"; God cannot be codified! His living, dynamic character demands that we hear him in our time.

THE GOSPELS

CANONICAL CONTEXT

The Gospels of the New Testament canon did not circulate in the early church as gospels *per se*; rather, Matthew was a *biblos* (1:1), Luke was a *diegesis* (1:1), while Mark was only the "beginning" of the gospel (1:1). John, a book some think should not even be considered a literary gospel, was written to secure and to disciple the faith of the Church (20:31). Whatever one thinks about their original intention, these four books have been clustered together by the canonizing community as Gospels so that the good news of God that was revealed in Jesus from Nazareth could be told. Further, while we might wish to argue about their authorship, they are left anonymous; these are not narratives written "*by* someone," but *about* our Lord, and that is what counts for faith.

The beginning point for New Testament ethics arises from an analysis of the Gospels' canonical position. The Church placed the Gospels *first* in the New Testament canon because the story of Jesus enshrined in them is of *primary* importance for shaping and informing the faith and life of God's people. The New Testament ethos arises from a soil fertilized by a single demand: *imitatio Christi,* "imitate Christ!" Even as he incarnated God's love and truth, so are we to do likewise. Yet, two qualifications are pertinent. Jesus' mission was to bear witness to his Father. Thus, in Matthew's Gospel, Jesus is confessed as the "Son of the living God" (16:16), while in Mark, he is the messiah of God, in Luke, the prophet of God, and in John, the Word of God. In each case, the vocation of Jesus is subordinated or understood in terms of his relationship to God. The New Testament ethos, then, while made concrete by the life of Jesus, is really a *theocentric* ethics: in imitating Christ, we are doing the will of the one who sent him. Further, as we will describe under Ethical Content, the evangelists interpreted *imitatio Christi* in differing ways with differing emphases. We should not seek to prescribe a specific content to the *imitatio Christi* formula; indeed, *to imitate Christ is not a prescription but a paradigm*—a pattern that is informed by *all* the Gospels, which are brought together to tell the good news of God in Christ.

Two further clues are recovered for New Testament ethics from the way the Gospels are arranged as a canonical group. Historical criticism has determined (although debated) that Mark was written first, and scholarship is inclined to begin there in telling the story of Christ. This ignores the canonical arrangement of the Gospels, which begins with Matthew and not with Mark. The *canonical* intentionality recognizes that the Gospels together link the Jewish Scriptures with the Christian Scriptures, Old Testament with New Testament, because there is fundamental continuity between the histories of Israel and the Church and between Torah and the Gospel. Indeed, there is continuity between the messiah of Judaism and rabbi Yeshua whose teachings and work founded Christianity; the story of Jesus fulfills the Law and the prophets (Matt. 5:17; Rom. 10:4) and thus it is pivotal for *all* of Israel. For this very reason, Matthew's Gospel is positioned first among the canonical Gospels because it brings together in a most deliberate manner the traditions of the Law and the prophets with the traditions of Jesus. Matthew not only seeks to authorize every claim he makes for his Lord by an Old Testament citation, but opens his Gospel with a genealogy that extends the story of Israel to the story of Jesus (1:1–17). God's will for Israel, his people, is posited in Jesus, his Son and Israel's "son of David."

The canonical Gospels are arranged dialectically as well: the synoptic tradition (Matthew, Mark, and Luke) interplays with the Johannine tradition. In fact, coming out of the synoptic Gospels into John's Gospel is like coming into a strange and foreign country where everything said and done is different from what is known before. But might the canonical intention be even as John Calvin suggested: "This Gospel is a key to open the door for understanding the rest;"[10] the questions and issues raised by the synoptic Gospels make John's Gospel intelligible to us, and even provide answers that the synoptics leave unattended.

ETHICAL CONTENT

Three concessions should be admitted at the outset.

First, no real consensus exists regarding the ethical content of any gospel. Each contains a complex of themes and demands, making it difficult to coordinate them all into simplistic slogans. And second, this is exacerbated by the nonsystematic character of the narrative. Yet, third, in their diversity, the canonical Gospels share a set of convictions about Jesus: his mission was messianic and his words and work are revelatory.

Matthew. The ethics of Matthew follows from his central conviction that Jesus is the "son of the living God" (16:16)—he is in fact the promised "Immanuel" in whom God stands with his people (1:23; 18:20; 28:20).[11] As God's Son, Jesus, knows his Father's will perfectly, and as Immanuel, he is able to communicate it concretely to his disciples (11:25–7). In this Gospel, Jesus assumes his vocation of Teacher, and as the "new Moses" he teaches God's new demands to those who repent.

The importance of Jesus' vocation to communicate concretely God's will to new Israel is underscored by his distinctive use of two motifs: *righteousness* and *fulfillment.* Both in his presentation of Jesus' baptism (3:15) and his discipleship sermon (5:17, 20), Matthew carries his important freight into critical interplay. J.P. Meier has suggested that the evangelist's intention lies in his moral concern that a disciple live a righteous (i.e., moral) life in order to fulfill God's "entrance requirement" for his promised kingdom of heaven.[12] Thus, the disciple should read the opening Sermon on the Mount (5–7) and the final Sermon on the Future (24–25) in the light of that norm. The Sermon on the Mount brings together Jesus' teachings on the "greater righteousness" (5:19–20)—words that give specific content to "God's will" (7:21–24). Read in this light, the disciple who truly repents and desires the "greater righteousness" seeks to live both pure in heart (5:3–12, 22, 28) and in deed (5:13–16); he obeys Jesus' reinterpretation of God's Torah totally (i.e., "perfectly," 5:48; 5:21–48); his piety reflects God's interests (6:1, 4, 6, 18) rather than the world's (6:19–34). It is a righteousness that is profoundly personal and spiritual (7:7–20).

Throughout the course of this sermon by the new Moses, he qualifies his words by the eschatological situation—"Repent! For the kingdom of heaven is at hand!" More precisely, this "greater righteousness," taught by Jesus, *fulfills* the law and the prophets (5:17–18; cf. 7:12). In Matthew's Gospel, fulfillment refers back to those promises of Israel's salvation and God's kingdom contained in the Jewish Scriptures—the "law and the prophets." At every point of Jesus' career, Matthew cites a biblical passage to underscore the point: Jesus fulfills the promises of God's salvation contained in the Law and the prophets. Yet, Jesus in turn points his disciples toward the future once again. Even as he fulfills the law and prophets, so now his demands—his Law—contain the promise of eternal life for those who obey them (5:19–20; 7:21–27; 10:32–39; 25:31–46). The righteous life and the future kingdom come together, then, as a new moral norm: obedience to the demands of the "greater righteousness" (Sermon on the Mount) yields the reward of eternal life (Sermon on the Future; cf. 25:46).

It should be noted in passing that Matthew's formula, "kingdom of heaven," is hardly a euphemism for "kingdom of God"; rather, it is crucial for the moral norm suggested previously. The values and demands of God's heavenly kingdom, brought to earth by Jesus, are now encountered historically and specifically. However, the Kingdom is still heavenly, even after Easter; its final eruption into human history is left in the future at the seond coming of Christ.[13] Matthew's futurism intensifies the prophetic nature of Jesus' teaching and his construal of the moral (i.e., righteous) life: the righteous life prepares one for the *future* kingdom.

When one reads Matthew's Gospel, one is struck with

the strong sense that discipleship is rooted in obedience to those *rules* established with the absolute authority of God's Son. One's spiritual fitness is checked against the standard left by Jesus whose ongoing presence is made concrete by the community's collection for his teaching (18:15–20). The very genre of this Gospel bears testimony to this. As has been shown, Matthew is structured by five long discipleship sermons;[14] it bears a catechism-like quality that reinforces a rule-ethic. The true disciple obeys Christ's teachings as set down by the gospel. Further, the eschatological character of the Matthean ethos qualifies this legalism in a positive way: God's saving grace that is found at Christ's return is executed on the basis of a righteousness that results from obedience to the demands of Jesus.

Luke.[15] Lukan theology and ethics are really quite different from either Matthew or Mark. The fabric of Lukan ethics is taken from the Old Testament theme of *Jubilee*.[16] We must clarify what Jubilee is. First, the Old Testament idea of Jubilee derives from the Holiness Code (Lev. 25; cf. Deut. 15) and construes Israel's relationship with Yahweh in sociological ways.[17] For instance, in order for Israel to be Israel, all property was returned to its original owner every fiftieth year, all slaves were released, aid was given to the poor and alien, and the land was stripped to lie fallow for the Jubilee year. These radical socio-economic reconstructions of the Promised Land only intended to function as an illustration of Yahweh's ownership of the land, and his gracious and merciful treatment of Israel. Indeed, Jubilee was used to teach Israel that its security was grounded in its covenant with God and in nothing else. Second, it was this representation of Yahweh's relationship with Israel that then shaped the way in which Israel hoped for its eternal promised land, the kingdom of God, brought to them by Messiah. The early church inherited this hope from Judaism, and we inherit it from the Gospel of Luke. In Luke's Gospel as nowhere else in the New Testament canon, the gospel of the Kingdom is given a social character; the love demand is presented in terms of community; to be righteous is not merely understood in terms of one's relationship with a righteous God (as with Matthew) but also in terms of one's relationship to the poor, the outcast, and the "public."

As with all the biblical writers, Luke's ethics follow logically from his fundamental convictions about God's Christ. Luke's Jesus is patterned after the Old Testament Joshua. Even as Joshua led Israel into the Promised Land, it is Jesus who leads new Israel into its promised land, the kingdom of God, by his death and resurrection. Even as the Old Testament Jesus (= Joshua) becomes in his canonical role a "former prophet" who announces that one day Israel will take possession of its land when it turns to its Torah (Josh. 23–24), it is the New Testament Joshua (= Jesus) who, as the prophet of God,[18] announces that "today" (4:21; 19:9; 23:43; cf. 2:11) Israel has entered into its promised land. Two ethical conclusions logically follow: first, if Israel has taken possession of its promised land, then a jubilary sociology that determines how life is lived in the land during the messianic age should be implemented. Second, since jubilary ethics is a reversal of things as they are, the implementation of Jubilee always comes with social criticism against the tyranny of things and of social class (which characterizes things as they are). Such a socio-economic reversal is a manifestation of God's grace, which has redeemed new Israel in Christ.

The social structures of the Lukan ethic are illustrated by his presentation of Jesus' inaugural sermon (4:18–19) and his discipleship sermon (6:12–49). Luke's use of these two traditions takes its theological cue from Isaiah 61:1–2, which interprets Israel's jubiliary institution in terms of the eschatological Prophet, who Judaism later taught would announce the messianic age (4:21).[19] Note that in both the

Nazareth scene (4:20–30) and in the discipleship sermon (6:20–26), Jesus speaks of a *reversal of fortunes*. Indeed, Isaiah proclaimed the same (4:18) for the "favorable year of the Lord" (4:19)—or eschatological Jubilee! Two points must be clarified at this point: first, Jesus specifies a *community* of disciples (6:20–22; "you") for *immediate* (4:21; "today") reversal of their fortunes, and second, Jesus specifies that the form and the condition of this eschatological reversal is realized by imitating God's mercy toward the helpless and the outcast (6:36). The social contour of Luke's *imatatio Christi* (10:25–37) follows from his conviction that Jubilee has come with Christ, and that "today" his disciples be the agents of the eschatological reversal.

While introduced to Nazareth (4:18–19; cf. 3:7–14; 7:18–23) and in the Sermon on the Plain (6:12–49), the Lukan ethic is thoroughly rehearsed in the "Special Section" of his Gospel (9:18—19:27). C. F. Evans has shown that Luke orders the traditions of Jesus' journey to Jerusalem with his disciples by using Deuteronomy 1–26 as a "template."[20] The ethical impression arising from this hermeneutic is made more important if Jesus is the new Joshua. Indeed, it was old Joshua who told old Israel that the way of securing the Promised Land was to obey the Law (Josh. 25:25–28)—the very law the new Joshua represents afresh to the new Israel! If new Israel is to secure the Promised Land, or kingdom of God, which the new Joshua will already deliver to new Israel on the cross and by way of the empty tomb, then it must obey his law. Logically it has a jubilary character to it. Thus, those who are enslaved or oppressed by the religious or political powers of the demonic dominion are to be released (10:25–27; 11:45–12:12; 14:1–24). Those who have wealth are to share it with those who do not; jubilary economics are rooted in grace, not greed and in sharing, not accumulation (11:1–8; 12:13–24; 16:9–18; 18:18–30). The socio-economic structures of the new community in the new promised land are shaped by a jubilary ethos that identifies the poor, that promotes justice and compassion, and that reverses those powers that are against God's reign. The net result is that God's gospel advances on earth.

One must also note the importance Luke attaches to the Spirit. Lukan ethics assume that the people of faith have already been liberated by God's mercy revealed on the cross of Christ. Obedience to the law given by the new Joshua intends to lead a people into the Kingdom more by *willing response* than by required demand. It is the engagement of the Spirit within the community that yields this obedient response. Not only does grace stand *before* the demand to obey, but the grace of God stands among and within his people in the Spirit, who then empowers their obedient and logical if not obligated) response of mercy (11:1–13).

John. The Johannine ethos is very much like his theology in character: it focuses on fundamentals. The essential fundamental of Johannine Christianity is that Jesus is the Word of the Lord; he is the revelation of God made flesh (1:1–18). When the Word enters the world, even his own kind (1:10–11) are provoked to an internal crisis: do we receive the glory and the truth of this one who so boldly ties his life to God's, or do we reject him? John's narrative is rooted in such an antithesis between those of darkness, who reject the Word of the Lord, and those of light, who receive him and so become children of God (1:12).

Such a decision about Jesus gives rise to the ethics of John. In his conversation with Nicodemus (3:1–21), Jesus concludes his discussion of "heavenly things" (3:12ff.) with an ethical equation (3:18–21): those who reject the Son practice wickedness. It is a kind of moral determinism found also at Qumran. Faith is the beginning of morality. To believe in truth is to practice it and to reject truth is to practice evil. *The condition, then, for moral behavior is to receive by faith the revelation of God incarnated in his Son, Jesus.*

The content John gives to the praxis of truth is equally as straightforward: "Love one another; even as I have loved you" (13:34). To practice the truth shed by the Light is to love as he loved; indeed, it is to love even as his Father loved and so gave his Son for the world (3:16). This "new commandment" seems at first consistent with Matthew and with Luke, who gives as Jesus' demand, "Love your enemies" (Matt. 5:43–44; Luke 6:27–28). Yet on closer analysis John's presentation of the love demand is different.[21]

First, John's Jesus demands that his disciples *love one another*. Rather than loving one's *enemies*—the most *inclusive* community of neighbors possible—Jesus is clearly referring to and thus restricting his commandment to the believing community. It is God who loves the world at large and who acts directly on their behalf by sending his Word into the world. In his consecratory prayer (17), Jesus brings the believing community into contact with the world, but only indirectly so; it is by their love for one another that the *world* is convinced of God's love for it (17:26). The sectarian character of the believer's love is further clarified by Jesus' commissioning of Peter (21:15–23). Unlike the synoptic commission, in which Jesus tells his disciples to go to the whole world (Matt. 28:19; cf. Acts 1:8), Jesus tells Peter to shepherd only the believing community. The Johannine ethos is focused on the household of faith—to build it up and to care for its needs (cf. Gal. 6:10).

This sectarian love is also an *active love*. John uses verbal forms of love to energize Jesus' demand; it is a love that remains restless until it shows itself! But this leads to a concern. There is already a great deal of ambiguity in this Gospel; perhaps this is because the teaching function has been left in the future as the special ministry within the believing community of the Paraclete (14:26; 16:13). While the demand to love one another is an urgent one, Jesus leaves it without detail; he leaves it to the future and to the promise of the Spirit. However, the Spirit comes to help the believing community love (14:15–16), dependent upon the Word (16:13) for ethical specificity. That John has given us a narrative of the Word foreshadows if not clarifies what the Spirit will disclose to the believing community. Thus, John brings the community to the *logos sarx egeneto* as its moral paradigm by which God's will is made known in contemporary conversation with the Paraclete.

PROPHETIC INTERPLAY

Two vital conversations arise from our brief treatment of the ethical content of Matthew, Luke, and John: the first within the synoptic Gospels between Matthew and Luke, and the other between the synoptic Gospels and John. As the Church joins in on these canonical conversations, she is informed as to the full extent of her *imitatio Christi* rule of life.

Matthew and Luke. Even within the synoptic tradition, where the lay of the literary land appears the same as one moves from Gospel to Gospel, we have recovered a diversity of ethical content between Matthew's Gospel and Luke's. The ethos of Matthew's tradition emphasizes the personal, laying stress on one's own righteousness, which emerges out of the disciple's relationship with God. It is an ethic that is profoundly futuristic, looking to the future eruption of the final kingdom as the goal of the righteous life. Further, the content of the moral life is rooted in the teachings of Jesus, who as son of God has entered into history as Immanuel with a new and final interpretation of God's will (i.e., Law). Matthew's ethos, then, is more legalistic in keeping with his Jewish church; and this casuistry forges a perception of the Christian life that is intimately connected with a certain set of teachings (18:15–20) as the criteria of acceptance both by God on his future day and by his community today.

There are many important and necessary features received from Matthew's Gospel in building a truly biblical ethics. There are certain situations, or certain stages in moral development, when rules effectively guide human conduct and insure right living. Paul Ramsey has long argued that moral ambiguity produces moral immaturity.[22] Indeed, any society or community must establish by law certain specific rules that mark out what is right or wrong in order to maintain its health. Such clarity, Ramsey argues, is itself moral and leads to heightened moral sensibility. Matthew connects a rule ethic with community in chapter 18 as the means of maintaining discipline and preventing chaos—whether religious or ethical.

Further, Matthew's Sermon on the Mount posits the disciple's ethic in the specific demands given by Jesus—demands that are inherently righteous (5:19–20) because they are taught by God's Son (7:21–24). Because they are inherently righteous, obedience to the demands of Jesus will yield a righteous life and will therefore gain his positive judgment at the end of time (25:46). The disciple is not left in a lurch; he knows precisely and concretely what the perimeter of God's will is and thus can do it and find eternal life.

While there is much to commend Matthew's rule-ethos, it can lead to certain problems if not corrected or balanced by other biblical moral paradigms. His emphasis on personal ethics can quickly collapse into a quiet pietism that tends to emphasize concerns of an exclusively private kind and dismiss (even argue against!) the importance of a social ethics: one's personal relationship with God and the moral maintenance of it is all that matters, while the active dismantling of structural-societal forms of evil only distract from the doing of God's will. Further, such moral pietism can lead to a life preoccupied with codes of rules both as a personal ethic and as a criticism of judging others. In its final and tragic form, a rule ethos can become self-damning, pathological, and devastating to spirit and mind.

Such abuses, which lie lurking in the Matthean scheme of things, are corrected by the Lukan ethos. Against Matthew's personalism, Luke's jubilary ethics exacts a more social perception of God's will. Moral actions are those that promote welfare for the needy neighbor. Grace is measured not only by God's saving mercies but by a public activism that turns divine mercy into acts of mercy to any and all in trouble, whether spiritually or socially. Indeed, Luke softens the futurism of Matthew's interpretation of God's reign while laying emphasis on its immediacy and its "worldliness": God's promised land has already broken into history through the work of God's new Joshua, who has led new Israel, the Church, there by way of his cross. God's Jubilee has come (Luke 4:18–21), and it is the Church's responsibility to live in conformity to the jubilary ethic in celebration of God's merciful redemption.

The Lukan ethos, geared toward proper response to social conditions met, tends to view the morality of an act and evaluate its moral good on the basis of result; if there is liberation from need, then the act that produces it is a merciful and thus good act. Such a "teleological" ethic can collapse into moral confusion, especially in less mature communities of faith. Without concrete boundaries set and shared by the community, there is nothing to defend or to judge against the inroads of competing and often perverting alternatives. The lack of moral means to get to moral ends leads to a lack of moral decisiveness and sometimes to a life that is something other than Christian. It is in this positive sense that Matthew's stress on moral rules can check and balance Luke's stress on moral ends—especially for recent converts who need a rule-oriented ethic to move out of a value system that is against the will of God.

Luke's social ethos can also dissolve into an exclusive concern for more public and less personal forms of justification and away from the Gospel's primary call for personal redemption. Matthew reminds us that faith arises from personal commitment; indeed, repentance demands that the disciple turn to God "poor in spirit" (Matt. 5:3) before God turns to those who are "poor" (Luke 6:20). Matthew's moral paradigm challenges any programme that fails to attend adequately to personal, spiritual needs at the expense of a social gospel. This seems especially pertinent in view of the current tendency to use Luke's Gospel to authorize a view of "liberation" that is exclusively social and political. The canonical Christ demands both polarities, the social and the spiritual, to exist as a dynamic whole. The people of God and the persons of God must be individually holy and collectively active in redeeming the world from both personal and public forms of evil. The *imitatio Christi* demand is perceived, then, as a self-correcting conversation so that the Church whose stress is personal and evangelistic is corrected by a countering stress that is public and socialistic. The reverse is also true: to imitate Christ means to replace exclusive commitments to social action with a balancing commitment for personal redemption and growth. God's grace is transmitted through obedient disciples in both arenas.

Synoptic and Johannine Gospels. Two self-correcting interplays emerge from the conversation between the synoptic and the Johannine traditions. We have already suggested that the Johannine use of the Lord's "love demand" is stripped of its complexity, the result being an intensification of its importance for the gospel. Indeed, the reader is forced two ways at once: toward Jesus as the Word of God and toward the Word's revelation of God's love for the world in his compassionate response toward human need and finally by his self-giving sacrifice on the cross. The crisis and cost of discipleship is abiding in the Word whose essential meaning is to love in that manner. It is the utter simplicity of this *imitatio Christi* formula in John's Gospel that cuts through the red tape of the more complex formulations in the synoptic material (i.e., the Matthean "rule-agapism" and the Lukan jubilary "principle-agapism") and bids us to focus on the Christ of God as our moral paradigm. Any specificity of what is meant to love like Christ for any moment of history in the light of any dilemma in history is left by John for that future when the *Paraclete* will clarify and contemporize God's will by bearing witness to his Word (14:25–31). John's "counter-punch" morality, dynamic and situational, tends to correct any efforts at codifying God's will before God can speak concretely to his people through his Spirit.

The second interplay takes up the sectarian character of the Johannine love demand along with the more universal character of the synoptic demand to love even one's enemy. John's election theology logically gives way to a more exclusive ethos that attends to the construction of a special community of faith that stands uniquely for God in a world that is against him. The building up of a household of God is the principal focus of Johannine ethics; thus, the true disciple is called to *share love with other disciples* even as the Son shares love with the Father (10:17). The synoptic tradition, on the other hand, calls disciples to *love the whole world*—even enemies—in response to God's love. Sectarian love and secular love are the two sides of Christ's demand that his true disciple love, and these two sides now bid the Church, who reads *both* as authoritative, to correct an exclusive grounding in either. The Johannine demand to love other disciples corrects the liberal tendency to focus on the world and on its structures, becoming another social agency whose compassion is institutionalized. John demands the Church focus upon the welfare of those believers who share in God's salvation; when the Church becomes merely a social agency rather than a spiritual community, it becomes something other than the Church. However, the synoptic demand to love all who need liberating, whether from social or spiritual bondage, corrects the conservative tendency toward moral provincialism that construes God's will only in terms of spiritual needs or personal discipleship. The *imitatio Christi* formula bids the Church to be concerned for the building of a spiritual house of committed disciples who then can minister beyond its walls to even the enemies of God as the revelation of his grace and justice. The oppression of the soul and of the society is dismantled by courageous and risky actions of love; such is the gospel's ethos.

The Acts Of The Apostles

CANONICAL CONTEXT

With the rise of historical criticism, scholars have merged Acts with Luke's Gospel as that evangelist's "history of Christian beginnings." While that may well have been Luke's original intention, the canonizing community had a different intention and separated Luke's Gospel from his treatment of primitive Christianity. In fact, it seems clear that the earliest canons of the Church did not include Acts but consisted of Gospels and Letters. At some point, however, before the fixing of the sacred text, the Church inserted Acts as a bridge between the Gospels and Letters in order to relate the two collections together[23] —a purpose different from what Luke had envisioned!

This new canonical purpose makes sense: Acts was

written by Luke as a fitting sequel to his Gospel, and therefore logically it should follow the Gospels; further, Luke intended Acts to argue for the Church's apostles and for Paul, whose letters follow. Yet, apart from these obvious justifications for positioning Acts between "Gospel and Apostle," as Marcion called the two divisions of his canon, we must ask ourselves whether Acts's function as a canonical bridge yields any important norms for how we should use the New Testament for ethics.

As the primitive church became institutionalized toward the end of the first century, the memories of her first apostles were fixed as her foundation (Eph. 2:20; Rev. 21:14; 2 Pet. 3:2). Their "authority" authorized the Church's confidence in the face of difficulty as well as her gospel in the face of other religious options. Those apostolic traditions, shaped by the letters they wrote, stand *after* Acts in the New Testament canon, for it is Acts that legitimates the Church's confidence in her early apostles and so in the letters they wrote. Indeed, Acts narrates how God's Spirit empowered them to bear witness of his Christ and his redemption. While Acts does not speak of the apostles' writing ministry, it does tell their story and roots it in God's action and truth, which then extends to their letters within the context of the canon.

It is further clear that Acts is positioned after the Gospels because the proclamation of the apostles and their "acts" follow from Jesus and are stamped with his name. Indeed, the Spirit who founded the Church at Pentecost is the Spirit of the risen Christ, who continues on as Lord of the Church. Thus, the canonical position of Acts underscores that the true foundation of the Church is not apostolic but christological: to imitate the traditions and memories of the apostles is to *imitatio Christi* (1 Cor. 11:1)! In fact, the apostles' paraenesis found in their letters is nothing but the representation of the life of Christ adapted to specific moments of history.

One further question of a more specific kind: might the position of Acts suggest that this work be read as a preface to the Letters, and thus as a hermeneutic that suggests how the Church should use them? It is not unimportant that Acts ends with Paul in prison, his Gentile mission left incomplete and the Lord's commission (1:8) left unfulfilled. *God's final victory is left to the future and to the ongoing community of faith that follows from Paul's missionary activity.* Indeed, the ethics of the Letters propose to facilitate God's final triumph so that the ends of the earth might bear witness to his salvation (Eph. 3:10); it is a "missionary ethic," which equips the Church to take the Gospel to those "ends of the earth" that Paul did not reach.

ETHICAL CONTENT

While it is important to treat the *canonical* intention of Acts as something different from Luke's historical intention, it is necessary to bring them together to recover a common ethical programme. Even as was true for his narrative of Jesus, Luke narrates the story of a primitive Church concerned with enacting a *jubilary ethos* (2:42ff.; 4:32ff.). Not only is the apostolic view of possessions a critical aspect of Luke's description, but Jesus' ministry of compassion and mercy for the outcast continues on in the "acts of the apostles" (3:1–10).[24]

In Acts, Luke's emphasis on the Spirit is drawn in full; here, the Lukan ethos is *pneumatic*. God's will is made concrete by the Spirit, and it is the Spirit who empowers obedience and redemptive consequences. The moral act is completely under the aegis of God's Spirit to insure the ultimate success of his Church's mission. This is necessary because the struggling community made difficult choices in the worst of circumstances. Luke's point is clear: the

Church survived because God is for his people and with them in the Spirit's power!

While laying stress on the sovereignty of God, who acts by his Spirit to make his will known and obeyed, Luke is careful to characterize those human features that are necessary in obeying God's will. The pragmatism of Paul, for instance, or the radical courage of Stephen whose directness cost him his life, or the risky obedience of Peter who followed divine revelation rather than civil direction all shape a *moral character* that for Luke is the requirement for acting in accord with the Spirit.

Finally, Luke emphasizes *evidence*. The claims of the gospel are justified by data; indeed, obedience to the Spirit is proven by the actions produced for all to see. Thus, Paul's life as well as his gospel are defended whether at Jerusalem before his peers or before his critics on the basis of what is produced. For Luke, morality, if not theology, is a historical, concrete affair; there is always evidence that allows for a verdict of truth or falsehood, purity or evil.

PROPHETIC INTERPLAY

Two important interplays emerge from a conversation between Acts and the rest of the New Testament. There is no question that Luke softens early Christianity's apocalypticism (Acts 1:4–8).[25] In reporting the preaching of the early apostles, we do not find an emphasis on the second coming of Christ, finding rather a community that becomes more and more concerned with an earthly task. This seems to conflict with the letters of Paul and Peter, which emphasize Christ's return as critical for ethics (1 and 2 Thess.). In moving the Church's ethos away from an overt concern with God's future, Luke grounds choices in the needs of planet earth. This is consistent with both a jubilary and a missionary agenda: the Church becomes God's agent in redeeming his creation from spiritual and social crisis. There is a real sense that a Church that is overly concerned with the future is less than concerned about the present; apocalyptic morality seems to sanction an escape from reality when choices become the insurance of a heavenly security.

A second interplay, detailed in critical scholarship, arises when Paul's Gentile mission confronts the sectarian interests of a Jewish church. While the predominant conflict between the Gentile and Jewish communities was theological, there is no question that ethical implications were also involved. James Sanders has suggested that the Gentile mission emphasized the *muthos* (or "story") of the Christian gospel, while the Jewish church emphasized in agreement with Judaism the *ethos* (or "ethics") of living as a Christian ought.[26] Although it is not true that Paul was antinomian, his essential emphasis was preaching the good news of God in Christ and not the "works of the Law" (cf. Galatians); in fact, to emphasize Moses over Christ was to destroy the very ground of grace that Christ established in his death and resurrection. The logic of Paul's gospel and the content of his mission to the Gentiles centers on his claims about Christ—the *muthos* of Christianity. Even Luke's catholicizing (and so unifying) tendencies do not completely dull the conflict that emerged between Paul and the Jerusalem church (Acts 21:17–26; 15:1–29; cf. Gal. 2:1–21). The interplay narrated by Luke functions as a preface, then, for the canonical conversation between Paul and the "pillars of the Church" (Gal. 2:9)—James, Peter, and John—that follows in their letters! Indeed, our fundamental convictions about Christ (*muthos*) *and* our life in imitation of him *(ethos)* are set in a dynamic and authoritative tension there, and we will await that discussion.

The Letters

Canonical Context

In reading the New Testament, the position of the Letters *after* both the Gospels and the Acts leads us to two conclusions. First, there could have been no Christian letters without God's revelation in Jesus from Nazareth. Second, there would have been no Christian letters without the missionary activity of the early apostles, since there would have been no communities of faith to write to!

It is striking that some of the letters, such as Hebrews and James, were not written as "letters" and have been retooled in order to fit that genre. A greeting has been attached to James to make a paraenesis (moral sermon) look like a letter; a benediction is added to Hebrews to make a theological pamphlet fit a collection of religious letters; and 1 John is left as a sermon without any effort to make it conform to the literary requirements of a "religious letter" form.[27] There are letters written to individuals placed in a Bible that serves churches, and letters written to churches that are read by individuals as God's Word to them. My point is *theological*. These letters were collected and grouped together as canonical letters in order to shape a particular response of faith in our God. That is, there are certain features of "the letter" that should be raised to a primary level of importance as we use them in discovering God's will for us. Let me briefly suggest three.

A letter is read *liturgically*. Even prior to canonization, many letters were used in worship to instruct early Christians. Letters often employ hymns, confessions of faith, homilies, catecheses, and other features of the oral liturgy of the primitive church, because they were meant to be used by the community of faith to shape both theological and ethical perceptions of life as an act of worship.

A letter is read *historically*. Letters were written to specific communities in light of their concrete problems or needs; the letters were shaped by and adapted to a particular time and place. Letters should be read the same way today; they should be adapted in useful ways to our ongoing situations so that God's will can be heard in relevant ways.

A letter is read *didactically*. The purpose of a religious letter intends to convey information about God and what a commitment to him constitutes both in theology and in ethics. In fact, moral maturity cannot take place in an intellectual vacuum; the Scripture's letters are to be read in light of that equation.

Most important to our treatment of the canonical letters, however, is the observation that they are divided into two groups—Paul's first, and then the general letters. The implications of this arrangement must not go unnoticed for two reasons. First, there is a kind of primacy given to Paul's letters, recognizing that the catholic Church rests upon his Gentile mission and so upon his gospel, which is enshrined in his letters. Second, however, even the early church recognized that reading Paul exclusively can lead to perversions both in theology (e.g., gnosticism) and in ethics (e.g., antinomianism). Thus, they added a second collection comprising letters from the "pillars of the Church" in Jerusalem who often collided with the historical Paul, and positioned it alongside of the canonical Paul in order to continue the conversation that began at the Jerusalem Council![28] The net result for the ongoing community is that no one can read *sola Paula* without being corrected and balanced by the general letters within a canonical context.

ETHICAL CONTENT

The Pauline Ethic. It is virtually impossible to systematize the moral programme of Paul;[29] he was a letter writer, a missionary-pastor more concerned with the spiritual vitality of certain communities of faith than with formal treatments of Christian ethics. We make a mistake not to keep this in mind at all times when working with the Pauline corpus. Most would admit, however, that *Paul's preaching held theology and ethics together with a kind of inner logic:* if one trusted in certain theological convictions, then a certain life would be yielded. When Paul described the moral life, he was not so much interested in setting out a code of rules; in fact, this would be logically inconsistent with his theological convictions! Rather, Paul was *illustrating* the kind of life that ought to spring from faith in Christ.[30] Thus, the various vice lists (Rom. 1:29–30; 1 Cor. 6:9–10) or virtue lists (Gal. 5:22–23; Col. 3:12–15), and even the extended paraenetic sections that often closed his letters should be construed as checklists against which the believing community could evaluate its faith as lived.

For Paul, the demands of the Christian life began even where his gospel began—a fundamental trust in the grace of God as revealed in the dying and rising of Christ for human sin. The gracious action of God in Christ, when embraced by faith, resulted in the believer's baptism into Christ's risen body. It is in this new context that a new life is found with new gifts and demands. Baptism shifts lordships from evil to divine, from demonic to Christ. The demands that one might find in either dominion—evil or divine—logically follow from its Lord. The believer imitates Christ because Christ is his Lord. There are three dimensions of this new existence in Christ that are decisive for understanding the logic of Paul's ethics; we will briefly take them up.

1. *The believer finds the Spirit in Christ.* God's will is made concrete in conversation between the Spirit of Christ and the community that is baptized into him. For Paul, even as the Church is charismatic, so her decisions are charismatic as well (1 Cor. 2). Thus, the new "law of Christ" (Gal. 6:2) is in fact the internal (1 Cor. 9:21) "law of the Spirit" (Rom. 8:2), who works within the believer's spirit to move his faith to acts of profound love (Gal. 5:6). The Spirit is *against* legalistic formulations of moral reality

(2 Cor. 3); rather, he works dynamically and historically to make the lordship of Christ concrete and specific for an ongoing people of God. To have faith in Christ is to walk by his Spirit (Gal. 5:16), and to walk by his Spirit is to take on the mind of Christ so that God's perfect will is known (Rom. 12:2) in ways that follow logically from trust in him (Rom. 12:1).

2. *The believer finds the future triumph of God in Christ.* Paul's gospel is apocalyptic;[31] his interpretation of moral reality follows logically from the salient features of that theological trajectory. Apocalyptic theology interprets existence *dualistically*. Personal and structural evil follows from an evil dominion while personal and structural good follows from Christ's dominion. Yet, Paul believed in an *imminent resolution* to this conflict at the second coming of Christ. His primary moral concern was making the community of faith ready for the inbreaking of God's triumph at Christ's parousia. Every action finds its ultimate value there, for every action will be judged then; obedience insures reward while disobedience insures punishment (1 Cor. 3:10–17; 2 Cor. 5:10). The entire motivational superstructure of Pauline ethics finds its essential content in his doctrine of imminence; the faithful obey in order that they might share in the glory and triumph of their God and Lord. In this sense, Paul's ethics are eschatological; his point is to illustrate what kind of life God will bless at the second coming of Christ.

3. *The believer finds freedom in Christ.* Paul gives unique stress to this dimension of the Christian life.[32] Some suggest that it arises out of his Gentile mission, since it is an ethical formula to which the Gentiles could relate. Others, however, find the idea of human freedom in the Old Testament presentation of a free and sovereign God. Whatever the source, the believer's freedom is a critical feature of Paul's ethics for at least three reasons: *First,* faith in Christ frees the believer from the results of

evil. For the first time, he or she is able to choose freely between the inherent demands of flesh and of Spirit (Gal. 5:11–18). The unbeliever, enslaved to evil, is unable to know God and so is unable to do his will (1 Cor. 2:14). Pauline ethics is for believers only! *Second,* faith in Christ frees the believer from social oppression (Gal. 3:28; Philem.). There can be no question that Christian freedom transforms human relationships; everything that causes wedges between people can be dismantled by the power of reconciliation that is in Christ. *Third,* faith in Christ frees the believer to accommodate himself or herself to those actions that yield spiritual profit (1 Cor. 6:12; 10:23). The limits of Christian freedom are not construed in terms of rules or codes of right conduct; rather, for Paul, the limits of right conduct are relational.[33] Indeed, because a believer lives under the lordship of Christ, everything condemned by other lordships is condoned; however, hardly antinomian (in spite of his critics), Paul carefully qualifies his moral freedom by moral ends. A believer is free to act only as a means to bring glory to God (1 Cor. 10:31) and to seek the spiritual good of others (1 Cor. 10:33). If this means to accommodate the overly scrupulous conscience of the "weaker brother" (1 Cor. 8:7–13) or the uninformed conscience of the nonbeliever (1 Cor. 10:27), Paul's advice is to become "a slave to all, that one might win the more" (1 Cor. 9:19). By so doing, Paul suggests that the community fulfills its *imitatio Christi* demand (1 Cor. 11:1).

The General Ethic. The ethics of the non-Pauline letters are more difficult to organize because of their greater diversity. We might ease our task by referring the reader to our discussion of the Fourth Gospel for the ethics for John's letters; still we are left with books written for different communities by different theologians in different ways! It is useful to note that commentators have recently understood Hebrews, James, 1 and 2 Peter, and Jude as addressed to a suffering people. Of course, many other New Testament books have a similar setting; however, no other group of books deals with the problem of *theodicy* with the force that this one does. Our beginning point, then, is this: *The general ethic is an ethic of suffering (Leidensethik), which in turn interprets the problem of theodicy as it enters into the realm of human existence.* Four features follow from such an ethical agenda.

A *Leidensethik* is *rules oriented.* The ethics of this collection is prescriptive because human suffering produces chaos and doubt, which in turn produces defections of theology (heresy) and morality (disobedience). The positive value of a rule-ethic is that it organizes God's will very clearly and concretely; rules organize the moral ambiguity caused by crisis into orderliness and coherence, and makes doing God's will more ready.

A *Leidensethik* emphasizes *human submission* to authority figures. This is true both within the community (Heb. 13:17) and to those outside (1 Pet. 2:13—3:6) as an extension of the believer's submission to God (James 4:7). Perhaps this emphasis suggests the institutionalizing of the Church, which could well have been provoked by an increase of suffering. The securing of definite lines of relationships enhances survival; establishment power structures will not tolerate anarchism, and anarchism is the tendency of oppression and hardship. Certainly, a compromise of the *imitatio Christi* and a corresponding conformity to a non-Christian ethos are resisted (1 Pet. 2:21); submission to external authorities as "aliens and strangers of the world" (1 Pet. 2:11) is reinterpreted precisely by the *imitatio Christi* formula. This new synthesis enhances both the survival of the present community as "institution" as well as its survival at the second coming of Christ (2 Pet. 1:10–11). One must remember when reading the General Ethic that it is fundamentally a *survival ethos.*

A *Leidensethik* arises in part from the *apocalyptic*

trajectory of primitive Christianity; the ethics of the general letters points to the future triumph of God at the second coming of Christ. In this sense, their suffering only reinforced what the believing community thought all along: human history is going nowhere but down, and those institutions that control history—even though submission to them is mandated for the sake of survival—can offer nothing salvific. To endure is primarily a "test of faith" (James 1:2–4); and it is a test passed by hoping in God (Hebrews), by rejoicing in God's sovereign control over history (James), by understanding God's revelation in Christ (2 Peter), and by obeying God's will rather than doubting that the Church will ever participate in his final victory over evil (1 Peter).

Finally, a *Leidensethik* perceives reality as a *pilgrim people.* Suffering represents those hardships that all pilgrims must bear on their way to the "shrine." Especially in Hebrews, much of the paraenesis one finds there represents those rules that prepare a people for a pilgrimage[34]—to break from existing ties in the world outside of Christ, to launch out on a journey toward their heavenly shrine, so to enter into the full blessing promised there by God. A pilgrim ethos stands at a distance—as aliens, as strangers, as foreigners—from the norms and values by which a nonbelieving world lives. There is an intensity to obey God steadfastly as a condition of enduring the pilgrimage through human existence and so enter into eternal life—the chief blessing awaiting the pilgrim people at their heavenly shrine. Every decision, every action prepares for and promotes that pilgrimage to the end (Heb. 10:32—12:29; James 1:2-4, 12; 1 Pet. 1:1, 6-9; 2:11-12; 2 Pet. 1:4-11).

PROPHETIC INTERPLAY

The ethics of the general letters are positioned within the New Testament canon to check and balance the ethics of the Pauline corpus. It is impossible to show this extensive interplay at every point; however, one such interplay—between Paul and James—continues to attract attention, and we will take up that interplay here. In many ways, it reflects the canonical conversation between Paul and the rest of the "pillars" of the Church.

Most treatments of Paul and James set them at odds with the other in recomposing what probably was a historical contest or misunderstanding between the two leaders or their disciples.[35] The net result would be "Paul *versus* James," for the two certainly bear two different kinds of *ethoi*. Paul's ethic builds upon human freedom and divine grace in such a way that tends toward antinomianism if not corrected by his own "law of the Spirit" and appeals to imitate the traditions of Christ. James, however, clearly builds upon doing works as the essential data of faith (2:8–13). Works, for James, follow from a law that liberates (1:25; 2:12), and whose content intends to care for the poor by treating everyone equally (2:9); indeed, he keeps the validity of the Torah open and refuses to subordinate it to the requirements of faith (2:14–26). It is in the important "faith and works" passage of 2:14–26 that James specifically takes up some of the "slogans" of Pauline Christianity. Specifically what concerns James here is an arrogant if not self-righteous commitment to *sola fide* (2:24) whose only manifestations are confessions of piety (2:15, 2:19). James's understanding of religious faith extends to points of human need (1:27); law is valid because it construes actions that liberate humans from need. Further, James wishes to make obedience to the "law of liberty" redemptive not only socially but eschatologically as well (2:13). This follows from the eschatological character of James's moral materials (paraenesis): to be blessed and receive the "crown of (eternal) life" (1:12) demands that one obey the Law (1:25), which sets forth those works that justify (2:24–5) at the endtime judgment of the coming Lord (5:7–9).

Against James, Paul argues that liberty and eschatological well-being result from faith in Christ alone (Rom. 3:21–31; Gal. 2:15–21). Further, he redefines and re-presents Torah in terms of Christ; in fact, he replaces Torah by Christ (Rom. 10:4) and argues against "works of the Law" (Gal. 3:10). "Good deeds" (Eph. 2:10; esp., Pastoral Letters) are the natural consequence of faith and certainly *not* its content, as James would have it. It is possible (and perhaps important) to ground these differences in Paul within the scope of his Gentile mission,[36] and it is certainly possible that James is not responding to the historical Paul but to a sectarian group of Paulinists who have taken his Gentile gospel to a radical and non-Pauline end. However, within the context of our common book there exists a real tension between the two, for the legalistic tendencies of James do not easily coexist with the antinomian tendencies of Paul.

The tension, when engaged canonically, becomes a self-correcting conversation that serves and shapes the Church in a positive manner. One need survey the history of the Church (esp. Protestant) to recognize her tendency toward a "Pauline canon within the Canon": it organizes ethics and theology around the central convictions of Paul's gospel. James is largely abandoned, or as in Luther's case, rejected as an "epistle of straw." The result often leads to the very thing James condemns—an orthodoxy that manifests itself by empty though well-meaning confessions of piety and a disregard for the social conditions of humans.

It must be admitted that in correcting this tendency toward a dead orthodoxy, the Church has often over-reacted by replacing personal forms of faith with an activism similar to the one advocated by James's law of liberty. Such commitments to an orthopraxy of a social gospel sometimes deny or at least lose interest in the story of God's grace revealed on Christ's cross, which can only lead toward legalism (however socially construed) and theological impoverishment. A religion emptied of its story and shaped only by society's needs is left open to (and unprotected from) those sets of ideas that pervert the story itself. This would mean, of course, the end of faith. It is a liability of any religion that places ethics over theology; it is this liability that is corrected by Paul, who places theology over ethics. Indeed, orthopraxy of the very kind to which James calls the Church must flow from a vital commitment to a gracious God who redeems a sinful world through the redeeming work of his Christ. Good deeds are crucial, but they must be a reflection of good news. Good news is central; but receiving it by faith should always be extended into a world desperate for social and spiritual salvation. The self-correcting dialectic of Paul *and* James leads the Church to a balanced, biblical ethic rooted in both divine grace and human responsibility.

Revelation

Canonical Context

Revelation is both the final book and the final canonical group of the New Testament. It as an *apocalypse* (1:1) that classifies both its literary genre and its theology; the New Testament contains no other writing like it, although there are bits of the Gospels (Jesus' apocalyptic sermon) and pieces of the Letters (1 Thess. 4–5; 2 Pet. 3) that carry similar language and theological materials. For this reason, perhaps, the early church did not easily accept Revelation as canonical. As late as the Reformation, Martin Luther resisted its authority even as he did James. Even today, many communities of faith shy away from using it because it seems too odd, too incoherent to be useful in informing faith and practice. When it is used by the church, it often is abused, creating an atmosphere of fear or fanaticism. We want to suggest, however, that in knowing *how* Revelation functions as the final book of the New Testament canon in turn helps shape our understanding of biblical ethics.

Logically, Revelation comes last because its content concerns the last days. The symbolic features of the book suggest that all reality ought to be organized by the future when "plain talk" rather than symbol will be the norm (cf. John 16:25; 1 Cor. 13:9–12). In fact, unlike Jewish apocalypses, Revelation speaks *only* about the "last things" begun with the exaltation of Christ and ending with the theocracy. Indeed, Revelation speaks of endings even as Genesis speaks of beginnings and thus even as Genesis begins the Church's canon, so Revelation ends it.

Yet, it seems more useful to speak of Revelation's canonical function in terms of *conclusions* rather than endings; the difference is a subtle one. When one speaks about conclusions, generally one refers to the last part of a story that gives meaning to the whole; whereas an ending refers to a final product or a finished story. Revelation is best understood as the conclusion of the sacred story that is told in order for it to find its whole meaning. Thus, where Genesis speaks of evil, Revelation speaks of exodus; where Genesis introduces us to promise, Revelation speaks of fulfillment; where Genesis introduces human history, Revelation describes the completion of humanity's salvation. The Babel narrative in Genesis describes the final spread of evil from personal (Caan) to the structures of the human community, and Revelation concludes the history of evil by indicting the evil dominion. Genesis interfaces the histories of Israel and creation, and Revelation paints the portrait of God's final triumph, which establishes new Israel in new Jerusalem; the garden of Eden, which introduces the believing community to God's dream and to its hope, is finally revisited as new

Israel enters once and for all the garden of new Jerusalem. Yahweh is victor!

In reading Revelation as canonical conclusion, theological and ethical materials emerge of a critical kind. Theologically, God is confessed not only as alpha but as omega; he is savior and judge; he is promise-giver and promise-fulfiller. The Church's future merges with God's dream for Israel and for his creation. *Maranatha* becomes the Church's confession because it marks out not only God's triumph but her own. Thus, ethically, the Church's ethos is written and lived against the future of God's story, which is told with promise and with certain hope of fulfillment. *Imitatio Christi* intermingles with the confession of *Maranatha* as a shout of victory; we boldly and courageously follow Christ to the garden of New Jerusalem, because we know the story's conclusion.

ETHICAL CONTENT

Two foci are critical for recovering Revelation's moral programme. In his greeting to the seven churches (chaps. 2–3), John encourages *faithfulness to the risen Lord.* The demand is crystal clear: whether suffering because of obedience or prospering because of disobedience, each church is called to imitate the various characteristics of Christ's life enlisted there. It is against that standard that all of humanity will be judged (20:12ff). This eschatological situation of judgment is the second focus. The dynamic of Revelation's ethics is this: *imitatio Christi* in order to escape God's judgment of the evil dominion and find his goodness on his coming day.

The imprint of Christ's life is discovered throughout the vision. Conversely, we see the gross and exaggerated descriptions of evil work as a kind of "vice list" that is to be avoided if life is to be found on the future Day of the Lord. The way to salvation is by heroic faithfulness and sacrificial obedience to the *imitatio Christi* demand. Because Revelation is apocalyptic, the reader expects its extensive treatment of evil. The evil kingdom with which the forces of God are engaged in cosmic and earthly struggle is at once systemic (chaps. 17–18) and personal (chap. 13). That is, evil is everything above and below that opposes God's salvation and corrupts his creation. Evil is deceitful, seeking to turn people away from God often in the most subtle and engaging manner (chap. 17). It should be noted that John's vision construes evil in structural ways as well as in personal ways—an economic system that demands allegiance to money and "things," or a political agenda that secures its shalom by violence and triumphantly lauds itself as "peace-maker," or a religious institutionalism that promotes ritual rather than devotion are part of an evil dominion opposed to God and his Lamb. Jezebel, Beast, Prophet, and Merchant and the systems they organize are against God's will and await their destruction on the future Day. They are paradigms of immorality that the churches ought to resist.

Thus, the moral paradigm arising from Revelation is essentially dualistic and fundamental: *imitatio Christi* and do not follow that or those who are against God's redemption of creation.

PROPHETIC INTERPLAY

Even today, scholars insist that apocalyptic carries no moral agenda with it;[37] it is so occupied with the End that it is unconcerned with ethical concerns that arise from the present. It is an "interim ethic" at best, emptied of any lasting importance for the Church. In fact, in more radical apocalyptic communities, the ethos can be antinomian and not merely amoral; an overt concern for the future results in almost no concern for the present, which is polluted and passing away—a fatalism that can collapse into self-righteous forms of narcissism. Such an escape from reality can lead the other way as well; it is not uncommon to find a legalistic concern for an imminent end built around codes of right conduct geared toward making one morally ready for Christ's return. In neither of these extremes does one find any commitment to human history or for a social ethic. Apocalyptic allows for an escape into the future and from present moral obligations.

There are checks to these abuses even within Revelation. John is a realist.[38] He could see in his world the imprint of evil; he could see a world that needed a dose of grace to control evil. This has already been found in the Lamb of God and will be realized at his future coming; however, this does not authorize ethical escape. John never removes the Church from the battle waged against evil. The Church is called to bear witness of God's grace and his final victory in the midst of evil—that is her moral task and obligation, and it is by obeying the *imitatio Christi* demand that the Church does precisely that.

What John empowers by his apocalypse is a reminder for those who experience the byproducts of the demonic dominion to trust in God's gospel, to hope for his Day, and to obey his will at all costs. Moral decisions are made and they are motivated in light of that memory.

One might wish to chide those who advocate exclusively an apocalyptic theology (Hal Lindsey); however, Revelation's emphasis on God's future triumph over evil does remind us that history has a conclusion and it is under the aegis of God. God's story is not preoccupied with the present moment or with the past work of the Christ and history of Israel. Further, the optimism of liberalism, the naive support of institutions, the construing of evil in personalistic rather than in systemic terms are all corrected by apocalyptic's historical pessimism. Unguarded optimism is unfounded when it is rooted exclusively in human or historical evolution; Revelation bids us to ground our perceptions in a reality where evil and good slug it out together and where evil sometimes seems to be winning. Revelation also bids us, armed with these realistic perceptions, to do battle against evil as preparation for God's final triumph.

Conclusion

This chapter has plowed new ground and there is much work that must be done to harvest its crop. We have resisted the temptation to work with a core of themes that tends toward prescriptionism and away from the dynamic and risk of decision making. It is hoped that our work provides a context for *reflection* upon the biblical materials. It occurs to me that moral reflection, according to Scripture's own hermeneutics, is *midrashic*. The demands of the new situation led the biblical writers back to their authoritative traditions (oral and written) to find God's new word and will for them. *This movement from context to text is the fundamental structure for biblical ethics;* it is a *method* and not a code of rules. Indeed, God's will might be construed in terms of rules, but they are rules that arise only from the conversation between context and text, canon and community—a conversation that is "quality-controlled" by God's Spirit.

Such a method for utilizing a truly biblical ethics as the authorized resource for decisions is not without a focal point that centers the ongoing conversation between community and canon. Our study has suggested that the diversity of the New Testament moral paradigms is qualified by a singular demand—*imitatio Christi*. To live as the Church ought means to imitate Christ. Specific content to the demand emerges from the ongoing conversation between community and canon as text is adapted to new contexts under the aegis of Christ's Spirit. The Church's ethos, then, is christological; as God's people the purpose of our decisions must always be to yield a life that brings glory to God and redemption to a needy world and so continue the mission of the historical Jesus, who is our risen Lord.[39]

Notes

1. Two words, *ethos* and *ethic(s),* will appear in this chapter, and we intend to make a subtle distinction between them. By *ethos* we are speaking about the *character* or atmosphere of a tradition or a community that yields a kind of moral logic where certain actions or decisions make sense. By *ethic(s)* we are speaking about the *characteristics* or norms that specify the content rather than the context of that moral logic.
2. Cf. James Barr, *Fundamentalism* (Philadelphia: The Westminster Press, 1978), pp. 50–59.
3. For an excellent survey and critique of canonical criticism, see Frank A. Spina, "Canonical Criticism: Childs versus Sanders," in *Interpreting God's Word for Today: An Inquiry into Hermeneutics from a Biblical Theological Perspective,* W. McCown and J. E. Massey, eds. (Anderson, Ind.: Warner Press, 1982), pp. 165–94.
4. For an interesting discussion between Childs (and Sanders) and those advocating the critical orthodoxy, see "Part Two," *HorBT* 2 (1980), pp. 113–211.
5. Spina, in discussing Childs and Sanders, suggests that Childs views Scripture as a literary *product* of the canonizing process, and it is this literary product that ought to be elevated by the Church as the singular object of exegesis. Its final arrangement as canonical literature, then, becomes normative, whereas Sanders finds the Church's unwritten hermeneutics within the *history* of the canonical *process;* 185ff. Sanders's insight lies behind the section titled "Prophetic Interplay," while Childs's insight lies behind what we have called "Canonical Context."
6. It will be assumed that the reader is familiar with a good New Testament introduction such as W. G. Kümmel, *Intro-*

duction to the New Testament (Nashville: Abingdon Press, 1966), for the various historical and literary features shaping each New Testament book.

7. James D. G. Dunn, *Unity and Diversity in the New Testament,* (Philadelphia: The Westminster Press, 1977), pp. 369–88 esp.
8. For this feature in the history of the canonical process, see J. A. Sanders, "Adaptable for Life: The Nature and Function of Canon," in *Magnalia Dei: The Mighty Acts of God,* F. M. Cross, W. E. Lembke, and P. D. Miller, eds. (Garden City: Doubleday and Co., 1976), pp. 531–60.
9. Cf. J. A. Sanders, *God Has a Story Too* (Philadelphia: Fortress Press, 1978).
10. John Calvin, *Commentary on the Gospel According to John* (Edinburgh: Calvin Translation Society, 1847), p. 22.
11. Most notably advocated in American scholarship by Jack Dean Kingsbury, *Matthew: Structure, Christology, Kingdom* (Philadelphia: Fortress Press, 1975), pp. 40–83, and his subsequent commentary, *Matthew* (Proclamation Commentaries, Philadelphia: Fortress Press, 1977), pp. 30–57.
12. John P. Meier, *The Vision of Matthew* (New York: Paulist Press, 1978), pp. 222–39.
13. Günther Bornkamm, "End-Expectation and Church in Matthew," in *Traditions and Interpretation in Matthew* (Philadelphia: The Westminster Press, 1963), and Kingsbury, *Matthew,* pp. 58–77, and *The Parables of Jesus in Matthew 13* (London: SPCK, 1976).
14. See Krister Stendahl, *The School of St. Matthew and Its Use of the Old Testament* (Philadelphia: Fortress Press, 1968), who suggests that Matthew's function is similar to Qumran's *Manual* and early Christianity's *Didache* in that it was used as a teaching tool for instructing young converts. The five extended sermons in Matthew (chaps. 5–7, 10, 13, 18, 24–5) might be understood as catechetical, addressing young disciples and stressing the essentials of Christian discipleship; cf. B. W. Bacon, *Studies in Matthew* (New York: Holt, 1930).
15. Due to considerations of space, Mark will be bypassed, even though recent studies have it carrying its own theological

and ethical agenda; cf. Eduard Schweizer, *The Good News According to Mark* (Atlanta: John Knox Press, 1970).
16. Robert B. Sloan, Jr., *The Favorable Year of the Lord: A Study of Jubilary Theology in Luke's Gospel* (Austin: Schola Press, 1977).
17. Robert North, *Sociology of the Biblical Jubilee* (Rome: Pontifical Biblical Institute, 1954).
18. Cf. Paul S. Minear, *To Heal and to Reveal: The Prophetic Vocation According to Luke* (New York: Seabury Press, 1976).
19. J. A. Sanders, "From Isaiah 61 to Luke 4," in *Christianity, Judaism and Other Greco-Roman Cults,* J. Neusner, ed. (Leiden: E. J. Brill, 1975), pp. 75–106.
20. C. F. Evans, "The Central Section of St. Luke's Gospel," in *Studies in the Gospels,* D. E. Nineham, ed. (London: Blackwell, 1955), pp. 37–53.
21. Contrast, for instance, the synoptic trajectory of the Lord's love demand as comprehensively set forth by John Piper, "*Love your Enemies,*" SNTS 38, (Cambridge: University Press, 1979), and the Johannine trajectory as summarized by Birger Gerhardsson, *The Ethos of the Bible* (Philadelphia: Fortress Press, 1981), pp. 93–116.
22. Paul Ramsey, *Basic Christian Ethics* (New York: Scribners, 1950), and his splendid article, "The Biblical Norm of Righteousness," *Interp* 24 (1970), pp. 419–29; critique of his "rule-agapism" is given by Dewey Hoitenga, "Development of Paul Ramsey's Ethic," GorR 11 (1970), pp. 282–90.
23. F. F. Bruce, *The Book of Acts,* from *NICNT* (Grand Rapids: Wm. B. Eerdmans Publishing Co., 1954), pp. 15–17.
24. Luke T. Johnson, *The Literary Function of Possessions in Luke-Acts,* SBLDS 39, (Missoula: Scholars Press, 1977); Walter E. Pilgrim, *Good News to the Poor* (Minneapolis: Augsburg, 1981).
25. The classic statement is by Hans Conzelmann, *The Theology of St. Luke,* (New York: Harper, 1960); but see A. J. Mattill, Jr., *Luke and the Last Things* (Dillsboro, N.C.: Western North Carolina University Press, 1979) for critique and moderation of Conzelmann's position.
26. J. A. Sanders, "Torah and Paul," in *God's Christ and His*

People, J. Jervell and W. A. Meeks, eds. (Oslo: Universitetsforlaget, 1977), pp. 132–40.

27. But, unconvincingly, F.O. Francis, "The Form and Function of the Opening and Closing Paragraphs of James and 1 John," *ZNW* 61 (1970), pp. 110–26; cf. W.G. Doty, *Letters in Primitive Christianity* (Philadelphia: Fortress Press, 1973), pp. 70–71.
28. It should be admitted that the arrangement of the critical text follows from the Vulgate; the history of canonical arrangements leading to the Vulgate shows much variety (cf. J. Moffatt, *Introduction to the Literature of the New Testament* (Edinburgh: T&T Clark, 1918), pp. 13–21. The Greek fathers ordered the Letters by historical considerations whereas the Latin fathers ordered the Letters by theological considerations; we continue to be shaped by those theological considerations that lie behind the Vulgate's arrangement.
29. So Victor P. Furnish, *Theology and Ethics of Paul* (Nashville: Abingdon, 1968).
30. Doty, pp. 37–39.
31. Christian Beker, *Paul the Apostle* (Philadelphia: Fortress Press, 1981) for a recent, full-scale treatment of Paul's theology and ethics as apocalyptic.
32. See Peter Richardson, *Paul's Ethic of Freedom* (Philadelphia: The Westminster Press, 1979).
33. See Ralph P. Martin, *Reconciliation: A Study of Paul's Theology* (Atlanta: John Knox Press, 1980), for the relational dimensions of Pauline theology.
34. William G. Johnsson, "The Pilgrimage Motif in the Book of Hebrews," *JBL* 97 (1978), pp. 239–51; also, his commentary on Hebrews (Atlanta: John Knox Press, 1981), for an extended treatment of pilgrimage motif and its ethical implications for the paraenetic sections of the book.
35. The literature treating the James and Paul debate over faith and works is enormous; the reader can find bibliographies in the standard introductions to James. While disagreeing strongly with his positions, I have benefited from Jack T. Sanders, *Ethics in the New Testament* (Philadelphia: Fortress Press, 1975), pp. 115–28. Not found in the standard bibliographies but an article worth reading is William Dyr-

ness, "Mercy Triumphs over Justice: James 2:13 and the Theology of Faith and Works," *Themelios* 16 (1981), pp. 11–16.

36. See Krister Standahl, *Paul Among Jews and Gentiles* (Philadelphia: Fortress Press, 1976). pp. 1-77.
37. Most notably, Jack Sanders, *Ethics,* who argues that the entire New Testament is "mothered" (Käsemann's word) by apocalyptic and thus has no lasting influence, ethically speaking, for the Church.
38. See the superb closing chapter, "The Theology of the Book of Revelation," in G. B. Caird, *The Revelation of St. John the Divine,* HNTC (New York: Harper and Row, 1966), pp. 289–301, for this idea.
39. I have greatly benefited from ongoing conversations with my friends and colleagues, Eugene Lemcio and Frank Spina, both of whom continue to sharpen my thinking in matters related to this chapter. Especially important for the future of New Testament studies is Lemcio's excellent article, "The Gospel and Canonical Criticism," *BTB* XI (1981), pp. 114–22. His own synthesis serves as a programmatic study both for New Testament theology and ethics, and has been decisive for the method suggested in this chapter.

Jerry L. Mercer (Ph.D., School of Theology at Claremont), professor of preaching, Asbury Theological Seminary

Counterforce: A Review of Wesley's Ethics

IT WAS DURING the first flush of a Kentucky winter—dark gray skies, biting winds, swirling snow—that a sizable group huddled inside to hear the proposed budget of the Department of Human Resources. With dwindling federal aid and a pinched state budget, things looked rough for at least seventy-five thousand people in the commonwealth. At mid-morning all the statistics, proposals, and vested-interest speeches took human shape as a woman rose to ask a question. She had the look of a person in need—mismatched clothes, plain drawn face with unkempt hair, underdressed for the weather. "I am a poor mother," she said, biting her lips to fight embarrassment and angry tears. "It took me two hours by bus to get here this morning. I have no money for heat. My children are cold. What do I do?" A short awkward pause followed. Then a department head stepped up and said, "Let me tell you the history of all these cutbacks." My heart sank. That woman wanted heat, not history.

The tension created by that woman at the hearing is something like the tension I felt doing this assignment. To merely rehearse the ethics of John Wesley might be somewhat stimulating for an occasional scholar or an informed layperson, but it would do nothing for the kinds of people to whom Wesley ministered—the distressed, disturbed, and oppressed. Teaching ethics for over a decade and a half has tended to make me a bit cynical. After all, philosophers, ethicists, and department heads have used up untold gallons of ink and tons of paper writing about ethical problems. For the Christian, it seems as though Jesus stated the matter rather succinctly when he said that we are to love God with all we are and love our neighbors as ourselves. But looking at the books that line our shelves, it becomes painfully clear that we have trouble understanding, or doing, what the Nazarene said. Our confusion about how to interpret the seemingly obvious command of Christ is testimony to the difficult moral decisions we face. Whether or not John Wesley, an eighteenth-century revivalist, can help us out of our dilemma remains to be seen.

Wesley: The Practical Man

Actually Wesley did not develop a system or theory of Christian ethics.[1] He hardly had time, though he certainly was interested. After 1739, Wesley seemed constantly on the move as he became engaged in teaching, preaching, forming societies, and writing tracts, letters, and sermons. His amazing energy is in some way commented on by all of his biographers I have read.[2] The clear focus of his ministry was threefold: first, to reform the British Isles;

second, to awaken the Church of England to the glories of its evangelical past; and third, to spread his understanding of God's holy love everywhere he could.[3] No one can accuse Wesley of having small goals!

The upshot of all this is simply that even Wesley had to sleep sometime, which meant that something of his Christian concern had to go begging. There were not enough hours in his day to allow him to do more than give selected advice on how Christians ought to behave. But this he did with as much fervor as he could muster. For example, the "General Rules" give us a hint of what he expected from "Methodists." The rules can be summarized easily: (1) Avoid all the evil you can. (2) Do all the good you can. (3) Attend the means of grace.[4] But under each of these concise headings is a formidable list of specifics. The details need not concern us here, for in some instances they are definitely eighteenth-century concerns. The larger teachings, though, are timeless.

The journals and sermons show that Wesley was no armchair quarterback.[5] He was active in relief work, particularly among the poor. He authored a fairly good book on home medical remedies, notwithstanding the dubious suggestion that applying electric shock to bald heads may grow hair. He was opposed to ruthless competition in business, unrestrained consumption of alcohol, profane language, and gambling (especially horse racing). He supported free speech and opposed slavery. He occasionally condemned war. He did have his blind spots, however. An overview of the sermons shows a deeper concern for overeating than sexual immorality. Though he gave advice on family relations, he apparently did not take it. His own tragic marriage is a reminder of a great man's humanity—and sinfulness.

COUNTERFORCE

Eighteenth-century England was a good testing ground

for anybody's ethics. Overcrowded slums in the cities and large families among the poor bred widespread poverty and illiteracy. Sports were brutal and workers suffered exploitation. Child labor laws were nonexistent and the children fared little better than the live geese used to clean chimneys. Mine workers entered the tunnels before daybreak and came out after sundown. Historian Dorothy Marshall observes that it was "a hard, harsh world for the mass of English people . . . a world singularly devoid of pity."[6] By almost any standard it was a society in desperate need of fellow-feeling and social justice. The upper class had its elaborate parties, fox hunts, and formally attired bare-bosomed ladies. The poor, which is to say the majority, lived in pubs that were generously stationed on garbage-strewn streets.[7] The counterforce proposed by Wesley for this ragged society was so simple that it must have seemed impossible, particularly in the light of a generally powerless national church. Wesley believed that positive change was possible if the love of God could be unleashed in the lives of sincere people.

While it is important to know that Wesley understood some of the problems of a society unable to keep its house in order, there was no way he could have anticipated a world like ours. The twentieth century, for all its technological advance, has been bathed in blood. Psychologist Bruno Bettelheim suggests that science has betrayed us, promising a better life but instead giving us mass death—typified by the death camps in Nazi Germany and the dropping of atomic bombs on Japan.[8] Author Carl Skrade says moderns have exchanged the biblical God of life for a contemporary god of death.[9] The idea of humanity turning on itself to destroy itself is now a commonplace theme in the arts, if not on Capitol Hill. One thing for sure: no one knows better than we how much the counterforce of love is needed today!

The crucial point for this essay is that while some of the

problems have changed and other have intensified, the way out of the morass is the same for us as for those who pondered Wesley's views. In general, Wesley's teachings were based on those of Jesus, and before him, the prophets, and before them, the Law. It is a depressing observation that most of us learn little or nothing from the past. Each generation seems destined to repeat (and magnify) the sins of the preceding one. This is why there is a tendency to lash out—to be irreverent—in a paper on ethics. We are frustrated because we seem unable to find a way of being that enhances our self-worth and benefits those around us. We care but don't care! We need an inner dynamic that will stabilize our fluctuating attitudes and energize our sympathies. Such, Wesley believed, was the gospel of love preached and lived by Jesus and the early church fathers. Such was what he proposed—and it seemed to work at times, if only in isolated instances.

Christian Existence

Wesley knew that doing flows from being.[10] So he did not often address the non-Christian world on matters of ethics except in his preaching of judgment. How can a "natural" person—one hardened to the reality of God's love—behave in a way acceptable to God? If one is bound by original sin, as Wesley believed, then the results of such a life are predictable. We know that a dead tree cannot produce live fruit. Nonetheless, Wesley believed that non-Christians did in fact exhibit compassion and perform righteous acts.[11] How? Because God in his mercy has given the world enough grace to enable it to live in relative peace. Such "prevenient grace" is necessary if sinful people are to live together above the law of tooth and claw, and if they are eventually to respond to the gospel and discover the well-spring of life.[12]

Properly speaking, then, pure ethics relates to the body

of Christ. Nonbelievers may do good but never properly do "good works," since these must flow from faith. But what matters if good is done anyway? It matters a great deal since, for Wesley, ethics is a part of the redemptive process, expressive of the social nature of divine love. Here we are talking about salvation, not in the short run, but in the long run. This is a style of life that draws its meaning from its Creator. Acknowledgement of the Creator and fidelity to his will are what keep ethical concerns from being only stop-gap measures. "Good works" are not so because the doer is good. To think this smacks of self-righteousness, a mind-set Wesley abhorred. No, good works are those works that link one's personal experience of undeserved mercy to the needs of others, and all to the glory of God. Good works are not options in the life of faith; they are the very stuff of faith.[13]

The extent to which Wesley and his immediate followers changed social conditions in England and America is a matter for historians to decide. What is important for us was Wesley's firm conviction that the Christian community must, as a matter of faith and salvation, enter redemptively into the lives of others. This process begins with individual commitment and speaks to the practice of social righteousness. Therefore, Christian life can be understood as a combination of "works of piety" and "works of mercy."[14] "Works of piety" are such as stoke the fires of faith. The most important of these "works," though surrounded by a host of others, is receiving the Holy Sacrament of our Lord's Supper. "Works of mercy" demonstrate nurture and care. The first of these is loving God with all you are. The second is loving your neighbor as yourself.

It would be interesting if, by some time-warp magic, Wesley could meet Mother Teresa of Calcutta. This lowly Roman Catholic nun who ministers to the dying is a good contemporary illustration of Wesley's ethical concern.

Born in Yugoslavia, Mother Teresa was raised in the warmth and security of a loving Catholic family. Her early devotion to the Church, inspired by the attractiveness of her own home life, turned her heart toward those who knew nothing of these advantages. After some searching she knew her vocation was to "the poorest of the poor" in India.

Mother Teresa seems to be an uncomplicated woman. Apparently she doesn't question Church authority (unlike Wesley), renounces typical Western standards of success without being judgmental, spends little time worrying about matters she cannot control, and lives each day in simple dependence on God while she lovingly embraces the castoffs of society. Her life revolves around the worship of God and the attempt to live out the implications of God's love in her chosen world of the streets and alleys of Calcutta.

Wesley would have understood this woman, for she embodies his own intense desire to see "works of piety" and "works of mercy" as one. They both would be in perfect agreement that Christian life and service operate solely on the basis of God's love. It is this incomprehensible divine love that provides the proper motive for service; indeed, it makes service to others attractive, regardless of their condition. It seems to me that if there is any hope for the Church and the world it will be in the recapturing of this holy love.

So, true discipleship stems from love—divine love—for such is the nature of the biblical God. Wesley did not believe in a passive God—a God who was not moved by human needs. Rather, he believed that God was vitally concerned and moved without prior invitation to involve himself directly in the life of his creation. He is a God whose heart melts at the pleadings of the wayward but whose blood runs hot wherever injustice and unrighteousness plague the lives of people. But even with the wicked,

God is patient beyond belief. This patience is not weakness because as surely as daylight follows darkness, the judgment of God will fall relentlessly on the workers of evil. God wants personal holiness and social justice. He bends over backward to favor those who long for him, but he mounts his terrible throne of judgment in preparation for those who spurn him—for to spurn the Creator means to take his creation lightly, and that is something God will not tolerate forever.

The Royal Law

In his sermon "The Way to the Kingdom," Wesley says that "true religion" has three dimensions: righteousness, peace, and joy.[15] By "righteousness" Wesley means that response to God's mercy that results in obedient living. Righteousness is God's love working in human attitudes and behavior. No wonder peace and joy flow from it! This great love has both God and the neighbor (understood as any person) as its proper objects. In a sermon dedicating City-Road Chapel, Wesley interprets the Methodist view of love.

> This love is the great medicine of life; the never-failing remedy for all the evils of a disorderd world. . . . This religion of love, and joy, and peace, has its seal in the inmost soul; but is ever showing itself by its fruits, continually springing up, not only in all innocence . . . but, likewise, in every kind of benefice—spreading virture and happiness to all around it.[16]

Love is a force for Wesley that, if not conquered, conquers all things. "Who," he reflects, "can tell the force of love?"[17] Here is the key thought to all Christian existence. If one is open to the living God, then *all* of life can be made new.

This love is never an academic matter; it must be experienced. This understanding of love binds together, in Wesley's thinking, salvation by faith and holy living. It is the increase of God's love in the human heart that enables persons to be pleasing to God and helpful to others. At its highest level it approximates even the love of God. "Christian perfection," Wesley writes, "is pure love filling the heart, and governing all the words and actions."[18] This is, in effect, the "royal law" (i.e., "In everything, do to others what you would have them do to you, for this sums up the Law and the Prophets").[19] Commenting on that saying, Wesley writes, "The whole (both law and prophets) is comprised in one word—Imitate the God of love."[20] This is the heart and soul of Christian ethics.

Wesley's concept of love comes primarily from two sources: the New Testament (particularly 1 John and selected teachings of Jesus) and early church fathers.[21] Wesley had a special affinity for the desert fathers and in following them he came to believe that there are two levels of love—one for the beginner in faith and one for the more advanced. For the desert fathers it would be the difference between the experience of a novice and that of an elder. All the while, though, during the process of learning more about the love of God and the limitations of one's self, both novice and elder were to live out the implications of love in their relationship with each other and, as far as possible, with the world. The essence of their faith was the singular desire to love and worship God and serve humanity. It was a semi-mystical experience of God that drove men and women to embrace a life-style of humility and service—odd at times, to be sure, but this experience always compulsively drove persons toward God.[22]

By temperament and conviction Wesley was a conservative. He accepted preseventeenth-century Protestant orthodoxy with few problems, except for his badgering of the Calvinists for their low view (from Wesley's standpoint) of holiness (personal righteousness). His main objection to their understanding of the operation of divine grace was not their denial of a two-step application of love (justification and Christian perfection), but the damming up of holy living in which he believed they frequently engaged. In spite of his own occasional rigidities, the dominance of love in Wesley's thought tends to allow for a kind of situational application. That is, there is a certain flexibility in love that precludes a too-narrow setting of boundaries. Love does not make its own rules. Love is the rule! Such love is cultivated in meditation and prayer, devoted to the God of Scripture, with an unbridled zeal to do good.

Foundations For Ethics

It is possible to suggest something of the sweep of this dynamic of love in five affirmations.

1. A real change takes place in anyone who commits his or her life to Jesus Christ. It is more than a change in position (imputed righteousness); it is a change in the person (imparted righteousness). This is the initial movement from sin (rebellion, pride) to saving grace. It is important to stress that human beings are not made acceptable to God on the merits of their lives or intentions. They are made acceptable to God on his terms (i.e., his own eternal love, which calls sinful people out of their condition and into his grace and peace).[23]

2. However, Christ's people still live with certain inner tensions that may impede spiritual progress and hinder holy living. Some of these tensions may be traced to emotional disorders, and for these a person ought to seek professional help. Others, though, are the result of ego-serving needs and require a better understanding and deeper application (or appropriation) of God's love. For example, most of us still tend to justify our behavior and resist humility; that is, we try to make ourselves look good when we are not and guiltless when we are guilty.

3. The evil (ego-serving drives) that hinders our freedom

to be in reality what we profess to be in faith can be negated by the power of God's love.[24] It is possible for great leaps of faith to occur and giant strides to be taken in experiencing God's love in our lives. For all of us, spiritual growth takes place as our self-justifications and questionable living are replaced with the nonself-seeking character of God's love. What is important here is to realize that spiritual freedom in love can be presently experienced in our lives. Love that is not self-conscious also frees us to be able to respond immediately and without deliberation to the needs of others. This is servanthood!

A note of caution is important here. God's call for us to participate in his love indicates his willingness to continually rid us of sinful tensions and replace them with that unbelievable love. However, it must be remembered that such transformation takes place in "vessels of clay." For example, in Wesley's tract "The Character of a Methodist," I think he may expect more of the Christian than is possible short of "the state of glory."[25] To admit our humanness is not to fault the grace of God but to face us at all times with the necessity of humility. The Spirit is constantly bringing sinful attitudes to our consciousness. Cleansing is in one sense a perpetual, if not happy, experience. Wesley suspicioned this when he suggested that even Christians mourn over their sins.[26] This attitude of Christian experience is important because we can never be sure of the purity of our motives. Therefore, to God alone be the glory!

4. Normally spiritual growth takes place best within a context of mutual love and support such as one finds in the body of Christ. The Church is a community of dedicated persons whose support and judgment can help us share God's love meaningfully with the world. The faithful help us with those disciplines that promote a sensitivity to God and people (i.e., prayer, contemplation, fasting, understanding Scripture, self-discovery, but above all, collective participation in the Holy Communion).

5. The love of God that brings freedom, as suggested numerous times already, operates not only in the realm of individual experience but also in the structures of society. After all, remembering Wesley's question "Who can tell the force of love?" the strong implication is that God's redemptive grace is offered to all and can be experienced by all.[27] The possibility of a righteous society always hides in the shadows of Wesley's understanding of love.

This notion of a just and righteous society represents either great faith in God's love or a delusion. Certainly as one reads the history of civilization—and the Church—it appears that to talk at all of redeeming the social order is to fly blindly into a brick wall. But at the very least it means this: that Christians are never satisfied with the status quo—that this is never the best of all possible worlds until we hear the heavenly voice say to all the earth, "Arise, shine, for your light has come, and the glory of the Lord rises upon you."[28] Wesley did believe in "social holiness." How far he would have carried it is another matter. Certainly his understanding of love forbids us to say to the divine power, "You can redeem everything—but this." And it also forbids us to turn away from human need.

What And So What!

Though fearful of "the world" (or social structures), Wesley lived his own style of monasticism right in the middle of it. He was definitely one of the secular clergy. It is true that Kingswood School (Wesley's contribution to private education) was located in a remote area, far from the temptations of city life. But his evangelistic thrusts and social ministries were largely directed at cities and towns. Early on, when the British Isles had been divided into ten districts to facilitate Methodist work, John and Charles were self-appointed as overseers of the London area. Wesley loved the city and wanted to bring God's grace to its people. Of course, much of his opposition came from them. I am convinced, contrary to some, that Wesley not so secretly hoped for a great urban revival.

One of Wesley's overlooked contributions in understanding the life of faith was his earnest attempt to keep vital Christianity within existing church structures. He was a Methodist in spirit only. He lived and died a priest of the Church of England. All of the structures he devised were disposable. Had the Church of England been receptive to the moving of God in the Wesleyan way, it never would have been divided, and the division subdivided and subdivided again! As a result of all this we presently have more than thirty distinctive churches, each claiming Wesley as some sort of father-in-God, yet totally unable to unify, each protecting self-interests in polity and shades of doctrine. It is no comfort that other traditions have no better track record. The splintering of faith into different groups has immense consequences for ethics, not the least of which is the reality that the Church is unable to effect change to the degree of its disunity.

The movement that best represented Wesley's concerns in the twentieth century was the social gospel movement, notwithstanding Walter Rauschenbusch's failure even to tip his hat in the Methodist direction. Admittedly, it is difficult now for us to appreciate the optimism engendered by the social gospel in this country. Although Rauschenbusch and his followers would be severely critized by the Niebuhrs for their dependence on late nineteenth-century continental rationalism, it was really the perfectionistic tendencies in the American spirit, born on the frontier by a Methodist midwife, that enabled the social gospel to challenge greedy capitalism at the turn of the century. The advances made then in better working conditions, collective bargaining, and education had Wesley's ethics for a great-grandfather.

In our time the zeal to do good received a serious setback with the eruption of World War I. Large-scale conflict with horrible weapons and widespread destruction "killed" any remaining perfectionistic tendencies in American theology. Sixty years later (after another world war and numerous limited wars—including Vietnam!) we have not been able to recapture the hope made popular by Wesley of personal *and* national renewal. Some Methodist groups have traded social renewal for premillennial eschatology and now seem content to "wait until Jesus comes."

The ethical concerns of John Wesley seem to be reappearing in what is popularly known as process theology. Process thought dares to insert the word *sainthood* into its working vocabulary of religious experience.[29] This sainthood is the result of a serious attempt to follow the call (lure) of God into the unknown future. It comes from impacting the mind with renewal attitudes and caring actions. It goes beyond classical liberalism in its total dependence on God's grace, accepting as it does the radical sinfulness of the human condition. Yet it hopes for the freedom to become a responsible, faithful person. Process thought has the world for its arena and personal and collective righteousness (justice) as its goal. Its naturalistic ground is decidedly weak compared with a biblical view of revelation, but in its response to the world it is very close to the teachings of our Lord and the energies of the Methodist tradition.

Agenda

Wesley was compelled to proclaim the saving grace of God, compelled because he believed that God's love could work miracles in the lives of persons and their societies. That his concerns, and those of his followers, seem to be highly individualistic at times may be somewhat justified on historical grounds. Nonetheless, the overwhelming implication of his theology of spiritual formation is that God's love can redeem all things—even the social order.

However, we are not now so optimistic. The continental theology of Karl Barth and Emil Brunner, plus the work of American thinkers like the Niebuhrs, have pulled moderns back to hard realities. Martin Luther King, Jr.'s movement from the theology of Walter Rauschenbusch to that of Reinhold Niebuhr is a parable of the times. We have seen too much. Experiences like those of the Jews in Hitler's Nazi Germany make us forever doubtful of human motives—and suspicious of human governments. The incredible abundance of nuclear arms in the world forces us to expect the whirlwind. Humankind seems bent on proving the early Freud right; that is, lodged deep in the human psyche is the desire to return to the void—to nothingness—and we seem determined to carry out that suicidal impulse.

The Church cannot watch this mad dash toward oblivion without saying something—doing something. We are tempted to do nothing but condemn. But Wesley, if not our Lord, will not let us do only that. God's grace is greater than human sin. The grave problems that face the world push the Church to return to its roots—complete trust in God's power and providence. We must, by God's help, emphasize the interior life, contemplation, and prayer. We must also, again with God's help, give ourselves to a life of servanthood—to good works. Only with these methods of the Spirit will renewal take place. Without them there is only darkness, and wailing, and gnashing of teeth.

One last word before closing. When my wife, Ruth, returned from a "working" missions trip to Belize, she brought home a poem on a poster she found crumpled up on a Sunday school room floor. The piece was written by Mawldyn Davies, a little girl about twelve years old. It is titled simply "Foodless Children."

Foodless children,
With stomachs puffed out,
Why do you have no food to eat?
Why do you beg?

Foodless children,
Suffering from starvation,
Why is your skin like paper?
Why do your bones poke out?

Foodless children,
Eaten up by disease,
Why not see a doctor?
Why not?

Foodless children,
You are so thin,
Your eyes are so appealing,
And you will soon be dead.

This is a Sunday school girl who has written this poem. No frills, no clichés, no overdrawn optimism—just life as she sees it. She is a "Methodist." A study of Wesley's ethics, or anyone else's for that matter, is justified only to the extent that his desire to meet people's needs becomes our mandate to help add a fifth stanza of caring love to the poem of this little girl.

Notes

1. Wesley's ethical concerns are communicated for the most part in his sermons and in selected tracts and "advices." Approximately one-third of the sermons are specifically concerned with ethics *per se*. His primary battles were theological, with special reference to the doctrines of original sin, assurance, and Christian perfection.
2. Still one of the best in terms of its emphasis on Wesley's ethics is Francis J. McConnell, *John Wesley* (New York: Abingdon Press, 1939), especially chapter 9, "Spreading Social Righteousness," pp. 231ff.

3. *Works of John Wesley* (Grand Rapids: Zondervan Publishing House, 1892), VIII, p. 299. Hereafter any reference to this source will be cited as *Works*.
4. *Works,* VIII, pp. 269ff.
5. It is impossible in this short paper to note the specifics of Wesley's ethical thought. For an introduction to his ethics I recommend the reading of his thirteen sermons on the Sermon on the Mount. At least there one can begin to grasp the theological and practical aspects of the Christian life. For an important book that attempts to relate some of Wesley's views to current problems, see Theodore Runyon, ed., *Sanctification and Liberation* (Nashville: Abingdon Press, 1981). Of special interest may be Dow Kirkpatrick's chapter, "A Liberating *Pastoral* for the Rich," pp. 209ff., in light of Wesley's conviction that the misuse of money was very high on the list of English sins (cf. "The Danger of Riches," *Works,* VII, pp. 3ff.; "The Use of Money," *Works,* VI, pp. 124ff.; cf. *Works,* VII, pp. 407–8; VII, pp. 244ff.).
6. Dorothy Marshall, *Eighteenth-century England* (New York: McKay, 1962), p. 243.
7. An interesting and highly readable book on social and cultural conditions in eighteenth-century England is J. H. Whiteley's *Wesley's England* (London: The Epworth Press, fourth edition, 1954).
8. Cf. Bruno Bettelheim, *Surviving and Other Essays* (New York: Alfred A. Knopf, 1979). This is a most important book by an internationally respected psychologist, especially in light of revived interest in the Holocaust.
9. Skrade's analysis of the modern mind-set is strengthened by examples drawn from the arts. Cf. Carl Skrade, *God and the Grotesque* (Philadelphia: The Westminster Press, 1974). Of particular interest to me is Ernest Becker's *The Denial of Death* (New York: The Free Press, 1973). This is a superb treatment of the human condition in the twentieth century.
10. Niebuhr suggests that Wesley held a "conversionist ethic." (Cf. H. Richard Niebuhr, *Christ and Culture* (New York: Harper and Row, 1951), pp. 218ff.) That is, converted people change social institutions; first, spiritual renewal of the individual, second, social renewal. For conversionist

themes in Wesley's thought, see "The Scripture Way of Salvation" (*Works,* VI, pp. 43ff.), "A Caution against Bigotry" (*Works,* V, pp. 479ff.), and "National Sins and Miseries" (*Works,* VII, pp. 400ff.).

11. For an interesting treatment of this theme, see Wesley's sermon "The Reformation of Manners" (*Works,* VI, pp. 149ff.). On the relation of faith to works, see William R. Cannon, *The Theology of John Wesley* (New York: Abingdon Press, 1956), pp. 145ff. Deschner has an important footnote discussing Wesley's view of the Law; cf. John Deschner, *Wesley's Christology* (Dallas: Southern Methodist University Press, 1960), pp. 112ff.
12. On "preventing grace" see *Works,* VI, p. 512.
13. Such "works" are never the ground of faith (*Works,* V, pp. 425ff.), nor do they store up merit (*Works,* VI, p. 148). However, they demonstrate sincerity (*Works,* V, pp. 210ff.) and cannot be omitted by the Christian (*Works,* VII, p. 131).
14. Wesley's theology of good works finds its clearest expression in the sermons "On Visiting the Sick" (*Works,* VII, p. 117) and "The Danger of Riches" (*Works,* VII, p. 3).
15. *Works,* V, pp. 78ff.
16. *Works,* VII, p. 424.
17. *Works,* VI, p. 117.
18. *Works,* XI, p. 401.
19. Matthew 7:12 (*New International Version*).
20. John Wesley, *Explanatory Notes upon the New Testament* (London: Epworth Press, 1958), p. 42.
21. On the influence of the early church fathers, see Albert C. Outler, ed., *John Wesley* (New York: Oxford University Press, 1964), pp. 9ff.; also Outler's chapter "The Place of Wesley in the Christian Tradition," in Kenneth E. Rowe's book by the same title (New Jersey: The Scarecrow Press, Inc., 1976), pp. 11ff.
22. The dynamic of Wesley's understanding of the life of love can be better understood after reading Thomas Merton, *The Wisdom of the Desert* (New York: New Directions, 1960), pp. 3–24. This helpful essay serves as a good introduction to the type of Christian thought that set the stage for Wesleyan mysticism, particularly with regard to the notion of Christian perfection.

23. Cannon's book (see note 11) attempts to understand Wesley's theology from the perspective of justification. See pp. 312ff. for a brief discussion of the concept of "real change," coupled with the doctrine of assurance. Helpful sermons would be "Salvation by Faith" (*Works,* V, pp. 7ff.), "Justification by Faith" (*Works,* V, esp. pp. 58ff.), and "The Marks of the New Birth" (*Works,* V, pp. 212ff.). The backdrop of justification, for Wesley, is the concept of original sin. See especially his tract on this subject in *Works,* IX, pp. 191ff.
24. I suggest a careful reading of the "Plain Account of Christian Perfection" in the *Works,* XI, pp. 366ff.; the sermon "Christian Perfection" (*Works,* VI, pp. 1ff.), and Harald Lindstrom's book *Wesley and Sanctification* (London: The Epworth Press, reprint 1956). Couple these readings with that suggested in note 22. These readings serve only as a meager introduction to a fruitful and controversial area of Wesley studies.
25. *Works,* VIII, pp. 339ff.
26. *Works,* V, pp. 253ff.
27. Wesley had a running quarrel with the Calvinists, who he thought restricted the saving grace of God. Cf. "On Predestination," *Works,* VI, pp. 225ff.
28. Isaiah 60:1
29. I have found the writings of John B. Cobb, Jr. very helpful at this point. Cobb's book *God and the World* (Philadelphia: The Westminster Press, 1969), pp. 115ff. is a good place to begin. Complementary readings from Cobb would be in *The Structure of Christian Existence* (Philadelphia: The Westminster Press, 1967), pp. 107-36 and *A Christian Natural Theology* (Philadelphia: The Westminster Press, 1965), pp. 246-51.

W. Stanley Johnson (Ph.D., Saint Louis University), professor of Christian history and thought, Western Evangelical Seminary

Christian Perfection as Love for God

THE MISSION to declare scriptural holiness challenges each generation to Methodism. It would be self-aggrandizing and false to imagine that only holiness voices proclaim such things, but it is not far-fetched to claim that certain nuances of expression habitually occur primarily within these circles. If one listens attentively, the terms *entire sanctification, Christian perfection, second definite work of grace, deliverance from inbred sin,* and *purity of heart* may be parsed from the grammar of holiness. This is all well and good, but after reexamining the bulk of Wesley's writings on perfection, it appears that his concept of love for God does not receive adequate treatment.[1] Although a recent rereading of holiness theologians[2] unveils a sketch of John Wesley's doctrine of love for God in relation to Christian perfection, the details and place of this panel in the mural of Wesleyan theology remains to be seen.[3]

The growing conviction that love for God is central to Wesley's idea of perfection stands in the uneasy company of a nagging suspicion that current theological literature and much preaching from the holiness pulpit have missed the Wesleyan and biblical emphasis upon love for God. The following material represents an attempt to clarify the nature and central role of the concept of love for God in Christian perfection according to Wesley's vision.

It must be acknowledged that a paranetic tone permeates this discourse. Mary Alice Tenney in her book *Blueprint for a Christian World* sets the stage for us as she describes the "dominant disposition" of the Methodist: "It was love-love to God, expressed in complete obedience to His will, and love for men, expressed in tireless service to all in need."[4] The Church today needs to review, reappropriate, and proclaim the privilege and responsibility to love God. This mandate cannot be overlooked without detracting from the vitality of the faith and life of our movement.

In the material that follows, we will consider first, the centrality of love for God in Wesley's concept of perfection, and second, the grounds of love for God. These grounds are God's prior love for humanity, human knowledge of God, and our love for and faith in God. Third, we will consider the nature of love for God under the following headings: love for God as passion and affection, love for God as changeable, love for God as an "expulsive power." Fourth, we will examine the God who is loved, and the relation of love for God to love for others.

Finally, I will propose two broadly stated implications of Wesley's concept of love for God as I conceive its application to the holiness movement today.

The Centrality Of Love For God In John Wesley's Doctrine Of Christian Perfection

One of the most crucial texts[5] in the literature of John Wesley quotes Jesus directly: "Thou shalt love the Lord thy God with all thy heart, and with all thy soul, and with all thy mind. This is the first . . . commandment. And the second is like unto it, Thou shalt love thy neighbor as thyself. On these two commandments hang all the law and the prophets" (Matt. 22:37–40).

Unlike the anthropocentric understandings of this text that dissolve the first commandment into the second[6] or dismiss it as hopelessly outmoded because it is linked to an ephemeral eschaton,[7] Wesley thrusts the first into prominence throughout the *Plain Account of Christian Perfection* and other key passages of this theological literature. In answer to the question "What is Christian perfection?" he responds,

> *The loving God* with all our heart, mind, soul and strength. This implies that no wrong temper, none contrary to love, remains in the soul; and all the thoughts, words and actions are governed by pure love.[8]

Wesley's "abridgment" of the twofold commandment is significant. He cuts across the grain of all theologians who produce anthropologies of love, forthrightly insisting that the Christian is perfected *primarily* in love for God. A *theology* of love is intended. To another question, "What command is there" for Christian perfection or entire sanctification? he answers,

> "Be ye perfect, as your Father who is in heaven is perfect." (Matthew v. 48) (2) "Thou shalt love the Lord thy God with all thy heart, and will all thy soul, and with all thy mind." (Matthew. xii, 37.) But if the love of God fill all the heart, there can be no sin there.[9]

There is nothing more important than love; indeed, Wesley affirms there is "nothing else."

> You should be thoroughly sensible of this,—"the heaven of heavens is love." There is nothing higher in religion; there is in effect, nothing else; if you look for anything but more love, you are looking wide of the mark, you are getting out of the royal way.[10]

Wesley's vision of love for God as the apex of Christian religion is clearly reflected in these representative passages. Wesley believes that faith in God leads to a knowledge of God and that both faith and knowledge become the ground for the self's genuine love for God.

REASCENDING FIRE

The *descent* of God's love to human selves makes possible the ascent of human love for God. Wesley sweeps aside any notion that love for God can erupt out of the resources of the *unaided* human self. His vivid imagery leaves no doubt about this: "The fire of divine love has this advantage over material fire, that it can reascend to its source, and raise thither with it all the good works that it produces."[11] In more traditionally biblical language the same truth emerges:

> We must love God, before we can be holy at all; this being the root of all holiness. Now we cannot love God, till we know he loves us. "We love him, because he first loved us." And we cannot know his pardoning love to us, till his Spirit witnesses to our spirit. Since, therefore, this testimony of his Spirit must precede the love of God and all holiness, of consequences it must precede our inward consciousness thereof, or the testimony concerning them."[12]

For Wesley, this does not imply that the love that returns to God is merely a product of divine cause. Anders Nygren errs seriously at this point when he asserts that the proper understanding of *agape* in the New Testament excludes the action of the self's love for God as an act of a free moral agent.[13] While Wesley grounds love for God in prior movement of divinity, he does not deny the properly active role of the self's love for God.

Love For God Requires Knowledge Of God

Love for God as Wesley understands it is an impossibility without the close fellowship and true knowledge of God himself. Wesley laments the religion of the world that substitutes "doing no harm," "doing good . . . being charitable," "using the means of grace" for genuine spiritual worship. He attacks this error forcefully:

> But will this satisfy him who hungers after God? No. . . . the knowledge of God in Christ Jesus; "the life which is hid with Christ in God;" the being "joined unto the Lord in one spirit;" the having "fellowship with the Father and the Son;" the "walking in the light as God is in the light;" the being purified even as He is pure;" this is the religion, the righteousness, he thirsts after: Nor can he rest, til he thus rests in God.[14]

Knowledge of God includes, for Wesley, an element of immediate encounter with God: "The soul could not . . . 'bide in the love of God' without a direct witness of the Spirit to sanctification."[15] Prayer becomes a matter of knowing God intimately. Wesley instructs converts to "see that it be thy one design to commune with God."[16] Such communion in the love of God experiences a continual sense of spiritual "presence."

> The life of God in the soul of the believer . . . implies the continual inspiration of God's Holy Spirit; God's breathing into the soul, and the soul's breathing what it first receives from God . . . an increasing presence of God, the loving, pardoning God . . . and an increasing of love, promise, and prayer.[17]

The "increasing presence of God" grounds love for

God, since he is "the Sole End as well as Source, of your Being."[18] The pure in heart enjoy "such a near approach as cannot be expressed. They see him; as it were, face to face, and talk with him, as a man talketh with his friend;—a fit preparation for those mansions above, wherein they shall see him as he is."[19]

The Relation Of Faith And Love

For Wesley, love must be grounded in trust of the beloved. The "victory that overcometh the world" is faith, but not bare faith. Wesley writes, "But here let no man deceive his own soul. It is diligently to be noted, the faith which bringeth not forth repentance, and love, and all good works, is not that right living faith, but a dead and devilish one."[20]

Wesley does not collapse love into faith. The significant, but erroneous, idea that "faith is love towards God, but a love of which the keynote is receptivity, not spontaneity"[21] is foreign to Wesley's thought. He speaks of love that "engrosses the whole heart," "takes up all the affections," and leads one to "desire God." Such love, Wesley says, leads believers to rejoice in him" and "to have such a possession of God as makes us always happy." Our Anglican "enthusiast," or so he was labeled by many more passive intellectuals, gained his reputation for zeal and fervor in part by believing that the true Christian is one who actively demonstrates love for God.

Love For God Includes Eros

Some theologians within Christendom have been wary of the identification of passion for God, eros, and love of God. Nygren is adamant that eros has nothing to do with Christian agape, while Kierkegaard emphasizes the *duty* of loving God ("you *shall* love").[22] Passions and feelings do not have permanence and fall short of the eternal character of love. Wesley does not share this degree of reservation about emotions, passions, and feelings. He continually pictures the Christian as one who desires God and who is in love with God in such a way that all the capacities or faculties of human personality are involved. When he explains what is "implied in the being altogether a Christian" he says;

> First. The Love of God. For thus saith his word, "Thou shalt love the Lord thy God, with all thy heart, and with all thy soul, and with all thy mind, and all thy strength." Such a love is this, as engrosses the whole heart, as *takes up all the affections,* as fills the entire capacity of the soul, and employs the utmost of all its faculties.[23]

Of such a Christian Wesley affirms, "All his desire is unto God . . . there is none upon earth that I desire beside thee."[24] This desire for God is one that not only involves all the passions and affections of the soul, but results in "a possession of God" that is true happiness:

> Now to love God in the manner the Scripture describes; in the manner God himself requires of us, and by requiring engages to work in us,—is to love him as the ONE God; that is, 'with all our heart, and with all our soul, and with all our mind, and with all our strength; '—it is to desire God alone for his own sake; and nothing else, but with reference to him;—to rejoice in God;—to delight in the Lord; not only to seek, but find, happiness in him, as our God and all;—in a word, to have such a possession of God as makes us always happy.[25]

In Wesley's way of thinking, the whole person participates in loving God. Various thinkers elevate intellect, or feeling, or will as the central human capacity, but Wesley refuses to reduce human nature to a single trait.

Affections Are Involved

The importance of the affections is noticed when Wesley

considers the marks of those who are only partially perfected in love for God. Carnal Christians, writes Wesley,

> know they do not love the Lord their God with *all* their heart, and mind, and soul, and strength . . . when they pour out their souls in secret to Him who seeth all the thoughts and interests of their heart, they are continually ashamed of their wandering thoughts, or of the deadness and dullness of their affections; yet there is no condemnation to them still, either from God or from their own heart.[26]

The affections are, for Wesley, an important indicator of the perfection of love. "Deadness and dullness" are evidence of less than perfect love. He certainly disagrees with any who propose to love God "disinterestedly."

Wesley asserts that the hunger and thirst for righteousness is satisfied only in love for God, adding, "Give me love, or else I die!" Wesley asks rhetorically if it is true that

> the keeping the outward commandment is all that is implied in loving God with all your heart, with all your mind, and soul, and strength, and in loving your neighbour as yourself? that the love of God is not an affection of the soul, but merely an outward service?[27]

He answers his question vehemently, "To mention so wild an interpretation of the Apostle's words, is sufficiently to confute it."[28]

The flame of revival kindled the feelings of many with the approval of Wesley. He would not deny his broad parish the strong feelings of an affectionate love for God. To those who feared such open piety he only affirmed the richness of his own devotional experience as one instance among many of his companions.

Love Endures But May Change

There is no guarantee that love for God will always remain the same. It may change, as Kierkegaard also notes in *Works of Love*. Speaking of the last days in his *Explanatory Notes*, Wesley quotes Matthew 24:12: "And because iniquity shall abound, the love of many will wax cold." He warns, "The generality of those who love God will, like the church at Ephesus (Revelation ii.4), leave their first love."[29] When one examines the comment he offers on Revelation 2:4 in the *Notes*, one sees how changeable love is.

> *But I have against thee, that thou hast left thy first love*-that love which all that church was so eminent when St. Paul wrote his epistle to them. He need not have *left* this. He might have retained it entire to the end. And he did retain it in part, or there could not have remained so much of what was commendable in him. But he had not kept, as he might have done, the first tender love in its vigour and warmth. Reader, hast thou?[30]

Love for God had been a chief mark of this early church. They lost it, but they needn't have lost it. Throughout the vicissitudes of the soul, human commitment to God on the moral level accompanies and stabilizes immediate states of feeling. Wesley writes,

> The mind itself may be deeply distressed, may be exceeding sorrowful, may be perplexed and pressed down by heaviness and anguish, even to agony, while the heart cleaves to God by perfect love, and the will is wholly resigned to him. Was it not so with the Son of God himself?[31]

The work of the Spirit penetrates deep into the marrow of the personality. The self's mind, passion, and moral nature all join in united expression of adoration and love to God. There is no aspect of human nature untouched by the perfection of love. The whole self is devoted to God.

Love For God Is The Dynamic Of Holiness

Love for God is the principle dynamic that, as a fire, burns up the dross of sin. Wesley instructs those who have not been perfected in love that "nothing should remain in thy heart but the pure love of God alone? Be of good cheer! Thou shalt love the Lord thy God, with all thy heart, and mind, and soul, and strength."[32] In the "Preface" to *Explanatory Notes upon the Old Testament,* Wesley describes a sequence that suggests that love works this cleansing process:

> This scriptural knowledge will lead you "to love him, because he hath first loved us;" yea, "to love the Lord your God with all your heart, and with all your soul, and with all your mind, and with all your strength." Will there not *then* be all "that mind in you which was also in Christ Jesus?" And in consequence of this, while you joyfully experience all the holy tempers described in this book, you will likewise be outwardly "holy as He that hath called you is holy, in all manner of conversation."[33]

In harmony with this, Wesley states, "We must love God, *before* we can be holy at all; this being *the root* of all holiness."[34] This is a work of the Spirit of God, who is never far from the conversation about love in Wesley's theology: "I rejoice, because the sense of God's love to me hath, by the same Spirit, wrought in me to love him, and to love *for his sake* every child of man, every soul that he hath made."[35]

"The expulsive power of a new affection" claims our attention as the chief dynamic of the sanctification of the soul. Love for God subordinates and reorders all lesser loves. This is Christian perfection for John Wesley.

PRAYERS DIRECTED TO THE TRIUNE GOD

If love for *God* is truly central to Wesley's definition of Christian perfection, we should expect to find his spirituality influenced in distinct ways. To test this, although not exhaustively, we study "A Collection of Forms of Prayer, Every Day in the Week," "A Collection of Prayers for

Families," and "Prayers for Children."[36]

A characteristic prayer of "A Collection of Forms of Prayer" illustrates Wesley's basic pattern. He first addresses *each* member of the Godhead—Father, Son and Holy Spirit—offering his "sacrifice of love and thanksgiving."[37] Then he summarizes his prayer to the Trinity as follows:

> Glory be to thee, O Holy, undivided Trinity, for jointly concuring in the great work of our redemption and restoring us again to the glorious liberty of the sons of God. Glory be to thee, who, in compassion to human weakness, has appointed a solemn day for the remembrance of thy inestimable benefits. O let me ever esteem it my privilege and happiness to have a day set apart for the concerns of my soul, a day free from distractions, disengaged from the world, wherein I have nothing to do but to praise and love thee. O let it ever be to me a day sacred to divine love, a day of heavenly rest and refreshment.[38]

The theme of love for the triune God is characteristic of this passage and most of Wesley's prayers. This consciousness of adoration of the Trinity is again explicit in the prayer for "Friday Evening."

> O God the Father, who canst be thought to have made me only to destroy me, have mercy upon me.
>
> O God the Son, who, knowing the Father's will, didst come into the world to save me, have mercy upon me.
>
> O God the Holy Ghost, who to the same end has so often since breathed holy thoughts into me, have mercy upon me.
>
> O holy, blessed, and glorious Trinity, whom in three Persons I adore as one God, have mercy upon me.[39]

Despite Wesley's definite Christological commitments, his own prayers show a love for God that is not "Christomonism." It would be saying too much to claim that Wesley's theology of perfection is Christocentric. On the contrary, a concerned reading of the texts of Wesley's prayers and his statements about love for God show a trinitarian awareness that pervades his thought and practice of devotion.

Love For God—The Root Of Love For Neighbor

One of the most regrettable confusions of our generation occurs frequently when love for neighbor displaces love for God as the "first and great commandment." Wesley speaks rightly on this issue:

> How excellent things are spoken of the love of our neighbour! It is "the fulfilling of the law," "the end of the commandment." Without this, all we have, all we do, all we suffer, is of no value in the sight of God. But it is that love of our neighbour which springs from the love of God: whether we do "love him because he first loved us."[40]

Wesley's total life and ministry proclaim the urgency and importance of loving service to neighbor, yet he sees the *root* of such love as "the love of God." In *The Plain Account* he declares, "One design ye are to pursue to the end of time,—the enjoyment of God in time and eternity. Desire other things, so far as they bend to this; love the creature, as it leads to the Creator."[41]

Nothing in the realm of being is exempt from its relation to God, including the love of neighbor. As we serve the neighbor, we do serve God; indeed, Wesley says, "We are to serve him [God] in our neighbour; which he receives as if done to himself in person, standing visible before us."[42]

Wesley, in a remarkable statement, identifies the creation with the Creator, showing that the true ground of love for and valuing of creation is mandated because God is reflected in his handiwork:

> The great lesson . . . is, that God is in all things, and that we are to see the Creator in the glass of every creature: that we should use and look upon nothing as separate from God, which indeed is a kind of practical atheism; but, . . . survey heaven and earth, and all that is therein, as contained by God

in the hollow of his hand, who by His intimate presence holds them all in being, who pervades and activates the whole created frame, and is, in a true sense, the soul of the universe.[43]

The substitution of love for neighbor as the ground of ethics or religion is not properly Wesleyan. If such humanism is perpetuated, it must not be done so in the name of John Wesley.

Implications Of Wesley's Concept Of Love For God

If Wesley's concept of love for God is taken seriously, it appears that certain adjustments need to be made. After due consideration, the following items of our theological agenda deserve careful attention:

1. Theology should be conceived as radically monotheistic. Proper attention needs to be given to Scripture, evangelism, the realization of the kingdom of God in society, individual self-love, development of academic integrity. But nothing supercedes the priority of "the increase among men of the love of God and neighbour." God is our "ultimate concern." Even love for the Father, or the Son, or the Holy Spirit is relative to the unity of the three persons of the Trinity and to the distinct identity of each person of the Trinity. In short, we will worship the triune God.

We will worship God and not sinlessness or love as ends in themselves. H. Richard Niebuhr remarks that "though God is love, love is not God." We may also affirm in sympathy with this, that though God is holy, holiness is not God. The subtle shift of focus from God to persons can be made to appear legitimate, but it is not.

2. Christian perfection is best defined according to Wesley's grounding concept as love for God that results in love for others and cleansing of the heart from the old inadequate dreams of an evil imagination that found root in a

fundamentally idolatrous attitude toward some thing, or person, or center of value other than God. The initial shedding abroad of love in the heart of the believer is followed by a crisis situation in which the self perceives the upward call of God in Christ Jesus and enters a new level of depth in his or her relationship of love for God. The difference is a matter of *degree* if the metaphor of love for God is to be consistent. But the difference is real and the degree of change is so significant that a new quality of life begins. Yet it is a beginning again. The second definite work of grace is, in a special sense, only the first step of a journey of growth that will never end. The fire of love returns to its primal source in God.

Notes

1. Love for God is not to be confused with love from God. Love of God is somewhat ambiguous, so the phrase "love for God" is used in this chapter to make the issue clear.
2. The past issues of the *Wesleyan Theological Journal, Insights into Holiness, Further Insights into Holiness, The Word and the Doctrine,* as well as selected works of holiness writers have been studied. These latter include Leo Cox, Eldon R. Fuhrman, George Allen Turner, Mildred B. Wynkoop, and others. Writers from other movements have also been included in this study: Harald Lindstrom, Ronald Knox, Albert Outler, Frank Baker, William Sangster, and Martin Schmidt. Subsequent references will represent other interpreters throughout this chapter.
3. I know of no satisfactory treatment of Wesley's views on this topic. Although the present study could be extended in various ways, it is presented with the confidence that Wesley's writings are represented fairly, although not exhaustively. Special attention has been given to Wesley's sermons and the *Explanatory Notes upon the New Testament* (Naperville, Ill.: Alec R. Allenson Inc., 1958).
4. Mary Alice Tenney, *Blueprint for a Christian World: An Analysis of the Wesleyan Way* (Winona Lake, Ind.: Light and Life Press, 1953), p. 17.

5. See Gene Outka, *Agape: An Ethical Analysis* (New Haven: Yale University Press), 1972, p. 1 and Leon Hynson, "Christian Love: The Key to Wesley's Ethics," *Methodist History,* XIV, No. 1 (October 1975), p. 45, for comments on the importance of this text.
6. Karl Rahner, *Theological Investigations,* V, pp. 439–459 and VI, pp. 231–249. Cf. Graeme de Graaff, "God and Morality," *Christian Ethics and Contemporary Philosophy,* Ian T. Ramsey, ed. (London: SCM Press Ltd., 1966), pp. 31–52, and Richard R. Roach, "Excessive Claim: Rahner's Identification of Love of God with Love of Neighbour," *Studies in Religion,* 5, No. 3, pp. 247–57 and No. 4, pp. 360–72.
7. Reference is made to Jack T. Sanders's claim in *Ethics in the New Testament* that "the command to love is so inherently anchored in the expectation of the imminent end of the age and of God's final victory that the failure of that expectation renders the call of love meaningless." Cited in O. Lamar Cope, "Ethics and the New Testament: A Survey of Perspectives 1970–1980. *Word and World: Theology for Christian Ministry,* p. 179.
8. John Wesley, "Plain Account of Christian Perfection," in *The Works of John Wesley,*" (Grand Rapids: Zondervan Publishing House, n.d., reprinted in 1972) p. 394; cf. *Works,* 11, p. 368 and many similar statements.
9. Wesley, *Works,* 11, p. 390.
10. *Ibid.,* p. 430.
11. *Ibid.,* p. 441.
12. Wesley, *Works,* 5, p. 115; cf. *Works,* 5, p. 127.
13. Anders Nygren, *Agape and Eros* (London: SPCK, 1957) Part I, "What we have here is a purely theocentric love, in which all choice on man's part is excluded" (p. 213). Cf. M. C. D'Arcy, *The Mind and Heart of Love: Lion and Unicorn: A Study in Eros and Agape* (New York: Henry Holt and Company), 1947, p. 312.
14. Wesley, *Works,* 5, pp. 268ff.
15. *Ibid.,* p. 420.
16. *Ibid.,* 5, p. 330.
17. *Ibid.,* pp. 232ff.
18. *Ibid.,* p. 208.

19. *Ibid.,* p. 281.
20. *Ibid.,* p. 22.
21. Nygren, *Agape and Eros,* p. 127
22. Soren Kierkegaard, *Works of Love;* (Princeton: Princeton University Press, 1946), pp. 40ff.
23. Wesley, *Works,* 5, pp. 21ff.
24. *Ibid.*
25. *Ibid.,* p. 381.
26. *Ibid.,* p. 92.
27. *Ibid.,* p. 220.
28. Ibid.
29. Wesley, *Explanatory Notes upon the New Testament,* p. 113.
30. *Ibid.,* p. 943.
31. Wesley, *Works,* 5, p. 399.
32. *Ibid.,* p. 96.
33. Wesley, ''Preface,'' *Explanatory Notes upon the Old Testament,* 1765, 1, p. viii.
34. Wesley, *Works,* 5, p. 115 (my emphasis).
35. Wesley, *Works,* 5, p. 141; cf. *Works,* 5, p. 211: ''This is the true circumcision of the heart. Let the spirit return to God . . . with the whole train of its affections.''
36. Wesley, *Works,* 11, pp. 203–72.
37. *Ibid.,* p. 203.
38. *Ibid.,* p. 203.
39. *Ibid.,* p. 230.
40. Wesley, *Works,* 5, p. 278. This study does not discuss self-love in Wesley's thought. However, it is worthy to note Wesley's comment in the *Explanatory Notes up on the New Testament* on Mark 12:35: "*And to love his neighbour as himself*—to maintain the same equitable and charitable temper and behaviour toward all men, as we, in like circumstances, would wish for from them toward ourselves, is a . . . necessary duty." Wesley does not clearly *promote* self-love here, although he does not disapprove of self-regard. A full-scale study of Wesley's concept self-love on the order of Oliver O'Donovan's *The Problem of Self-Love in St. Augustine* (New Haven: Yale University Press, 1980) would be useful, but I am not convinced that Wesley

says enough on the topic to make such a work possible. If the material is present in Wesley's writings in quantity and/or kind to allow such a study, it would certainly be useful to augment the serious consideration of Wesley's doctrine of love in general.

41. Wesley, *Works,* 11, p. 368.
42. *Ibid.,* p. 440. Austin Farrer accords with Wesley's theological understanding of regard for neighbor as we see in the following statement from Farrer's article "Examination of Theological Belief." "The regard we owe him. And yet he is no mere channel through which regard is paid to God, for God is regarded by regard for what He regards, and what He regards is the man" (From *Faith and Logic,* Basil Mitchell, ed. [London: George Allen and Unwin, 1958], p. 20).
43. Wesley, *Works,* 5, pp. 283ff.

Part II
Contemporary Issues

Harold B. Kuhn (Ph.D., Harvard University), professor emeritus of philosophy of religion, Asbury Theological Seminary

Abortion

THE QUESTION of whether a pregnancy once begun may legitimately be terminated artificially and with intent has been with the human race from time immemorial. With the coming of the Christian message into human history and human experience, the issue has taken on new dimensions, the more so with the burgeoning population of the world and with the development of 'refined' techniques for the interruption of pregnancy. Coupled with this has come the more modern emphasis upon individualism, and upon a hedonistic interpretation of right and wrong, to which the inconveniences and discomforts of pregnancy seem somehow to be elements so hostile to "the good life" that there have come imperious demands upon society to relax the historic safeguards that have been set about fetal life, in favor of what is called, rather ineptly, "abortion on demand."

The issue has become more and more murky in our century, as the matter of the public notice given the subject has been considered within wider parameters. Humanity's control over the processes of nature has been extended to a degree seldom envisioned a century ago, and with this, there has come increasing pressure from within society for what is called "Life Control." In this connection, much has been made of what is called "the quality of life" as opposed to the more traditional emphasis upon "the right to life." This introduces the larger question of *rights,* upon which the issue of rights at both ends of the human life-spectrum is very much under discussion.

From the time of the life of our Lord to the present century, there has been continuous regard for the sacredness of life. Against the Roman patrician ideal, in which the power of continued life or immediate death to the newborn lay in the whim of the *pater familias,* the Christian evangel has insisted that God is both Lord of life and Lord of death, and that arbitrary taking of life, particularly at the fetal level, is to be condemned upon theological grounds. This attitude came, understandably, to be embodied in the legal codes of many Western nations, including our own. It has been correctly noted that up until two decades or more ago, the United States of America was one of the most difficult nations in which to get an abortion. Many secular issues contributed to this fact, notably that of the 'youth' of our nation, which began in a nearly empty environment and whose development was intimately geared to an ever-increasing population. Yet even here, the matter of the Christian conscience was a prominent factor.

Seen from the perspective of our national history, the current situation in which our land has become one of the easiest countries in which it is possible to arrange for a 'legal' abortion appears as a radical departure. This fact is in reality only a epiphenomenon, which rests upon a complex of strands of argument that touch deeply the total fabric of human life. Among these are the growing sense of individualism in a society threatened by totalitarianism; the expansion of public and private permissiveness; the loss of the sense of "the sacred" in general, and of the sacredness of life in particular; the spread of secularity within our society, emanating especially from our institutions of higher learning; and the growing hedonism with which a bored society seeks to compensate for the many pressures upon the human psyche that are attributed to the spread of technology.

In this connection, it must be said with great regret that the rising tide of demand for legal freedom from the securing of legalized abortions is in some significant part caused by the loss of the ability of the Church to project into the social structures of the time her historic message with respect to the sacredness of life. It is fateful that even today, considerable segments of the Church have become permissive with respect to the abortion question. In many cases, at least, this is rationalized by church persons on the grounds of compassion, or by reason of an appeal to a supposed *quality* of life that allegedly is impossible for children developing from imperfect fetuses.

In some respects the issue is becoming increasingly clear in our time; in others it is beclouded by slogans and by an appeal to exceptional cases. Situation ethics has entered into the lists in favor of unlimited abortion upon this basis and appears to have offered a great deal of aid and comfort to the forces favoring "abortion on demand." Supporting the demand for complete legalization of abortion, frequently concealed by the euphemism that abortion is strictly a matter between the pregnant woman and her physician, many voices are being raised. On the other hand, the voiceless unborn are being represented by a wide spectrum of "pro-life" organizations, as well as by a good number of highly respectable and highly placed individuals concerned for what is increasingly called "the right to life of the fetus."

A Historical Perspective

In the Greco-Roman world, into which early Christianity was projected, abortion and infanticide were frankly employed measures for the regulation of population growth. The measures were frequently crude and callous, as would be expected in a culture in which these measures found public endorsement and support. With respect to abortion, the early church felt conscience bound to stand in opposition to the conventional wisdom of the Greco-Roman paganism. John Noonan gave expression to this opposition in his words.

> Although therapeutic and social reasons for abortion were known by the best doctors and philosophers, these reasons were never mentioned (i.e., by the writers of the early church) as justification. All the writers agreed that abortion was a violation of the love owed to one's neighbor. Many saw it as a failure to have reverence for the work of God the Creator. The culture had accepted abortion. The Christians condemned it. Ancient authorities and contemporary moralists had approved, hesitated, made exceptions, but the Christian rule was certain.[1]

This general Christian rule prevailed for nearly nineteen centuries, and it is only recently that major Christian writers have become, to some measure at least, tolerant of a libertarian attitude toward abortion.

In the world of antiquity, abortion and infanticide were, in general, justified from a common base. Typically, the *pater familias* was held to possess the full legitimate authority to deal with new life. Historians record that when a newborn child was brought to the father of the patrician class, he looked it over carefully. If it pleased him, the child was forthwith cared for well, with nothing being too good for it. If it did not please him, he simply broke the child's back over his knee and left it to die.

Many or all today would condemn the practice of infanticide, while at the same time defending with eloquence the elimination of incipient life within the uterus. The distinction between abortion and infanticide was, of course, clear in such a society. Today, genetic and fetal research tend to close the gap between the two.

The border line separating abortion from infanticide is most clearly crossed in the practice of hysterotomy, a surgical operation that differs from caesarian section only in intent. Recommended by advocates of liberalized abortion as a licit means for employment during the third trimester of a pregnancy, it has a callousness that should shock even the most liberal type of mind. The fetus, removed from the uterus during this stage of pregnancy, is a live human being, whose destruction (passive or active) is one of the horrors of the delivery room. The prognosis for the viability of the child thus violently removed from the uterus is frequently strongly affirmative, as actions of compassionate nurses have demonstrated.

Abortion by the insertion of a strong saline solution into the fetal membranes, usually also employed in the third trimester, does in some cases lead to the birth of a badly scorched, but viable fetus. It is a small wonder that the saline solution thus employed is sometimes called "the abortionist's napalm."

If it be questioned that the foregoing paragraphs are properly included in this historical perspective, it may be said that the advocates of the extreme forms of "abortion on demand" approach very closely the classical view of antiquity concerning infant life. Once abortion becomes legal, and once it is accepted as the broad right of all those involved in pregnancy, there seems to be little to restrain the callousness that marked the world of Greco-Roman paganism. It is to the credit of the impact of the Christian message that for nearly two millenia abortion was treated with general repugnance and that strong safeguards, whether legal or psychological, were erected around the unborn.

It must be said in fairness, that through the centuries intervening since the time of our Lord, there have been honest differences of opinion with respect to the point at which life begins. Following the precepts of Aristotle, the Middle Ages received certain tendencies toward permissiveness with respect to abortion through Thomas Aquinas's writings. The Church at that time permitted abortion prior to what was called "fetal quickening."[2] In 1588, however, the pope issued an encyclical forbidding all forms of abortion.

Mention should be made of the contrasting view concerning abortion within the Jewish tradition. Orthodox and conservative Judaism held that life began with conception. Liberal Judaism has held that life begins just at, or just prior to, birth. This has led to a view within the liberal tradition that permits abortion on a wider scale, at least during early pregnancy.[3] This latter view was presumably based upon the question of viability, that is, the point at which the life of the fetus is capable of being self-sustaining. Mention of the bearing of current techniques for lowering the time of viability will be made later in this chapter. It needs to be pointed out in passing that such passages as Exodus 21:22–24 suggest that life in the uterus is in reality an issue of personal being, as does also the passage relating to the prenatal life of the prophet Jeremiah.[4]

Seen from the perspective of history, the question of abortion has been variously treated. Classical paganism, lacking a doctrine of creation, dealt with the question on a pragmatic basis. The general tone of society with respect to human life tended to govern the public attitude toward the unborn and the very young. The tendency was toward the extension of the power of the patriarch in the structure of the family to the question of the survival of the unborn or the newly born. In the overall consideration, reverence for human life was a consideration subordinate to societal and familial arrangements.

The coming of Christianity introduced a new and ennobling concept, that of the worth of the person as created in a high image, the *imago dei*. It is not easy for those of us who live within a general context of Christendom to realize the profundity of the influence of the Christian Evangel upon the estimate of fetal life, and as well upon the entire question of child life. It is only when there occurs a serious breakdown in the impact of Christianity upon Western society that one can perceive the negative effects of such a breakdown.

Verbal And Linguistic Aspects Of The Abortion Question

Parallel to the vast increase of communication and communication systems, there has come a vast extension of the verbalization of the issues connected with the permission to terminate fetal life. Sloganeering has reached into this issue, and in all too many questions, clichés and catchwords have become powerful elements in the public treatment of the question of abortion. It is essential that such slogans be not only recognized, but also subjected to scrutiny of their import.

In the polarization of society with respect to the question of abortion into the *pro* and *anti* phases, there has come a similar dichotomy with respect to the verbalization of public attitudes. On the one hand, there is the familiar motif of "right to life" as an inclusive term for the opposition to the practice of abortion. This term is not to be despised, for it encases as a silent corollary the view of the high value of human life. One of the "inalienable rights" guaranteed by the United States Constitution is "the right to life." The term has come to involve much more than the mere right to be visibly alive. In current usage, it has been extended to imply respect, even reverence, for fetal life as its development has become increasingly well charted by medical research.

Over against this more general interpretation, the proabortion forces have sought to modify this in terms of the word *viability,* by which is meant the point at which the fetus is capable of existing on its own.[5] It is true, of course, that viability is a relative term. Some fetuses are, during especially the third trimester of pregnancy, better able to survive outside the uterus than others. More significant still, the advance of technology is pushing the point of viability further and further back, so that neonatal techniques are capable of sustaining the life of the premature fetus from as early as twenty to twenty-two weeks.[6]

Advocates of right to life welcome researches that do push the point of viability ever further back as movements within human experience serve to enhance the appreciation for incipient human life. This does not, of course, settle the question of when human life actually begins. Much is made by preabortion advocates of the United States Supreme Court's inability (or unwillingness) to make any definitive pronouncement at this point. Mention of this matter will be made at a later point in this chapter.

In any case, the right to life advocates have on their side the general thrust of the Christian message, that human life is something precious and worth safeguarding. The issue at stake here is of course, when *human life* begins, or more precisely, at what point in the career of the fertilized human ovum may it properly be said that claims of the conceptus as possessing human life, and thus possessing the *right* to pursue development in the usual course of a human pregnancy are valid. Certainly biological life exists at the point of the meeting of sperm and ovum. The collection of cells that issues from this meeting is without doubt living; is it a living human organism?

The issue at this point is whether fertilization of the ovum of a human female is a *real beginning* of humanity. Here seems to be the major point of tension for both the right to life and the right to choice advocates. The phenomenon of identical twinning seems, many feel, to introduce a new dimension if not of uncertainty, then certainly one demanding some kind of answer to the question of the precise moment at which the conceptus may be considered to enter the area of the inception of individual humanity. It is reasonably well established that twinning of this sort occurs at a point prior to the implantation of the fertilized ovum in the uterine wall, and that after this point, fission of the same is no longer possible. Some feel that this is the point at which the embryo begins a stable life in itself, so that *life* that is manifested from this point on is a phenomenon that moves steadily onward to the production of a full-grown infant.

Others will suggest that some physical phenomenon in the experience of the incipient fetus, such as the establishment of cerebral or cardiac action, may be regarded to be the point at which the embryo becomes in a proper definition of the term, a fetus. The issue here is whether the question of when human life begins can be determined upon the basis of any specific biological criterion. Some base their negative conclusions at this point upon the fact that the rate and stages of development among the unborn as well as among those already born are slightly different in each case. It may be questioned, however, whether this range of individual differences is so manifestly great that *no* determination may be made upon the basis of the line of biological development.

One is at times tempted to wonder whether the age-old issue of heredity or environment is most largely determinative for the understanding of the human organism. Until very recently, environment has been regarded to be the major force shaping us all. The science of genetics has had something of an uphill pull against the conventional wisdom of the present century. It seems reasonably certain, however, that the identification of what is called the genetic code has given the edge to the view that from the moment of conception, the fertilized ovum moves steadily forward toward the genetic determination of the infant ready to enter the outside world (i.e., a production that is shaped by factors existing from the beginning).

It is not surprising that the issue of the beginning of life should be clouded by both pragmatic and emotional considerations. Right to life advocates naturally feel that abortion, at whatever stage in pregnancy, involves the destruction of a human life, whether or not the precise moment when life may be said to be present can be determined. On the other hand, those who argue for elective abortions maintain that, at certain stages of the development of the fetus, the right of women to control over their own bodies takes precedence over the right of the fertilized ovum to proceed in normal course toward the viable human infant.

The right to life movement has become a controversial and powerful factor in the politics of our time. What concerns the Christian, however, is not whether the movement possesses a certain degree of power, but rather, where lies the evidence sufficient to enable the Christian conscience to make a fairly defensible yes or no decision.

Major Personalistic Issues

At this point we turn to the question posed by those who hold that the element of *choice* takes precedence over any supposed *right* of the conceptus to pursue its course of development without being interrupted artificially in its progress from fertilized ovum to fully developed infant. This is, of course, a deeply personal issue.

It is undeniable that choice is a legitimate element in any

discussion of ethics, including Christian ethics. And the right to the determination of the uses to which the human body is put belongs to the larger issue of freedom to choose between genuinely alternative courses. It must be remembered that the question is frequently not a simple and univocal one. The structures of human life are such that many considerations enter into the what and where of freedom of choice. There are, however, points in most elective situations in which the die is cast, and onward from which the results are at a certain moment determined.

The alcoholic, for example, had a long span of time in which he or she could choose to drink or not drink. However, it seems evident that following a certain series of choices in favor of alcohol, the individual is no longer free thus to decide. There is something to be said in favor of the position that there is a point at which the human woman surrenders the right to full control over her body.[7] The question becomes, of course, the identification of that point. A strong case can be made for the view that with respect to the matter of body-choice, this point is that moment at which she consents to sexual congress. From this moment onward, certain risks exists, and we believe these risks should be recognized as determinative and of the nature of commitment.

It is precisely at this point that those who call themselves crusaders for choice demur. They insist that if women are ever free to control their own lives, they must hold abortion to be their right. Many thus feel that the law of the land, dating from the 1973 decision of the United States Supreme Court, in the case of *Roe v. Wade,* is ethically correct. By this ruling, it is understood that women have a constitutional right to have an abortion, up to and through at least the third month of pregnancy.

This decision by the Supreme Court seems to have rested, in principle, upon the negative factor of the inability of the justices to determine the point at which life really begins as human life. This is, to be sure, a highly debatable question. What is at issue seems to be, however, whether fetal life may not be *life on the way to human personhood.* The issue is put succinctly by Dr. and Mrs. J. C. Wilkie:

> Is the fetus human life? This is the question that must first be considered, pondered, discussed, and finally answered. It cannot be brushed aside or ignored. . . . Upon its answer hinges the entire abortion question. . . . If this growing being is a human being, then we are in an entirely different situation than if it's just protoplasm. If human, he or she must be granted the same dignity and protection of life, health, and well-being that our Western civilization has always granted to every other human being.[8]

One must not allow the simplicity of this statement to obscure its validity. Dr. C. Everett Koop, a pediatrician, offers forceful confirmation to this position in his volume *The Right to Live, the Right to Die,* in which he traces the development of the fetus, from the eighteenth day onward. From that date, cardiac action already exists. At forty-five days, brain waves can be picked up by the electroencephalograph, while fingerprints exist on the fetal hands at eight weeks. He traces, in succession, the development of the glandular system, the endocrine system, the growth of hair and nails, and the ability to respond to light and sound.[9]

In light of this, *viability* (which is a proposed criterion for the presence of human life) loses much of its relevance as indicative of an answer to the question, When does human life begin? Viability is, as noted previously, a highly relative term, the more so as more sophisticated techniques are developed for use in the neo-natal wards of our hospitals. In other words, it seems clear that altogether too much emphasis has been laid, especially in the "choice" discussions and by its advocates, upon the argument that, since the majority of persons cannot find a precise point at which it can be said that a human life exists in a fetal development, such a point does not exist. And it is this last assertion upon which the argument for unregulated elective abortion rests.

It would be helpful, as the Reverend Paul W. Kirkpatrick notes,[10] if the precise status of the fetus at each stage in its development could be decisively determined. In such a case, "the controversy over abortion would be well on the way to settlement."[11] The issue at this point might well be stated thus: Are we to give the benefit of the doubt to the developing fetus, as the prolife advocates insist, or are we to give it the benefit of *no* doubt at all?

Nor is it helpful to argue, at this point as at many others, that in case of reasonable doubt, the wish of the pregnant woman takes precedence over all other considerations. In such a situation, rights must be balanced, namely that of the mother and that of the unborn child. Again there arises the question of control over the woman's body. Here again is raised the question of freedom. It is significant that in some areas of the United States, "reproductive freedom" appears on the masthead of some proabortionist literature.

It needs to be noted that proabortionists tend to maintain that the insistence that at the point of agreement to sexual congress constitutes the voluntary surrender of a large measure of freedom over the woman's body (i.e., for at least three-fourths of a year) is a product of male chauvinism. Here again there is room for definitions. If the fact (upon which few would disagree) that pregnancy does involve more for the woman than any man can really understand constitutes male chauvinism, then the argument seems to be conclusive on the side of free elective abortions. It is possible, however, that much more than masculine *macho* is at issue here.

The question of freedom in relation to the question of abortion does rest upon individual feminist grounds insofar as it is regarded to be an issue of privacy. Control of the body of the woman is not, let it be said, something to be pushed aside lightly. Intensely human considerations are at stake here. This suggests that those who approach the question from the privacy angle frequently do so upon humanitarian and compassionate grounds. No sensitive person can brush aside thoughtlessly the questions that arise in this connection. One thinks at once of the indigent woman, trapped in poverty, to whom another pregnancy looms as the cause of deepening personal crisis. As a human being, she feels totally incapable of coping once more with diapers, lack of privacy in cramped quarters, and the loss of dignity that accompanies being on welfare.

Nor can the sensitive Christian view without concern the case of the adolescent girl who finds herself pregnant before realizing what has really happened, and who has been battered by peer pressure to "join the adult crowd" through sexual congress. She *and* her parents must certainly face the issues with which such a pregnancy confronts them as a family. This is not to say that abortion should be regarded as the primary way out of such a situation. It does indicate that Christian compassion needs to enter into the cluster of elements that comprise the problem. But it is much too facile to consider the aborting of the fetus as the first resort, or to suppose that this is but an issue of an hour or so in the abortion mill or the hospital.

It is understandable, *given* the climate of permissiveness that has come to be dominant in much of today's thinking concerning reproductive matters, that the young couple whose life-style is geared to two incomes should regard a surprise pregnancy as presenting a crisis to which abortion is the only answer, or even a simple answer. However, a couple who accepted the vows of marriage should also have long since made a place in their thinking in which, if even the best of contraceptive measures should fail, they would immediately welcome the life that is incipient within the wife and make whatever arrangements are necessary to be ready for its coming.

From the foregoing, it may be concluded that there *may* be cases in which Christian compassion renders the privacy argument to be one stemming from more than mere selfishness, although this element must not be ruled out. The real issue is, whether inconvenience or even personal hardship are factors of such importance that they outweigh the right of the fetus to continue living along the course that is properly called the road to human personhood. There exist, of course, other situations of unwanted pregnancy that constitute what may be called "gray areas." One thinks of pregnancies resulting from violent or felonious connections, such as rape or incest, to which may be added cases in which the health of the prospective mother is at stake.

These situations do—and perhaps should—anguish the Christian conscience. Some of us, in the pursuit of, for example, the refugee ministry at the end of hostilities in World War II, have talked with the shattered young women who were raped, not once but many times, and not merely due to individual human lust but by deliberate planning of invading armies desiring to terrorize and humiliate captured areas, and know what psychic lesions such violation of womanliness leaves. It is no small thing for such women to feel totally incapable of bringing a child so conceived to full term, and then to live for years haunted by the visible issue of experiences of such a violent sort. Certainly society has an obligation to render all possible assistance to victims of such "man's inhumanity to man," quite possibly arranging for the adoption of such children at birth, providing of course that the mother so chooses after careful consideration of the total picture facing her.

With respect to pregnancies due to incest, it needs to be said that the taboo (if we may properly use the term here) against incest is one of the most deeply etched upon the collective consciousness of the race. From the genetic point of view, it cannot be passed over lightly, in view of what is known concerning the compounding of, especially, dominant traits that incest may cause. Here is an issue that demands, we are persuaded, much more attention than has been given to it to date. The Christian movement is in need of information from sources informed in the area of genetic research at this point.

The questions raised by the occurrence of felonious pregnancies are such as to involve necessarily the issue of human compassion. There is a third issue that some Christian moralists consider within the category, namely that of the unwanted child. Here the issue is whether a pregnancy that would incontestably produce a child who will be irrevocably unwanted should not be terminated by abortion of the fetus. Certainly the prominance given to research into "the battered child syndrome" has brought to light important data with respect to the reception of the child by its parents, especially the mother. On the one hand, we have those who say that there are really no unwanted children, but that each child brings into the world with it a certification of acceptance. This view is certainly too simplistic.

It would seem that this issue is too complex to form the basis for a decision with respect to the acceptability of abortion as a preventative of the so-called unwanted child. The depth of maternal—and paternal—sentiments is such that mere surface indications of noninfant-acceptance are scarcely sufficient as a basis for a firm justification of the termination of a given pregnancy upon grounds of emotionally loaded pronouncements of prospective parents. It should be noted here that very many prospective mothers do, in the early stages of pregnancy, wish that they were rid of the whole procedure. If all, or even many, of such transient feelings were followed by action, early abortions would be numerous indeed.

The issue of the justification of abortion upon the basis of threat to the health of the prospective mother is likewise one involving perplexities and uncertainties. It should be noted at the outset that removal of the fetus in case of ectopic or tubal pregnancy that clearly jeopardized the well-being of the woman involved, involves no question of "whether or no." Other cases in which possible danger to the prospective mother is involved are not so clear-cut. Usually such perils are considered under two rubrics: physical peril and psychological danger. Of these two, the latter is most fully fraught with ambiguities.

Now, those who hold that physicians do as a rule tell the woman what they believe she wants to hear are grossly unfair to the medical profession. There are indisputably cases in which carrying an infant to full term does involve serious physical threat to the prospective mother. It can be said, however, that the advance of medical techniques is rendering the number of such perils to be increasingly small. Threats to psychological health are more difficult to determine, and are certainly worthy of recognition and respect. The mere threat to commit suicide if abortion is denied can scarcely be taken as *prima facie* evidence of a case in which psychological grounds justify an abortion. The integrity of the medical profession will need to be the major element. The availability of increasingly sophisticated methods of monitoring a borderline pregnancy, plus the relative safety of caesarian section, greatly reduce the number of actual perils involved in even complicated pregnancies; and it is difficult to make the fear of possible complications in case of a full term (or of pregnancies well into the third trimester) a facile justification for terminating a pregnancy.

Thus far, special attention is given to the private and personal dimensions of the case for an abortion. It is hoped that sufficient room is made for exceptions to the rule of no-abortion in order to save the mother's life.

However, it needs to be said again that the argument in favor of such exceptions has lost considerable ground in the face, not only of the increase in medical technology's ability to surmount such physical perils, but as well, in the growing concern for sensitive persons to maintain the *equal* rights of both mother and child.

Some have charged that those who hold a reasoned position against unlimited abortion are harsh absolutists. As noted previously, there are gray areas within which decisions must be made in given cases. But even in those instances in which an abortion *may* be permissable, it must be recognized that *abortion is an evil,* and as such to be undertaken only in such cases as present *unmistakably greater evil* if events take their usual course. The writer is aware that this last proposition is not universally accepted, and that many thoughtful persons hold that anything that inhibits a major evil is by that much *good.* While feeling the force of this argument, the writer feels that the latter argument is fraught with ambiguities greater than the one stated above. Certainly the area within which an abortion may be permissable, if at all, is a relatively small one, one which proabortion advocates refuse to recognize as being minor.

Some Sociological Issues

In the discussion of the more permissive attitude toward abortion, there has been a major emphasis upon the privacy argument (that is, the argument based upon the woman's control over her body at all stages in life), to the neglect of the interest of society as a whole in this entire issue. That is to say, many of the arguments of proabortionists are social in nature. Mention has been made of the appeal to the motif of quality of life as justification for the abortion of fetuses whose prognosis for what is usually regarded to be "the good life" is poor. Those who propose an affirmative reply in such questions do, in many cases at least, assume that they are adequate arbiters of the goodness of life for others.

At this point, attention should be drawn to the fact that historical records are full of instances in which even gravely handicapped persons have made outstanding and even indispensable contributions to human civilization. Even in less spectacular cases, handicapped persons themselves will, if consulted, value for themselves the gift of life quite as highly as do the rest of us. Greatness frequently emerges from unpromising backgrounds and out of the midst of what would seem to others insuperable handicaps. Today even victims of rather advanced forms of Down's Syndrome (Mongolism) who would have in another generation been confined to the back room of the house as causes of shame to the entire family are today occupying useful places in the life of society as self-supporting workers.

The societal issue of the sexual freedom of women is, of course, given great prominence today. Any male consideration of this question will inevitably bring charges of male chauvinism and of the unfeeling quality of the person giving attention to it. It should be acknowledged at the outset that the male of the human species cannot really understand the feeling of entrapment that pregnant women, even at best, do experience. Those going through such experiences are not always deeply impressed by any statements to the effect that the Almighty has by wise providence laid his heavy burden upon the female of the human species. It is difficult to contemplate the quantity and intensity of suffering that the reproduction of the race has imposed upon women through the millenia of history. Nor does it help greatly to say that the Creator has given women a high degree of ability to endure suffering—and perhaps also the ability to forget labor pains quickly at the joy of having given new life to the world. Suffering is suffering, whenever and to whomever it occurs. But whether the bare question of feminine comfort should be extended as a determinant for the legitimacy of abortion is one of the most highly debatable issues of the time.

With the development of relatively safe (and when conscientiously applied almost 100 percent effective) methods of contraception, the question of sexual freedom for both women and men takes on a new dimension, namely that of responsible and serious attention to the matter of conception. With a few exceptions, moralists, whether Christian or secular, today view as licit many or most of the methods of contraception. A quiet revolution has occurred at this point in our century, due first to the development of the Latex processing of rubber, and second, to the development of anobulant steroids, with the result of the availability of a wide range of oral contraceptives. Consultation with the patient's physician can now result in the prescription of that blend of steroids that will produce a minimum of side effects and bring the practical elimination of most if not all of the perils of the Pill.

With the foregoing development, the force of sociological justification of abortion as a method of population control has been greatly reduced, particularly in our Western world. With the increasing availability and reliability of adequate contraceptive methods, this social argument for the availability of abortions to pregnant women becomes increasingly unconvincing. In this connection, it may be useful at this point to observe that Roman Catholic moralists have in the past not been as far wrong as some of their Protestant counterparts believed when they linked together contraception *and* abortion. While the two elements are by definition separate elements, yet today they are moving more and more closely together *at one point*. It was noted earlier that abortion by hysterectomy brought together more and more closely contraception and infanticide. Today some pharmaceutical developments that are regarded as being contraceptive in nature are in reality abortifacients. Outstanding among such developments are those relating to the use of prostaglandins.

Ground has already been broken for the development of do-it-yourself abortions in the so-called morning-after pill that is designed to prevent the implantation in the uterine wall of the already-fertilized ovum. And while the total effects of the interuterine device (IUD) are not yet known, it may prove true that it is also an abortifacient, in that it may, repeat *may,* render the uterine wall inhospitable to the fertilized egg. In any case, the next breakthrough at this point may be an abortifacient based upon some variety of the prostaglandins, which can be used privately, perhaps in suppository form, by the individual to induce abortion.

Such a development, unless it is somehow regulated by legal means, may open the door to abortions on a wide scale, and if so, it may reasonably be expected to support a trend, which is already growing, to regard abortion as a simple backup method to contraception, with a consequent carelessness in the employment of legitimate contraceptive methods—or in a total lack of their use. Already we find public figures suggesting that abortion is an acceptable reserve supplement to other contraceptive methods, particularly to the diaphragm, from which there continue to be unexpected and unexplainable failures. The extension of this mentality can scarcely be regarded by Christians as other than a tragic breakdown of the wall that properly separates contraception from abortion.

The long-range consequences of the easy acceptance of abortion, in whatever form, are treated euphemistically by some of its advocates. One of the favorite terms employed to describe a culture in which abortion is taken for granted is "the Century of the Wanted Child." We read, for instance, that

> the right to abortion is the foundation of Society's long, long

> struggle to guarantee that every child comes into the world wanted, loved and cared for. The right to abortion along with all birth-control measures, must establish the Century of the Wanted Child.[11]

Personal choice in both contraception and abortion is thus held to mark the inauguration of a new era of total control over fertility, an era in which the unwanted child will be a thing of the past.[12] This position reflects a total absence of reference to God and to his laws and rests upon the concealed premise that the fetus is part of the woman's body and thus subject to as much of her personal control as would be a diseased tonsil.

At this point, it may be observed that the argument that abortion belongs to the just and prior claim by a woman to exercise control over her body needs to be seen in relation to the claim of the fetus to be protected in his or her rights to bodily integrity. John Finnis has a penetrating observation at this point, one that deserves to be taken into serious consideration.[13] And when all is said and done, the primary objective in the procedure of abortion is the killing of the fetus. In proabortion literature this last phrase is studiously avoided. The usual euphemism is "the removal of the contents of the uterus," an expression that scarcely covers the actual intent and objective of the act. Nor does it seem that the inability to reach a generally agreed upon cut-off point at which the zygote ceases to be a simple combination of reproductive cells and begins to be a human being justifies an assault upon the body of the fetus.

This prompts the observation that those who advocate abortion on demand on the grounds of woman's alleged right to control over her own body have made a decision that is open to question.

> Feminists shift the emphasis away from the unborn child to the mother. . . . The fetus is deliberately misrepresented in order to justify his extermination.[14]

> Feminists emphasize the mother's rights in a country where the individual's rights and liberties are treasured, and carefully guarded . . . Feminists fan the flame by contrasting the *right* of the woman to control her own reproduction by means of contraception and abortion without interference by the state.[15]

The latter statements place the focus of the issue upon the state, whose concern to limit abortions is regarded as infringement interference, probably unwarranted upon the rights of all women.

What is lacking here is, above all, any seeming concern for fetal rights, and as well, a complete disregard for the effect that widespread legal abortions will have upon public sexual attitudes. Dr. Everett Koop observes that "already here in our community, the advertising media make pregnancy a loathsome thing."[16] It goes without saying that the thrust of proabortionism is seldom or never made within the context of the Christian understanding of such issues as Creation and Providence. This enables the use of the term *fetus* in impersonal ways, with scarcely a thought of its being an unborn child.

It is difficult to maintain that the public good is well served by an increasing callousness to the divine interest in child life, even in its uterine stage. The denial of legal status to the unborn cannot fail to form a basis for chipping away at the safeguards that are set by law about existing persons, and more especially the deformed and the senile. David Granfield, in his volume *The Abortion Decision,* after tracing the ways in which jurisprudence has historically recognized the rights of the unborn, observes,

> We have seen how property law, criminal law, and tort law bear enduring witness to society's recognition of the rights of the unborn. The question is: Can we deprive this voiceless minority of its vested rights? Should not these traditional

rights continue to be protected in this age of liberty and equality?[17]

Turning to the practical outworking of the legalization of abortion in the United States, Paul Kirkpatrick notes in his unpublished paper that

> the pro-abortionists in Great Britain told the people, in the days before our Supreme Court decision, how legalized abortion would curb illegitimacy, prostitution, venereal disease, and other social ills.

He goes on to quote from the volume *Thou Shalt Not Kill:*

> Unfortunately, the excellent records of the first five years of liberalized abortion under the National Health Service in Great Britain have revealed an increase in illegitimacy, venereal disease, prostitution, and in pelvic inflammatory disease from gonorrhea, as well as in sterility of previously aborted mothers and subsequent spontaneous abortions or miscarriages. Ectopic pregnancies . . . have doubled since abortion has been legalized.[19]

While the citation of the aftereffects of liberalized abortion practice in Great Britain may not tell the full story, it remains that the alleged freedom that abortion on demand provides does not guarantee "the real fruits of liberty" in a society.

Relatively too little attention has been given to the question of the psychological effects of abortions upon the women who undergo them and particularly those who do so for reasons of mere convenience or whim. The study of postabortion reactions has been too largely confined to psychological investigators whose outlook is conditioned by the view that moral sanctions are cultural and human-made.[20] Their conclusions tend to be that if guilt feelings follow an abortion it is due to wrong and morbid attitudes toward morality, and that such sentiments are mere "minor negative feelings" without any real psychological significance.[21] If persistent negative psychological effects continue, it is concluded that these existed prior to the decision to abort and were causal to it. Such conclusions are in the nature of rationalizations, and all too frequently the proposed solution is not the awakening of the public conscience so that the practice of abortion may be increasingly avoided but a hardening of the public and private conscience to the practice. As a radical sample, it may be noted that one psychologist has coined a new term for abortion, referring to such practices as "life-rationing activities."[22]

As a side thought to the question of the effect of abortion upon the feminine psyche, it should be noted that some women who have undergone such a procedure for *bona fide* justifiable reasons very soon seek to establish a new pregnancy. Sensitive and spiritually minded women have shown themselves to be especially compulsive at this point.[23]

From the foregoing, it appears that the effects of the abortion experience, both from the standpoint of the individual and of society, are serious and persistent. While euphemisms and circumlocutions may conceal the real nature of the practice, it still remains that human life is at stake. As recently as 1967, the First International Conference on Abortion, which drew largely from a secular segment of people, said, "We can find no point in time between the union of sperm and egg and the birth of an infant at which point we can say that this is not a human life."[24] It is principally during the past decade that attempts to minimize the individual and social consequences of abortion have become successful. And all too largely the public thinking has shifted "the truth that the unborn child is the victim of the abortion to the fact that the mother not wanting a pregnancy . . . is the victim of pregnancy."[25]

Conclusion

From the foregoing, it is evident that the question of

abortion is a complex one, with many facets. While it has many sociological implications, it finally resolves itself to an intensely person-centered issue. The prospective mother must share the stage with the unborn life no less in the abortion situation than in the whole breathtaking drama of the development of the human person, including birth. Prudential and compassionate elements do, it is true, play a role in the entire discussion, but these must yield precedence to the fact that while every human being is finite, yet he or she possesses tremendous worth as God's creation, and has been endowed with almost infinite possibilities.

The proabortionist argument fails to take due notice of this and in so doing sets those who advocate it as every women's right in a position "to assault God by destroying the pinnacle of his creation, the creature made in his image—man."[26] It needs to be noted in passing that these are the words not of one of the clergy, but of the surgeon-general of the United States.

A clear corollary of the doctrine of Creation as understood by the Christian faith is precisely this: that those who *oppose* unrestricted abortion (abortion on demand) are not depriving women of their liberties, but are seeking to incorporate in human living the highest insights into the worth of all human beings. Against the supposed liberty that the proabortionist hail, there is the deeper liberty that follows the reverencing of God's investment in human beings—not merely in perfect specimens of humanity, but including even the handicapped, the genetically limited, the humble and unheralded "ordinary persons," for all of whom Jesus Christ died.

If it be asserted that this is an argument that has weight only for Christians—and certain kind of Christians at that—a case can still be made for the position that abortion, for whatever reason, involves serious consequences for those who undergo it and those who assist that procedure, whether by legal consent or whether by illegal aggression against the fetus. The last word has not been said concerning either the deep psychic lesions that abortions inflict upon the women who undergo them, or the deeper consequences for physicians or para-medical persons who perform them. However, case studies abound that indicate that these consequences are far reaching and serious.

It is worthy of note that the edict of the United States Supreme Court issued in 1973 (case of *Roe v. Wade*) was underlain by the announced inability of any agency to define precisely where human life begins.[27] It is significant indeed that a decision of such wide implications should be based upon a thesis so negative in its form—really upon an appeal to ignorance. Surely it is the height of imprudence to proceed upon a course so precarious as is indicated by the slogan "abortion on demand" when so much is at stake in today's society. We may well take heed to the words of Malcom Muggeridge, a convert from secularist humanism to Christianity, and who cannot be accused of being either sociologically naive or humanly insensitive:

> For we can survive energy crisis, inflation, wars, revolutions, and insurrections, as they have been survived in the past; but if we transgress against the very basis of our mortal existence, becoming our own gods in our own universe, then we shall surely and deservedly perish from the earth.

It is noteworthy that the British journalist utters these words in direct connection with the questions of abortion and of euthanasia, which he believes "must surely attend on its heels."[28] Abortion as a broad option in a society thus appears not as a movement for liberty but as an option that places society at war with the God of nations and the God of the universe.

Here at last is the crux of the situation. Is the question of unlimited abortion (which is the goal of the proabortion forces in our time) one with which only the individuals immediately involved are concerned, or is it an issue that goes to the very heart of our civilization? After all, life is not easily sectored into prenatal-postnatal but is rather a continuum—a continuum in which the creative will of God is involved. It is a reasoned conclusion that no considerations of human convenience and human caprice are of sufficient weight to afford a safe guide in any course that ignores the divine role in human affairs, a role that is ignored and set aside when humans become the arbiters of life at and from its inception.

In the last analysis, our society must come to grips with several problematic issues, among which are the following:

1. Is the destruction of human fetuses a necessary step toward the liberation of human persons, and more especially, of women?
2. Is the destruction of human fetuses any less defensible when such a result is accomplished by so-called legal and sanitary methods?
3. Is there no other answer to the question of a burgeoning world population than that of an unlimited taking of incipient human beings?

Moreover, a society that recognizes, even in a rudimentary manner, the claims of God upon human life, must come to grips with the immeasurable worth of human life, and with the sovereign design of a God whose purposes alone give meaning to such preciousness. Thus the question of abortion as it is envisioned as an elective option to all prospective parents is ultimately a spiritual issue. Legislation, if enlightened, may undergird the mandate of "Thou shalt not kill" as applied to incipient human life no less than to the lives of existing persons. However, the only adequate basis for a society in which the entire continuum of life is safeguarded must be rooted in the individual and societal expression of persons whose consciences are *in*formed by the principle that God alone is Lord of life and Lord of death.

Notes

1. John A. Rasmussen, "Abortion: Historical and Biblical Perspectives," in *Concordia Quarterly,* 43 (January 1979), p. 23.
2. Leroy Augenstein, *Come, Let Us Play God* (New York: Harper and Row, 1969), p. 116.
3. *Ibid.,* p. 117.
4. Jeremiah 1:5.
5. Richard L Ganz, *Thou Shalt Not Kill: The Christian Case against Abortion* (New Rochelle, N.Y.: Arlington House, 1978), p. 9.
6. Clifford E. Bajema, *Abortion and the Meaning of Personhood,* p. 22.
7. Anne W. Kuhn, "Women's Liberation: Some Second Thoughts," in *The Asbury Seminarian,* vol. 31, no. 3 (July 1975), p. 5; Paul W. Kirkpatrick, "The Problem of Abortion," Unpublished Paper, Asbury Theological Seminary, December 1981, p. 6.
8. Dr. and Mrs. J. C. Wilkie, *Handbook on Abortion* (Cincinnati: Hiltz Co., 1971), p. 4.
9. C. Everett Koop, *The Right to Live, The Right to Die* (Wheaton, Ill.: Tyndale House, 1976), pp. 29ff.
10. Paul W. Kirkpatrick, "The Problem of Abortion," p. 5.
11. Richard L. Ganz, *Thou Shalt Not Kill,* p. 156.
12. Betty Sarvis and Hyman Rodman, *The Abortion Controversy* (New York: Columbia University Press, 1973).
13. John Finnis, "The Rights and Wrongs of Abortion," in Marshall Cohen, et. al., eds. *The Rights and Wrongs of Abortion* (Princeton, N.J.: Princeton University Press, 1974), p. 109.
14. Richard L. Ganz, *Thou Shalt Not Kill,* pp. 153ff.
15. *Ibid.,* pp. 154ff.
16. C. Everett Koop, *The Right to Live, The Right to Die,* p. 67.
17. David Granfield, *The Abortion Decision* (Garden City, N.Y.: Doubleday and Co., 1969), p. 154ff.
18. Paul W. Kirkpatrick, *The Problem of Abortion,* p. 14.
19. Richard L. Ganz, *Thou Shalt Not Kill,* p. 13.
20. *Ibid.,* p. 29.
21. *Ibid.,* p. 31.

22. *Ibid.*, p. 34.
23. Sarah K. Chatterji, ed., *Legalization of Abortion: Studies on National Legislation*, No. 3 (Madras India: 1971), p. 40.
24. Quoted in Koop, *The Right to Live, The Right to Die,* pp. 43ff.
25. *Ibid.*, p. 45.
26. C. Everett Koop, "*A Physician Looks at Abortion*" in Richard L. Ganz, *Thou Shalt Not Kill,* p. 39.
27. Everett C. Koop, *The Right to Live, The Right to Die,* pp. 36ff.
28. Malcom Muggeridge, *Human Life Review,* 1:3 (1975), p. 6, quoted in Ganz, *Thou Shalt Not Kill,* p. 112.

William S. Sailer (S.T.D., Temple University, Philadelphia), professor of systematic theology, Evangelical School of Theology

Homosexuality

SEXUALITY: THE BIBLICAL NORM

THE BIBLE is not a Victorian book. The very first reference to human beings (Gen. 1:26–28) says not only that they bear God's image but that they are "male and female" as well. Part of their mandate to exercise dominion over creation was to be fruitful and fill the earth. Adam's need for companionship was satisfied only by Eve, who was flesh of his flesh and bone of his bone (Gen. 2:22–23).

Without embarrassment Scripture records that Isaac caressed his wife—in public (Gen. 26:8). The joy of a bridegroom over his bride parallels God's own delight in his people Israel (Isa. 62:5). Fornication and adultery are condemned. But the sexual side of human existence is never portrayed as ignoble in itself. On the contrary, Scripture ingenuously portrays the physical joys of the marriage relationship between a man and a woman (Song of Sol.; Pro. 5:15-19), and employs the marriage figure to describe the relationship between Yahweh and Israel as well as that between Christ and the Church.

Depreciation of sexual expression among human beings stems more from Greek speculation than from biblical revelation. In general, Greek philosophy reckoned material substance to be evil (and eternal!) and therefore something to be avoided or negated as much as possible. The former Neo-Platonist, Augustine of Hippo, reflected more his Hellenistic than his biblical heritage when he concluded that sex, even within marriage, is necessarily tainted by sin and that it is the mechanism whereby depravity is visited upon each new generation.

Sexual expression that exploits or dehumanizes another person, even though it may go by the euphemism of "making love," always violates the biblical standard. Such sexual exploitation may—and does—happen even within marriage. But this does not negate the fact that a life-long monogamous relationship between a man and a woman is the proper context for physical sexual expression and the procreation of children (Matt. 19:4–6).

This biblical-theological creation motif regarding human sexuality provides the only valid and comprehensive standpoint from which to consider the question of homosexuality. And it is precisely at this point that many recent defenses of an epicene life-style fail. When pro-gay writers appeal to biblical evidence at all, they usually cite specific references to homosexual practice, and this in an attempt to show that these no longer apply or that they speak only to unloving, debased types of homosexual behavior. The force of the pervasive biblical understanding of human sexuality is ignored in an apparent effort to blunt the impact of the specific teaching of Scripture regarding homosexuality.

Scripture makes five direct references to homosexuality

(Lev. 18:22; 20:13; Rom. 1:26–27; 1 Cor. 6:9–10; and 1 Tim. 1:8–10) and alludes to it in four other places (Gen. 19:4–9; Judg. 19:22–26; 2 Pet. 2:1–22; and Jude 3–23). Since "many have taken in hand" to analyze these passages, we will refrain from repeating what others have already said.[1] Instead, we will concur with the judgment of others that the Bible nowhere condones, but rather uniformly condemns, homosexual practice.

We will note in passing, however, that an unwitting corroboration of this thesis is provided by a number of writers who feel compelled to reject biblical authority outright in order to defend a gay life-style. Thomas Maurer, for example, asks, "Why don't we have the courage and the candor to admit that the attitudes and opinions expressed by these ancient writers are thoroughly reprehensible and repugnant?"[2] In more restrained fashion, W. Norman Pittinger observes that "it would be absurd to use [the biblical] condemnation in a way that would imply that they were a precise disclosure of the will of God. . . . God never makes verbal pronouncements about moral duty, as many good people seem to think he does."[3] If Scripture supported, or at least failed to condemn homosexual practice, such caveats would be superfluous. Hence, we are emboldened to assert that there is at least a *prima facie* condemnation of homosexuality in the Scriptures.

We cannot, however, rest our case at this point for at least two reasons. First, there are those who reject our thesis, and scholarship demands that these objections be considered. Second, a condemnation of homosexuality—even one based on Scripture—cannot be the end of the matter. Homosexuals and lesbians are persons—persons made in the image of God and persons for whom Christ died. Therefore we must consider the Church's responsibility toward the gay subculture as well as the justness of legal and social attitudes toward homosexuals.

Reactions to the Biblical Norm

1. *Rejection.* As noted earlier, there are those who simply dismiss the biblical teachings out of hand. At bottom this reflects a total rejection of the Christian ethic—at least as traditionally understood to involve a word revelation from the Almighty that includes moral principles and rules designed to guide the people of God particularly, and others as well, regarding proper human conduct.

a. *Pragmatism.* According to this view, ethical decisions must be made on the basis of the latest scientific evidence available. Moral standards are no more than community opinions forged over the centuries, and as times and conditions change ethical maxims must be updated and revised. The views of John Money illustrate the application of this approach to sexual matters.

> There are no absolute standards of right and wrong—only a series of approximations as new data, new events, new artifacts and new people require the updating of old standards. . . . There is no absolute criterion by which to evaluate a bisexual cultural tradition as either superior or inferior to a monosexual one. The very existence and cultural viability of a bisexual society does, however, require that we in our society do not set up exclusive heterosexuality as an absolute norm. An exclusive heterosexual society is neither superior nor inferior to a bisexual one.[4]

This view reflects the pragmatic dictum that the good is what works, and it shares the weaknesses of this approach. Since space limitations do not permit an extensive critique of this philosophy,[5] a reediting of the thesis with the words *slavery* and *freedom* inserted at appropriate places will have to suffice: "The very existence and cultural viability of a *slaveholding* society does, however, require that we in our society do not set up *freedom* as an absolute norm. A *free* society is neither superior nor inferior to a *slaveholding* one." Someone might object that slavery dehumanizes other persons. But this introduces another (absolute?) norm and negates thereby the original premise, namely, that existence and viability of a practice determine its acceptability.

b. *Argumentum ad misericordiam.* An appeal to pity or sentimentalism is found in a wide spectrum of opinion regarding homosexuality. It is used by writers claiming to be evangelical and, on the surface, it may appear biblical. But upon further examination it turns out to be a basically secular approach that in reality negates the scriptural norm.

(1) *The homosexual as neighbor.* This approach appears patently in Scanzoni and Mollenkott's book *Is the Homosexual My Neighbor?*[6] This titular question has, of course, a biblical ring. And the biblical answer is: certainly the homosexual is my neighbor! However, in posing the question in this fashion, the authors subtly divert our attention from the biblical position toward one based upon secular sentimentalism. Through this appeal to our emotions and, perhaps, our sense of guilt as well, we are manipulated into admitting that since we indeed have a neighbor responsibility to the homosexual, we must condone his behavior—at least within certain limits.

An emotional argument deserves no more than an emotional response. May we not legitimately inquire when Scanzoni and Mollenkott will publish a series of sequels to their first volume? Some suggested titles might be *Is the Rapist My Neighbor? Is the Child Molester My Neighbor? Is the Klansman My Neighbor?* On the basis of the emotional "logic" of the first volume, we would have to conclude that these indeed are our neighbors, too, and therefore we must be nonjudgmental regarding rape, child abuse, and racism.

(2) *The homosexual as nice.* Again the Scanzoni and Mollenkott volume provides material illustrative of this appeal to pity. Two chapters in their book introduce us to homosexuals and lesbians who have excelled in the arts,

the sciences, and politics, or who have demonstrated a capacity to love on a deep level.[7] It is only following these chapters that any serious consideration is given to the teaching of Scripture regarding homosexuality. Somehow the reader is not greatly surprised by the handling of the biblical data nor by the conclusions reached. Again, responding in kind, we should remember that some murderers have demonstrated outstanding artistic ability and upon occasion a rapist turns out to be an otherwise upright and respected member of the community.

(3) *The homosexual as faggot.* This appeal to pity turns upon the current slang designation of homosexuals as "fags" or "faggots." Although these street expressions are apparently of recent origin (*Webster's Third New International Dictionary*, 1963, mentions it; the Second Edition, 1933, does not), several authors have tried to connect them, without supporting evidence, to an alleged medieval practice of burning homosexuals at the stake along with heretics and witches.[8]

The editors of the *Oxford English Dictionary,* however, know nothing of this proposed etymology. The OED does list an older dialect use of *faggot* as "a term of abuse or contempt applied to a woman." While this might provide a connection between *faggot* and *homosexual,* a more likely candidate is the more recent use of *fag* for a British school boy compelled to perform menial tasks for upperclassmen.[9]

The attempt to connect *fag* to medieval persecution of dissidents, then, appears to be nothing more than a myth concocted in order to stir up sympathy for long-suffering homosexuals and to instill guilt feelings in their detractors by subtly identifying the homosexual with the martyrs of the ages. But as Lewis Smedes has pointed out, "Compassion toward homosexual people is not a substitute for moral judgment on their actions. Empathy with people is not a basis for objective moral judgment on their conduct."[10]

Although we must not underestimate the effect of emotive argument on public and ecclesiastical opinion, we must not give the impression that this is the only type of defense employed in favor of homosexuality. There are approaches with more substance and with more apparent biblical foundation. To these we now turn.

2. *Realignment of the biblical norm.* Here we will examine several approaches that attempt to demonstrate that the Bible itself, when properly interpreted, requires us to reconsider its teachings on human sexuality and to reject the traditional interpretations of passages that seemingly condemn homosexuality.

a. *The appeal to love.* This approach, popularized by Joseph Fletcher in the mid-1960s, has exerted a widespread influence on contemporary moral attitudes. It insists that the ultimate norm of Christian decision making is love and nothing else. "Love . . . shoulders aside all codes," wrote Fletcher. "The Christian ethic reduces law from a statutory system of rules to the love canon alone. Love is a 'jealous' law to itself. It does not share its power with other kinds of law, either natural or supernatural."[11]

This appeal to love is of special interest to Wesleyans. At first sight, at least, there seems to be an affinity between Fletcher's situationism and John Wesley's notion of Christian perfection, which he defines in terms of perfect love. For Wesley, "scriptural perfection is pure love filling the heart and governing all the words and actions." It is nothing more or less than "pure love reigning alone in our heart and life."[12] One attaining this state of pure love might err in his actions. "Yet where every word and action springs from love, such a mistake is not properly a sin."[13]

Despite Wesley's bold affirmation of the potency and centrality of love, situationists do not as a rule appeal to him for support. This is as it should be. For there is a great gulf fixed between the approaches of Wesley and Fletcher. And although an extended analysis and critique of situation ethics lies beyond the scope of this chapter, a brief comparison of eighteenth-century Methodism with twentieth-century act-agapism may serve to forestall the mistaking of superficial similarity of language for substantial agreement in theory and practice.

The shared emphasis on the indispensability of love provides a convenient focus for comparison, since the term plays a central but radically different role in the two approaches. For Fletcher, love is generic, a natural capacity within the reach of every person. For Wesley, love is a specifically Christian grace received through faith. For Fletcher, love is autonomous, a law to itself that provides its own content and guidelines in a given ethical situation. For Wesley love is structured and guided by God's positive law revealed in Scripture. For Fletcher, as noted previously, love is the antithesis of law, "both natural and supernatural." For Wesley, love is the inner *motive* that impels the believer to obey, to carry out, the revealed commands of God.

A section from a 1750 sermon, "The Law Established by Faith; Discourse II," aimed at the antinomians of his day, summarizes Wesley's understanding of love:

> And by faith, taken in its more particular meaning for a confidence in a pardoning God, we establish his law in our own hearts in a still more effectual manner. For there is no motive which so powerfully inclines us to love God as the sense of the love of God in Christ. Nothing enables us like a piercing conviction of this to give our hearts to him who was given for us. And from this principle of grateful love to God arises love to our brother also.[14]

Wesley correctly understood love as an inner drive urging the Christian to perform the revealed will of God, and not as an autonomous principle rendering the law of God superfluous. On the other hand, Wesley's balanced biblical understanding prevented him from viewing the divine command as a heteronomous code mechanically imposed upon the Christian from without.[15] Rather, the law of God resonates harmoniously with the renewed heart of the believer. In the same discourse, Wesley observes,

> We then establish the law when we declare every part of it, every commandment contained therein, not only in its full, literal sense but likewise in its spiritual meaning, not only with regard to the outward actions which it either forbids or enjoins, but also with respect to the inward principle, to the thoughts, desires and intents of the heart.[16]

Because of this reciprocity between heart and precept, Wesley has no need to dread legalism as Fletcher apparently does. In another context Wesley warned, "Do not stupidly and senselessly call this 'legal'—a silly, unmeaning word. Be not afraid of being 'under the law of God,' but of being 'under the law of sin.' "[17] Submission to the law of God prevented Wesley from succumbing to the subjectivism and utilitarianism that plague modern situation ethics. Fletcher, on the other hand, mired in utilitarian circularity, can say only that "love is doing what is in the neighbor's best interest."[18] Wesley, settled upon divine revelation, can meaningfully characterize love as "fulfilling of the positive, likewise, as well as of the negative law of God."[19]

Recently Walter Wink applied the modern love ethic particularly to the question of homosexuality. For him, "there is no biblical sex ethic. The Bible knows only a love ethic, which is constantly brought to bear on whatever sexual mores are dominant in a given country, culture, or period."[20] A curious argument follows to support this contention. Wink cites more than a dozen Old Testament sanctions regarding sexual practices. Since we no longer feel bound to observe many or even most of these, he concludes that there is *no* sex ethic in the Bible. This queer logic seems to say that an ignored command is a nonexistent command!

There are, however, other possible ways of handling the

Old Testament sex ethic. We could, for example, accept it *in toto* as God's will for today and continue to observe all of it. Or, more in keeping with sound principles of biblical theology and progressive revelation, we may distinguish between temporary, ceremonial-pedagogical provisions and permanent commands that reflect the moral will of God as binding on all persons at all times and in all places.[21] While this latter approach has its own problems and gray areas—as Wink points out—it is by no means the impossible task he tries to make of it.

Wink, however, prefers to view the biblical record as a one-dimensional collection of rules, a seamless robe to be taken or left in its entirety.[22] Hence, he argues that if we wish to reject homosexuality on the basis of Leviticus 18:22, we must also regard as unclean those persons who touch semen or menstrual blood (cf. Lev. 15:16–24).

Despite an appeal to a *biblical* ethic of love, however, it is not difficult to spot important similarities between Wink's approach and that of the thoroughly secular approach of John Money. The coating of "love" is not thick enough to prevent Wink from admitting that

> approached from the point of view of the Spirit rather than of the letter, the question ceases to be "What does Scripture command?" and becomes "What is the Word that the Spirit speaks to the churches now, in the light of Scripture, tradition, theology, psychology, genetics, anthropology and biology?"[23]

If we stop asking what Scripture commands, however, are we not left to wonder what role, if any, remains for Scripture to play? We suspect that its voice is largely muted amid the din arising from the natural and social sciences.

b. *The appeal to grace.* Some homophile theologians frankly admit that Scripture catalogs homosexuality as sin—but along with pride, bad temper, gossip, and gluttony. We may not, then, single out sexual sin for special censure; we must recognize that every believer is *simul justus et peccator,* at the same time righteous and a sinner. And because our gracious God forgives his penitent heterosexual children all their trespasses for Christ's sake, they in turn should reflect this divine love and receive, without censure, their gay brothers and sisters.

This appeal to the grace of God has a certain surface validity. Christians standing in the Reformation tradition do not distinguish mortal from venial sins. And no one, not even the most mature, may count the blood of Christ as no longer necessary.[24]

Closer scrutiny, however, reveals flaws in this line of reasoning. First, it appears to minimize the regenerating and sanctifying power of the Holy Spirit in the lives of believers. If Christians may *legitimately* defend the works of the flesh simply because others in the household of faith are similarly afflicted, it would mean the virtual end of all effort toward sanctification that Scripture clearly commands.[25]

Second, this defense of homosexuality rests upon a highly unstable foundation. It is difficult not only spiritually but psychologically as well for a believer to openly defend—in herself or himself or in another—a habitual violation of a biblical command on the basis of the foibles of fellow Christians or the infinite grace of God. One of two things will likely happen. Either the convicting power of Word and Spirit will lead to a change of behavior, or the biblically proscribed behavior will ultimately be considered innocuous. Hence the purveyors of "cheap grace" must realize that they stand on a slippery slope. This homosexuality-is-a-sin-but-we're-all-sinners approach easily glides over to the position that some homosexuality at least is not condemned by Scripture. "The gay believer today is no longer *simul justus et peccator, . . .* he is simply *justus.*"[26]

c. *The appeal to normalcy.* In 1973 the American Psychiatric Assocation removed homosexuality from its list of recognized personality disorders. This, of course, has lent credence to the growing gay rights movement that insists that "gay is good." A similar trend has surfaced in ecclesiastical circles as well. In this case the biblical witness is often summoned to testify on behalf of the gay life-style. The following three lines of thought may be discerned:

(1) *Homosexual rape as sin.* Traditionally the account in Genesis 19 of the divine judgment upon the notorious city of Sodom was regarded as a weighty, if indirect, condemnation of homosexuality (cf. the term *sodomy*). Recently, however, this understanding has come under fire. D. Sherwin Baily, for instance, suggests that the intent of the men of Sodom was social, not sexual. Hence their insatiable insistence on checking out the credentials of Lot's visitors rendered them guilty of nothing more than inhospitality.[27] We agree with Derek Kidner that Baily's thesis will not stand serious scrutiny[28] (cf. Lot's offering the men his daughters) and we mention it here only because its ghost lingers on in later citations.[29]

Somewhat more plausible is the suggestion that the culpable design of the men of Sodom was homosexual violence or gang rape. This is certainly a valid analysis of the ancient scenario—as far as it goes. Some, however, infer from this that the townspeople of Sodom were "quite likely" primarily heterosexual, that they engaged in occasional homosexual acts as a means of humiliating their enemies by forcing them to assume the role of women.[30]

However likely that interpretation may be, it is far more likely, in the context, that the lives of the Sodomites were characterized by habitual homosexual practice and *therefore* their hostility toward the strangers took this particular form. The intent of the story is surely to present the characteristic behavior of Sodom as deserving the impending divine judgment. It would be strange, then, to choose an infrequent activity as a paradigm of the city's evil life-style. Further, it must be noted that the city was destroyed not on account of the specific behavior of its people toward Lot's guests, but because of habitual gross wickedness epitomized by their behavior on this occasion.

To conclude that only forceful homosexual rape is condemned in this pericope is, further, to isolate it from the creation account and the institution of heterosexual marriage found in the earlier chapters of Genesis. God's judgment came upon Sodom because its residents were violating their basic humanity as created in the divine image. In the light of this, then, we must reject as inadequate the notion that only homosexual rape is in view here.

(2) *Homosexual idolatry as sin.* In the so-called Holiness Code (Lev. 17–25) God spells out certain aspects of religious and moral purity he expects of his people who are to be holy because he is holy (Lev. 19:2). Among other requirements, God requires a repudiation of homosexual practice. "You shall not lie with a male as with a woman; it is an abomination" (Lev. 18:22). "If a man lies with a male as with a woman, both of them have committed an abomination" (Lev. 20:13).

Because these warnings occur among ceremonial prohibitions that Christians no longer observe, some argue that the prohibition of homosexual activity per se need not be observed either. The real sin in view is idolatry, compromising the true worship of Yahweh with the pagan practices of Israel's neighbors.

In response to this, it may be pointed out once again that there is a distinction in Scripture between temporary, ceremonial laws and permanent moral prescriptions. The former have been fulfilled through the obedience of Christ and no longer bind the believer. The latter, including the disallowance of homosexual practice, still convey to us the divine moral standard. "Therefore, we recognize the category of temporary ceremonial law in the Old Testament. However, there is no good reason to assign the prohibition of homosexuality to it. They do not anticipate the person and work of Christ for salvation in any sense."[31] Further, this condemnation of homosexual practice is reiterated in the New Testament. In addition to Romans 1, there are the statements in 1 Corinthians 6:9–10 and 1 Timothy 1:9–10 condemning homosexual activity in the lives of the people of God.

(3) *Homosexual perversion as sin.* In Romans 1:26–27 Paul describes the degraded behavior of sinful men and women who exchange natural sexual functions for unnatural homosexual and lesbian relationships. But some have argued that, unbeknown to Paul, there are persons so constituted that for them homosexual attraction is not an unnatural perversion. For such persons homophilia is perfectly normal; indeed, heterosexual desire would be unnatural. Hence, only the pervert, not the constitutional homosexual, would fall under the Apostle's scathing denunciation.

This alleged distinction between perversion and inversion leads logically to a consideration of the biological and/or psychological origins of homosexuality. Is it genetically based, a result of early family and social conditioning, or is it a deliberate (and presumably sinful) choice on the part of the individual? Since even a cursory analysis of the data marshaled in an attempt to answer these questions lies beyond the scope of our present investigation, we will observe only that the evidence at present for a genetic origin of homosexuality appears quite weak.

Any remaining uncertainty or confusion regarding the genesis of homosexual tendencies need not greatly concern us here. This is not really germane to Romans 1, and its intrusion into the discussion derives from basic misunderstandings of the text. First, there is the mistaken notion that Paul speaks of homosexual behavior that is *unnatural* or against the nature of the individual involved in it. Rather, Paul considers this behavior to be against nature in general and against human nature in particular. Lovelace points out,

> Paul's statement that homosexual practice is "against nature" does not mean that it is against the "natural orientation" or inner drives of an individual. He distinctly says that the desires and actions of those mentioned in verses 26, 27 are homosexual *and* in harmony with one another. "Against nature" simply means against God's intention for human sexual behavior which is plainly visible in nature, in the complementary function of male and female sexual organs and temperaments.[32]

In the second place, an attempt to provide an inversion/perversion escape hatch on the basis of Romans 1:26–27 fails to recognize the creation context of Scripture in general and of Romans 1 in particular. As David Field has well stated,

> In writing about "natural relations" Paul is not referring to individual men and women *as they are*. His canvas is much broader. He is taking the argument back, far more radically, to man and woman *as God created them*. By *unnatural* he means "unnatural to mankind in God's creation pattern." And that pattern he clearly understands to be heterosexual. So the distinction between pervert and invert (which Paul would hardly have made anyway) is by-passed. The "exchange" he has in mind is not just the capricious sex swapping of the pervert in his search for fresh stimulation, but the divergence *all* homosexual behavior represents from God's creation scheme. When set in the context of creation, all homosexual relations are "unnatural relations."[33]

Interestingly, Scanzoni and Mollenkott make much of the social and religious contexts of Romans 1 in an effort to justify "natural" homosexual relations, but they fail consistently to mention the far deeper and broader context of creation. Furthermore, once these authors have established (to their satisfaction) the invert-pervert distinction, they make little or nothing of it. It is the homosexual *per se* who is my neighbor. In the final analysis, invert and pervert alike escape the maledictions of Romans 1.

The Homosexual As Person

Besides teaching the sinfulness of homosexuality, the Bible also commands us to show love and concern to all—enemies, Greeks, barbarians. And Jesus' ministry to taxgatherers and prostitutes certainly provides a pattern for his church to minister to the outcasts and subcultures of every age. It is clear that Christians have only haltingly followed their Lord in this ministry of compassion. A number of reasons for this, particularly as it relates to reaching homosexuals, may be isolated.

1. *The problem of fear.* From the homosexual community itself comes the neologism "homophobia" or fear of homosexuals. This fear often lurks beneath the level of consciousness in many heterosexuals. To reach out to the homosexual, then, is really to engage in a threatening cross-cultural ministry. And the culture shock can be as severe as any encountered in a foreign land.

Even reaching out to a lone homosexual, one who is not aligned with the gay subculture, can prove challenging. There is always the fear of contamination. A straight male, for example, might understandably feel uncomfortable sharing on a one-to-one basis with another fellow who might find him sexually attractive. Discretion would certainly be advised in selecting places to meet and so on. And apparently this fear is not entirely groundless. There have been instances in which reoriented homosexuals began evangelistic ministries to their former culture only to be taken in again by the gay life-style.

2. *The problem of hatred.* Although no one has come up with a convenient label for it, there seems to be a deep-seated hatred for homosexuals as well. It is apparent in the derogatory street labels attached to gay persons: fag,

pansy, fairy, and others best left unmentioned. Although this hatred abounds in the secular world, it is by no means confined there. It is prevalent also in the Church—either consciously or subconsciously.

Part of the dynamic behind this negative feeling may be the Bible's strict censure of homosexual activity. However, feelings seem to run much stronger here than they do in the case of thieves or murderers—even though these are condemned by Scripture as well. Homosexuals are discussed in whispered tones of disgust as purveyors of unpardonable and irreversible perversity. A balanced biblical approach to the homosexual, however, requires that we see him or her as a fellow sinner still within reach of the grace of God.

3. *The need for caution and compassion*. Ministering to the gay subculture may well be a specialized calling best carried on by persons with specific spiritual gifts. It took a Hellenized Jew like Saul of Tarsus to break down the pro-Semitism of the early church and reach the Gentile world for Christ. So it may take persons with special knowledge—perhaps even experience—of the gay world to reach homosexuals for Christ in a biblical manner.

This does not excuse the rest of us for allowing our fear and/or hatred of homosexuals to go unchecked. Through obedience to the Word of Christ we can change our attitudes toward other subcultures, be they black, Hispanic, neo-Nazi, or gay.

Especially worthy of our compassion is the "constitutional homosexual." While a genetic origin for homosexuality has certainly not been proved, there do seem to be persons who, perhaps as a result of early childhood experience, find themselves unaccountably oriented sexually toward other persons of the same gender. Heart-rending confessions by gays of evangelical persuasion reveal tremendous struggles with fears, guilt feelings, and fruitless attempts at reform.[34] Of course, this does not make their gay orientation "natural" or place it outside the strictures of Romans 1. Their situation is nonetheless something different from the bisexual or the person who consciously takes the homosexual path to satisfy lust. But even these latter persons remain within the circle of Christian love and concern.

Our compassion must also extend to the families of homosexuals. Parents, siblings, and other relatives of gay persons often carry great burdens of shame and even of guilt. And such persons may be more numerous and nearer at hand than we might think. One recent study indicates that on the basis of an estimated 10 percent of the male population being homosexual and 5 percent of females lesbian, a congregation might have a sizable group of gay persons in it.[35] Perhaps it is illegitimate to attribute to the Church the same percentages found in the general population. But there can be no doubt that homosexuality is a far greater problem in the Church than evangelicals often recognize.

The love we are called upon to show the homosexual might be termed "tough love." Despite the contemporary calls to sentimentalism and cheap grace, the biblical standards simply will not allow the evangelical Christian to condone a gay life-style. In the final analysis—however distasteful this may seem to practicing homosexuals and their sympathizers—the biblical demand is for the homosexual to change his or her orientation or else to remain celibate. Only a misguided weak sentimentalism would allow homosexuals to flaunt or promote their peculiar life-style within the Christian fellowship.

Another side to tough love calls for the Church to cast aside its ingrained fear and hatred of homosexuals and to permit repentant gay persons to become participating members of the Christian fellowship. Tough love must be willing as well to reach out with compassion to the practicing homosexual and say I love you—even as you are.

Former homosexuals testify to the fact that encountering genuine nonjudgmental love in a caring Christian was the turning point in conquering their gay orientation.[36]

The Homosexual and Society

The Church exists within the context of the world. There are civil laws as well as ecclesiastical disciplines. After examining the teaching of Scripture concerning homosexuality and the proper attitude of Christians toward gays, attention will now be given to the proper attitude of society toward homosexuality.

1. *The extremes.* To begin, we will examine two extreme positions. The first is avowedly secular; the second claims a biblical base. From a balanced biblical perspective, however, both are unacceptable. The truth, in this case at least, lies in a mean position between the extremes.

a. *The gay liberation movement.* At one end of the spectrum stands the gay rights movement. After generations of closeted existence, many homosexuals and bisexuals are today announcing, even celebrating, their sexual predilection. Not only is homosexuality okay in their eyes; it is downright respectable and even superior to heterosexuality. From a hidden persecuted minority, homosexuals in a few short years have become a visible and vocal part of mainstream Western culture.

In evidence of this, we may mention the paid radio spot announcements aired in the spring of 1981 by the Gay Liberation Front of Philadelphia. The thrust of the message was this: we are a part of society, we are here to stay, and we are going to help shape the moral standards of the community. In February 1981 a full-page situation-wanted ad appeared in *The Christian Century.* The ad, placed by "an open and responsible gay person," implied that a gay orientation would help to equip the applicant for a position in the field of human service, dealing with "alienated adults, including aging, handicapped, rural, poor and single people.''[37]

Reflecting this positive appraisal of homosexuality, the Roman Catholic scholar John J. McNiell cites the need to provide a positive self-image for homosexual believers. To provide this the Church must accept not only the individual homosexual, but the gay community as well. ''Homosexuals, especially the young, have a desperate need of models of what it means to live out a full human life as a homosexual.''[38] McNeill's even more pointed affirmations of a homophile life-style are summarized by Lovelace:

> Most remarkably, McNeill argues that the homophile community has a God-appointed, providential role in alerting the rest of the Christian community to the dangers of male dominance in the traditional family pattern, to the positive values in the narcissist phase of psychological development of which homosexuality may be an arrested expression, to the need for accepting our own homosexual tendencies through reconciliation with exclusive homosexuals, to the need for homosexuals as ''catalyzers of heterosexuality,'' to the possibility of disinterested intersexual relationships, to the validity of teaching and artistic gifts among males, and to the refinements of religious sensibility for which homosexuals have special proclivity.''[39]

You've come a long way baby! Once a victim of intolerance and ignorance, then a fellow sinful recipient of the Savior's grace, the homosexual has now metamorphosed into a savior of family, Church, and society.

b. *The Chalcedon school.* At the other extreme stands a contemporary movement within Reformed theology, the so-called Chalcedon school, which calls for an almost complete application of the personal, religious, and social morality of the old covenant to our contemporary situation.[40] This approach demands that not only the biblical ethical *standards* be maintained, but that the corresponding biblical *sanctions* be imposed upon every violator of divine law. Hence not only murder, but adultery, blasphemy, and homosexuality remain capital crimes, and every civil magistrate in this and every other age has a scriptural mandate and obligation to enforce the whole moral law of God by imposing the retributions specified by Old Testament law. While the sacrifice of Christ on the cross exempts us from performing the Old Testament sacrificial rituals, no corresponding New Testament revelation frees us from the precepts and penalties of the Mosaic moral system.

Modern secularists will, of course, judge that legislation abhorrent in our age and in antiquity as well. Evangelicals, however, must not respond in the same fashion. If we accept the divine inspiration of Scripture, we must admit that this was indeed a divinely legislated moral code intended for the well-being of God's people under the Old Testament theocracy. Further, we must not look upon it as a lower level of moral perception that moderns have transcended. Present-day burgeoning crime statistics, crowded prisons, unpunished felons, and terrorized law-abiding citizens eloquently attest the failure of modern criminological theory and the bankruptcy of our almost sacred myth of criminal rehabilitation. We might, in fact, look back nostalgically to an age when restitution was required of lawbreakers and habitual criminals were removed from society by execution or banishment. We cannot then ignore the Chalcedon formula on the basis of a misguided, humanistically inspired emotionalism. The question remains, however, Does the entire legal-penal code of the Mosaic system apply in the age of the new covenant?

As much as we may wish to commend the Chalcedon spokespersons for attempting to establish a thoroughly biblical base for all life, we must answer our question negatively. There are serious deficiencies in this approach. First of all, it fails to take seriously enough the progressive revelation found in the Scriptures and the substantial differences (in spite of a basic continuity) between the old and new covenants. In effect, Chalcedon follows the opposite path from dispensationalism. Instead of insisting upon an almost total dispensational discontinuity between Christian and pre-Christian administrations, Chalcedon allows virtually no distinction at all. In this way it fails to recognize the uniqueness of the theocratic Davidic kingdom (and its earlier Mosaic expression) that set Israel apart from the other nations upon earth. As M. G. Kline has pointed out, "while the Bible says Israel was separated from the other nations to be a unique, holy kingdom [Chalcedon], says that God's kingdom Israel was just another civil government." This is tantamount either to a "denial of the holy status of the Israelite kingdom" or, put the other way, a "sacralizing [of] the other nations."[41]

While the secular state remains a divinely sanctioned institution (Rom. 13:1–4; 1 Pet. 2:13–14), it no longer functions as did Israel's kings of old as a guardian of exclusively private morality or piety. It is to punish social evil and maintain an environment within which law-abiding persons may pursue their callings in tranquility.

In addition to these general biblical-theological considerations, we may note further that the New Testament does mandate a type of sanction against violations of the law of God that does indeed differ from that found in the earlier dispensation. Paul, for example, upholds the right of the state to impose the death penalty upon evildoers (Acts 25:11), but neither he nor the other apostles impose it themselves. God, not Peter, capitally punished Ananias and Sapphira for lying (Acts 5:1–11). And disfellowshiping, rather than stoning, was imposed by Paul as punishment for the incestuous adulterer in the Corinthian church (1 Cor. 5:1–3). In this age, the followers of Christ are to love their enemies (Matt. 5:44), seek by moral suasion and preaching to bring them to faith in Christ (Matt. 28:19–20;

2 Cor. 5:20), and leave retribution for personal immorality and impiety to the final judgment (Acts 17:31).[42]

2. *The biblical mean.* Occupying middle territory between enemy flanks is seldom prudent in warfare or debate. Nevertheless, we choose this position not because of any affinity for Aristotle's ethic of the golden mean but in an endeavor to develop a biblically based social ethic with respect to homosexuality.

Responding to the fire from the right flank, we reassert our conviction that it is *not* the business of the civil government in the age of the New Testament to exact piety or private, personal morality from its citizens. It is, of course, true that personal morality can and does influence society. Widespread drunkenness weakens the social fabric and decreases productivity among the citizenry. But so do lack of sleep and gluttony. Yet few would wish to have a nation's police power diverted toward a vain attempt to ensure an 11 P.M. bedtime and a 2500 calorie per day diet for every adult citizen. *Mutatis mutandis,* what consenting adults do in the privacy of their bedsheets lies beyond the punitive jurisdiction of the state. The constitution guarantees to everyone the right to life, liberty, and the pursuit of happiness—without defining the what or the how of the latter—so long as it does not interfere with another citizen's equally valid rights.

We cannot, however, base a Christian social ethic on such an abstract "liberty ideal" that tends to sanction any behavior so long as it does not hurt someone else. The ideal itself provides no grounds for concern about others, nor can it define what is meant by hurting someone. Is this physical only? Or does it also include psychological and moral hurt as well? At this point we agree with Greg Bahnsen, an adherent of the Chalcedon school, when he observes, "The liberty ideal must be evaluated as insufficient in itself and in need of a Christian foundation to be valid. Therefore it cannot undermine the conclusion that we should decide whether homosexuality is a crime on the basis of God's infallible Word.''[43] Bahnsen then proceeds to criminalize homosexuality not because of any real or imagined negative social consequences but because it was (and remains) a punishable crime under biblical law. Any other approach to the problem, Bahnsen asserts, quickly places us at mercy of subjective feelings or the kaleidoscopic views of psychological and sociological theorists.

Bahnsen's solution does have a certain attractiveness. As M. G. Kline admits, ''The exegetical task of determining the specific sphere of the state's legal domain may be more difficult for us than it would be if we could subscribe to Chalcedon's simplistic equation of Israel's theocratic law with state law.''[44] But for reasons noted previously, we must conclude that Bahnsen's insistence upon the criminalization of homosexuality does not in reality derive from a proper exegetical base.

Training our guns now on the left flank, we must voice objection to the attempts of the militant gay liberation movements to normalize and legalize homosexuality. At this point, the issues do significantly impinge upon society and therefore become a legitimate concern of the state as well as of the Church. Western civilization—indeed world civilization—is predicated on marriage and the family. While for Christians these are divine institutions, they are at least traditional arrangements for the majority of humankind. Militant homosexuals, on the other hand, are avowedly antifamily. And although few families approach perfection, the political and communal alternatives currently being promoted raise more visions of Orwell's *1984* than of Eden.

In the light of this threat to the family, then, the state has the duty to refuse legal recognition, so persistently sought today by the gay community, of a homophile lifestyle. To enact specific civil rights legislation on behalf of homosexuals would be tantamount to social and judicial recognition of a homosexual life-style. The same would be true of civil marriages contracted between homosexuals or lesbians. To deny legal marriage between gay persons is not, as often charged, to rob such persons of their civil rights. They already have the right to cohabit if they so desire. And suitable legal instruments already exist to protect the property rights of individuals entering into such arrangements. They may draw up legal contracts of various sorts to spell out how mutual property is to be divided in case the arrangements are terminated. To allow for homosexual "marriage," on the other hand, would cheapen, if not destroy, traditional marriage by calling virtually any live-in arrangement a "marriage."

Another concern raised by the militant gay rights movement is the protection of the young. According to psychological studies, many children go through a "homosexual" stage in which they experience an infatuation with persons of the same sex. Usually this phase passes and the young person goes on to develop normal heterosexual attractions. But if, during these vulnerable years, a child is provided with homosexual role models and is counseled that gay and straight life-styles are equally viable options, an enormous growth in the homosexual segment of society would almost certainly result. Especially in these days of McLuhanesque hot and cool media, this offensive by gay activists is not a mirage. Novels and TV programs can provide subtle hints that the gay way is as normal as lefthandedness or brown eyes. Allowing openly avowed, vocal homosexuals to participate in the teaching, acting, and sports professions would have a similar impact upon impressionable young persons.

In the final analysis, then, the gay rights movement, if successful, would deprive a large segment of the population of *their* civil right to maintain traditional (and biblical!) family and sexual mores. It is not improper, therefore, for

Christians and other persons of like mind on these issues to use social and legislative means to stem or even reverse the tide toward moral anarchy. The charge of imposing one's moral and religious values on others will not stick. Every attempt at social legislation of any kind of necessity reflects some moral or religious world view and necessarily involves imposing strictures on other persons who happen to disagree with the legislation.

True, ours is a pluralistic society. For generations we have lived and worked together as Catholic, Protestant, Jew—and atheist. However, the persons feeding into this religious and ethnic mix had, for the most part, shared common basic social and psychological assumptions regarding marriage, family life, and social decency. Now the question arises, Can a society be almost totally pluralistic, sharing virtually no common values and goals, and yet remain a *society* in any meaningful sense of the term? Any society, it would seem, be it the Sierra Club or a local sewing circle, must have some significant shared beliefs and interests—or it will cease to function as a social unit.

American society can—and over the years has—tolerated small minorities that have been out of step with the mainstream drummer. But when these minorities become significant militant segments of the population, will the comradeship—the root meaning of *social*—necessary for cooperative living be strong enough to prevent disintegration?

Summary

A balanced study of the biblical teaching regarding sexuality and homosexuality makes it impossible for one committed to biblical authority to accept homosexuality as a normal alternative life-style. The biblical mandate directs us as well to love and minister in Christ's name to homosexuals, sharing with them the liberating power of the gospel. In this age of the new covenant, it is not for the state to ferret out and punish consenting adult homosexuals. The state, as a divine institution, does have the right and obligation to protect the family and the young and therefore must refrain from enacting legislation that would normalize or encourage the spread of the gay life-style.

Notes

1. See for example Richard F. Lovelace, *Homosexuality and the Church* (Old Tappen, N.J.: Fleming H. Revell, 1978), pp. 87–116; and Greg L. Bahnsen, *Homosexuality: A Biblical View* (Grand Rapids: Baker, 1978), pp. 27–61.
2. W. Dwight Oberholtzer, ed., *Is Gay Good? Ethics, Theology and Homosexuality* (Philadelphia: The Westminster Press, 1971), p. 135.
3. W. Norman Pittenger, *Time for Consent,* 2nd ed. (London: SCM Press, 1970), p. 43. The denial of verbal revelation remains a watershed dividing Neo-Protestant from evangelical theology. For an able critique of this modern existentialist, noncognitive concept of revelation, see Gordon H. Clark, *Three Types of Religious Philosophy* (The Craig Press, 1973) pp. 82–101.
4. John Money, "Issues and Attitudes in Research and Treatment of Variant Forms of Human Sexual Behavior," in *Ethical Issues in Sex Therapy and Research,* W. H. Masters, V. E. Johnson and R. C. Kolodny, eds. (Boston: Little, Brown and Co., 1977), p. 126.
5. For an extended critical analysis of pragmatism, see Gordon H. Clark, *Thales to Dewey* (Boston: Houghton Mifflin Co., 1957), pp. 498–533.
6. Letha Scanzoni and Virginia Ramey Mollenkott, *Is the Homosexual My Neighbor? Another Christian View* (New York: Harper & Row, 1978.
7. *Neighbor,* pp. 12–42.
8. For a recent example. see Walter Wink, "Biblical Perspectives on Homosexuality," *The Christian Century* (1979), vol. 96, no. 26, p. 1082.
9. *The Oxford English Dictionary* (London: Oxford University Press, 1933), vol. IV, pp. 19–20.

10. Cited in *Evangelical Newsletter* (January 13, 1978), p. 3.
11. Joseph Fletcher, *Moral Responsibility* (London: SCM Press, 1967), p. 17.
12. John Wesley, "Thoughts on Christian Perfection," in *John Wesley,* Albert C. Outler, ed. (New York: Oxford University Press, 1964), p. 293.
13. "Thoughts," p. 285.
14. *John Wesley,* p. 229.
15. This is how Norman H. G. Robinson in *The Groundwork of Christian Ethics* (Grand Rapids: Wm. B. Eerdmans Publishing Co., 1971), pp. 153–54, views the "fundamentalist" ethics of A. A. Hodge. In the light of ethical studies by Carl F. H. Henry, John Murray and others, it is interesting that Robinson dipped back one hundred years to find an evangelical ethic to characterize (caricature?).
16. *John Wesley,* pp. 223–24.
17. "A Blow to the Roots," *John Wesley,* p. 382.
18. Fletcher himself characterizes his own approach as a variation of J. Bentham's utilitarianism in *Situation Ethics* (London: SCM Press, 1966), p. 95. For an able critique of Fletcher's position, see J. Charles King, "The Inadequacy of Situation Ethics," *The Thomist,* 1970, vol. 34, no. 3, pp. 423–37.
19. *John Wesley,* p. 230.
20. "Biblical Perspectives on Homosexuality," *The Christian Century* (1979), vol. 96, no. 26, pp. 1082–1086. For a fuller, and far more profound, analysis of the biblical concept of love, see Leon Morris, *Testaments of Love: A Study of Love in the Bible* (Grand Rapids: Wm. B. Eerdmans Publishing Co., 1981).
21. See, for example, John N. Oswalt, "The Old Testament and Homosexuality," in Charles W. Keysor, ed., *What You Should Know about Homosexuality.* (Grand Rapids: Zondervan), pp. 17–77.
22. See N. H. G. Robinson's discussion in *Groundwork,* pp. 152–54.
23. "Perspectives," p. 1085.
24. See J. J. Escher, *Christliche Theologie* (Cleveland: Thomas & Mattill, 1899), pp. 461–62.

25. See Lovelace's discussion of "cheap grace" in *Homosexuality and the Church,* pp. 71–75.
26. *Homosexuality and the Church,* p. 75.
27. *Homosexuality and the Western Christian Tradition* (New York: Longmans, Green & Co., 1955), pp. 1–28.
28. F. D. Kidner, *Genesis* (Downers Grove, Ill.: Inter-Varsity Press, 1967), p. 137.
29. See, for example, *Neighbor,* p. 55.
30. *Neighbor,* p. 56.
31. Bahnsen, *Biblical View,* p. 39.
32. Lovelace, *Homosexuality and Church,* p. 92.
33. David Field, *The Homosexual Way—A Christian Option?* (Downers Grove, Ill.: Inter-Varsity Press, 1979), p. 30.
34. See, for example, Alex Davidson, *The Returns of Love* (London: Inter-Varsity Press, 1970). A common theme in such testimonials is the lament "I prayed for deliverance and nothing happened." For a full-orbed statement of the power of the gospel to transform homosexuals (and homophobiacs as well) see *Homosexuality and Church,* pp. 129–42, and R. F. Lovelace, *Dynamics of Spiritual Life: An Evangelical Theology of Renewal* (Downers Grove, Ill.: Inter-Varsity Press, 1979).
35. The Kinsey Report, *Sexual Behavior in the Human Male,* cited in *Homosexuality and Church,* pp. 29–30.
36. Tom Minnery, "Homosexuals Can Change," *Christianity Today* (1981), vol. 25, no. 3, p. 174.
37. *The Christian Century* (1981), vol. 98, no. 4, p. 139.
38. *Homosexuality and Church,* p. 53.
39. *Homosexuality and Church,* p. 53.
40. For extended presentations of this approach, see Greg L. Bahnsen, *Theonomy in Christian Ethics* (Nutley, N.J.: The Craig Press, 1977) and R. J. Rushdoony, *The Institutes of Biblical Law* (Nutley, N.J.: The Craig Press, 1973).
41. Meredith G. Kline, "Comments on an Old-New Error," *The Westminster Theological Journal* (1978), vol. 41, no. 1, p. 178. For a more appreciative but still critical appraisal, see John M. Frame, "The Institutes of Biblical Law," *The Westminster Theological Journal* (1976), vol. 38, no. 2, pp. 195–217.

42. It might be argued that since the apostles lacked political muscle they were compelled to settle for lesser penalties in cases of impiety or personal moral wrongdoing. However, one would expect that they would have at least stated the ideal and counseled patience on the part of the Church until such time as an ecclesiastically controlled government might be established. But such counsel is not found in the pages of the New Testament.
43. *Biblical View,* p. 118.
44. "Old-New Error," p. 189.

Lane A. Scott (Ph.D., Emory University), professor of theology and ethics, School of Theology, Azusa Pacific University

Divorce and the Remarriage of Divorced Persons

ACCORDING TO THE BIBLE divorce represents a distortion of God's creation. The Creator's intent is that husbands and wives shall unite in enduring marriage relationships. God's attitude toward divorce is expressed poignantly in Malachi 2:16, " 'I hate divorce,' says the Lord God of Israel."[1] Yet divorce marks the world God created, and the Bible indicates that God permits it under certain circumstances.

While Christians have always faced the possibility of failure in marriage, the likelihood of encountering divorce is much greater today. The incidence of divorce in the society at large has reached staggering proportions. One of every three marriages is terminated in the courts.[2] Because most persons who divorce marry again, there is also a much greater chance now that many Christians will have to decide whether to remarry. Given these significant increases in the rates of divorce and remarriage, there is a pressing need for clarity on the biblical view of both issues. Understanding the scriptural positions will not in itself provide the dynamic for positive and enduring marriages, but knowledge of God's design and purpose in the creation of men and women as sexual beings is foundational to the faith commitment that does establish a true marriage.

Unfortunately evangelical ethics at the present is emitting strangely mixed signals on the morality of divorce and remarriage. Working from the same commitment to the authority of Scripture, evangelical writers have reached almost diametrically opposed conclusions.[3] Robert K. Johnston describes the current evangelical dilemma in his insightful book *Evangelicals at an Impasse*. According to Johnston, evangelicals need to give more careful consideration to the fundamental ingredients of their moral arguments, that is, to exegesis and the interpretation of Scripture, to the relation of revelation and reason, and to the question of the proper starting point: revelation or observation.

While one would expect some differences among evangelical moral positions, it is hard to believe that the infallible Word of God really presents utterly conflicting teachings on issues as fundamental as divorce and remarriage. Surely all sides will gain from the greater clarity that continued study provides.

The task of presenting an evangelical ethic of divorce and of remarriage is defined in part by evangelicalism's commitment to the full authority of Scripture. The Bible reveals God's will and purpose for marriage and it provides a number of explicit texts on divorce and remarriage. God's creation-design and his will as made known in the

Scriptures are the sources of the norms for an evangelical position.

The initial phase of the task, accordingly, is the interpretation of Scripture. Proper attention must be devoted to the fundamental principles of hermeneutics. Of special importance in regard to the interpretation of the explicit texts on divorce and remarriage are the principles of historical context and the larger biblical-theological context. Evangelicals generally have recognized the importance of the historical frame of reference that governed the writing of Scripture. Drawing conclusions on the significance of specific elements in the historical context for the meaning of a given text is perhaps the most difficult assignment facing the ethicist.

Equally important to the work of interpretation, though, is the task of interpreting particular Scripture texts in the light of the whole Bible. The necessity of following this latter principle becomes apparent when one considers that the explicit texts on divorce and remarriage are almost without exception brief statements consisting of pointed prohibitions. Most contain little, if any, didactic or explanatory material. To understand the purpose for the prohibitions in these texts, their intended applications, and the limits of the same, one must interpret them in light of the great theological principles that they reflect.

The task of developing an evangelical ethic must move beyond interpretation to application. Life situations today differ from those in biblical times. Marking the way for responsible Christian living in the marital relationship requires the explication of biblical principles in light of the realities of modern social life.

In keeping with this brief description of the ethicist's task, section one of the essay presents the basic biblical texts on divorce and remarriage and points out the more pressing hermeneutical issues. In the second section, historical Christian positions are briefly surveyed. Section three utilizes insights from the historical positions and presents an evangelical interpretation of divorce and of remarriage.

The Biblical Texts On Divorce And Remarriage

The primary texts on divorce and remarriage are Deuteronomy 24:1-4, Matthew 5:31-32 and 19:3-9, Mark 10:2-12, Luke 16:18, and 1 Corinthians 7:10-15. The confines of this essay do not permit the presentation of exegetical studies of these texts. Excellent studies are available elsewhere for the interested reader.[4] In this section the most important points set forth in the seven texts listed previously are summarized.

Deuteronomy 24:1–4 is the single Old Testament record of legislation concerning divorce. It reads,

> If a man marries a woman who becomes displeasing to him because he finds something indecent about her, and he writes her a certificate of divorce, gives it to her and sends her from his house, and if after she leaves his house she becomes the wife of another man, and her second husband dislikes her and writes her a certificate of divorce, gives it to her and sends her away from his house, or if he dies, then her first husband, who divorced her, is not allowed to marry her again after she has been defiled. That would be detestable in the eyes of the Lord. Do not bring sin upon the land the Lord your God is giving you as an inheritance.

It is important to note that the provision in this passage does not require divorce or even sanction it. The law contained in the text simply provides that if a man divorces his wife, he cannot take her back if she has been married in the meantime to another man. At the same time it is certainly true that the wording of this text indicates a toleration of divorce. As John Murray has written, "This is just saying that a certain freedom in the matter of divorce was tolerated and when that freedom was exercised a civil or ecclesiastical penalty was not thereby incurred."[5]

The teachings of Jesus on divorce and remarriage may be summarized under the following headings:

1. Divorce is contrary to the divine action that establishes marriage as a permanent bond. In response to the Pharisee's question, "Is it lawful for a man to divorce his wife for any and every reason?" Jesus replied,

> Haven't you read . . . that at the beginning the Creator 'made them male and female,' and said, 'For this reason a man will leave his father and mother and be united to his wife, and the two will become one flesh'? So they are no longer two, but one. Therefore, what God has joined together, let man not separate (Matt. 19:4–6).

The central point that Jesus makes here is that God, the Creator, who designed humankind for the 'one flesh' union, works in his creation to unite marital partners in a permanent bond. In answer to the Pharisee's question Jesus, in effect, says that God establishes it as such and wills that marriage be permanent.

2. Divorce was permitted under the Mosaic law because of sin. The Pharisees were obviously bothered by Jesus' response to their question. "Why, then," they asked, "did Moses command that a man give his wife a certificate of divorce and send her away?" (Matt. 19:7). Jesus' response was, "Moses permitted you to divorce your wives because your hearts were hard. But it was not this way from the beginning" (v. 8).

Of first importance here is that Jesus relates the Mosaic provision for divorce to the Fall. Like law generally, the divorce regulation came in after the Fall (Gal. 3:19). As we have just seen, God's command expressed in creation is that marriage be permanent. The provision for divorce, therefore, is not to be viewed as a divine sanction for putting one's marital partner away. Rather, it carries the force of God's toleration of that which he doesn't will as the pattern of marriage. Surely, Jesus intends that the continuance of marriage in certain cases entails such a hardship on one or both parties that, in mercy, God permits divorce.

It must be noted, too, that in this passage Jesus does not abrogate the Mosaic provision for divorce. He clearly associates adultery with remarriage after divorce (with the exception of divorce for infidelity), but there is no word here or elsewhere in his teachings that may be understood as the abrogation of the Law.

3. A husband or wife who divorces his or her spouse, except for unfaithfulness, and remarries commits adultery. The express words of Jesus on the subject as recorded in the synoptic Gospels are as follows:

> Anyone who divorces his wife, except for marital unfaithfulness, causes her to commit adultery, and anyone who marries a woman so divorced commits adultery (Matt. 5:32).

> Anyone who divorces his wife, except for marital unfaithfulness, and marries another woman commits adultery (Matt. 19:9).

> Anyone who divorces his wife and marries another woman commits adultery against her. And if she divorces her husband and marries another man, she commits adultery (Mark 10:11–12).

> Anyone who divorces his wife and marries another woman commits adultery, and the man who marries a divorced woman commits adultery (Luke 16:18).

In these texts Jesus describes the sin of adultery from five different perspectives:

1. A man who divorces his wife for reasons other than unfaithfulness causes *her* to commit adultery (Matt. 5:32).

2. A *man* who divorces his wife for reasons other than unfaithfulness, and marries another woman, commits adultery (Matt. 19:9, Luke 16:19).

3. A *woman* who divorces her husband and marries another man, commits adultery (Mark 10:12).

4. A *man* who marries a *divorced woman* commits adultery (Matt. 5:32, Luke 16:18).

5. A man who divorces his wife and marries another woman, commits adultery *against her* (Mark 10:11).

Of singular importance in these passages is the exception clause. Because it occurs only in Matthew's Gospel many scholars view the exception as a redaction. Solid arguments are lodged both pro and con.[6] From the perspective of the evangelical view of inspiration, however, the reduction position is problematical. Taken at face value the words of Jesus in Matthew 19:9 describe divorce because of unfaithfulness as the one instance in which remarriage of the divorcing party does not constitute adultery.

To these passages from the Gospels may be added two passages from Paul. The most important text occurs in 1 Corinthians 7. Paul first addresses the situation in which husband and wife are both believers:

> To the married I give this command (not I, but the Lord): A wife must not separate from her husband. But if she does, she must remain unmarried or else be reconciled to her husband. And a husband must not divorce his wife (1 Cor. 7:10, 11).

Paul knows of the teaching of Jesus concerning the divine sanction of marriage as a permanent bond. This command from the Lord he now makes known to the Corinthians: they are not to separate or divorce. But, as Murray notes, "Paul recognizes human nature is perverse, that even Christians act perversely and not withstanding the wrong of separation or dismissal the parties to marriage may violate right and perpetrate wrong."[7] Should such a situation arise, the Christian husband or wife is to remain single or become reconciled with the spouse. Paul does not mention adultery as an exception to the command of the Lord.

The situation of mixed marriages calls for a different response on the part of believers:

> To the rest I say this (I, not the Lord): If any brother has a wife who is not a believer and she is willing to live with him, he must not divorce her. And if a woman has a husband who is not a believer and he is willing to live with her, she must not divorce him. For the unbelieving husband has been sanctified through his wife, and the unbelieving wife has been sanctified through her believing husband. Otherwise your children would be unclean, but as it is, they are holy.
>
> But if the unbeliever leaves, let him do so. A believing man or woman is not bound in such circumstances; God has called us to live in peace. How do you know, wife, whether you will save your husband? or, how do you know, husband, whether you will save your wife? (1 Cor. 7:12–16).

Believers married to unbelievers are not to divorce their spouses. Paul views mixed marriages as genuine one-flesh unions. True, such marriages lack the character of marriages between believers in which husband and wife both acknowledge Christ as Lord and receive from his hand the grace to live in agape. Nevertheless, mixed marriages do have a sanctifying character. It is difficult to know precisely what Paul means in this regard, but Hans Conzelmann rightly states Paul's general thought, "Through the believing partner, the marriage between a pagan and a Christian is withdrawn from the control of the powers of the world."[8] Given this fact, Paul's exhortation is that if the unbelieving partner is willing to live with the believer, he or she must not divorce the unbeliever.

On the other hand, in case the unbelieving spouse leaves, the believer is not bound. The interpretation of Paul's words here depend on the meaning of the phrase "is not bound." It has been argued that Paul means the believer is not bound by the obligations or duties of the marriage. In other words, the believer is free to live in separation from the unbelieving spouse. But according to this interpretation the believer is not free from the bond of the marriage and consequently is not free to remarry. However, a very strong case has been made for the view that Paul's expression "is not bound" should be understood as meaning "is released from the bond of marriage."[9]

First, the Greek term Paul uses can certainly express the idea "is not bound in marriage."[10] Second, Paul omits in verse 15 the words "remain unmarried," which he had used in the case of the separation of two believing marital partners. Third, there is a finality in Paul's words concerning the unbelieving spouse's departure, "let him do so," which suggests that Paul has more in mind than merely separation. The force of his words imply the dissolution of the marriage. If this is the case, remarriage is a legitimate option for the Christian who divorces a deserting partner.

These seven texts speak specifically to the issues of divorce and remarriage. They are, therefore, fundamental source material for an evangelical ethic of the two problems. But our ethic must not rest on these texts alone. For one thing, a valid understanding of the texts themselves depends upon their wider biblical-theological setting. The New Testament doctrines of grace and law, for example, bear directly upon the interpretation of the divorce-remarriage legislation found in Deuteronomy 24:1–4, as well as upon Mosaic law generally. But beyond these texts there is a biblical doctrine of human sexual relationship that is an essential source for the development of an evangelical ethic. For insight into the theological interpretation of the biblical view of divorce and remarriage we turn to the history of Christian thought on these issues.

Divorce And Remarriage In The History Of Christian Thought

The early church appears to have established a uniform position on divorce and remarriage. That rule is described by D. S. Bailey, who states, "The testimony of the Church, both eastern and western, during the patristic age is conclusive both in its universal allowance of divorce (that is, separation *a mensa et thoro*) for adultery, and in its unconditional condemnation of remarriage during the lifetime of the partner dismissed."[11]

A reading of the church fathers shows that as a whole they did not deal with the issues of divorce and remarriage from the perspective of a theology of marital relationship. Most of them were satisfied simply to appeal to the biblical texts that they understood as permitting divorce in the instance of adultery but forbade the remarriage of either spouse thereafter.[12]

An exception to this pattern is found in St. Augustine who, while not differing fundamentally from the position owned by the fathers generally, does interpret marriage theologically. The African father describes marriage as a sacrament, though he did not mean by that concept that the marital union has an indissoluble metaphysical reality. Bailey says of Augustine, "He defines the substance of this sacrament (*res sacramenti*) as consisting in the requirement that 'the man and the woman who are joined together in matrimony should remain inseparable (*inseparabilites perseverent*) as long as they live.' "[13]

By "sacrament" Augustine means that marriage symbolizes the union between Christ and the Church. It is important to note that in Augustine's view it is not the indestructible nature of marriage that makes it a fitting symbol of Christ and the Church. Rather, *scripture* declares marriage to be the sacrament that signifies the union between Christ and his people; therefore, the marital bond ought not to be broken, lest the symbol of the greater union be destroyed.

Augustine's conception of marriage as a symbol of Christ and the Church gave it a positive meaning, enhancing the significance of the nuptial union. But on divorce and remarriage his voice is in agreement with the age as a whole: divorce is permissible in the case of adultery, but remarriage during the lifetime of the divorced partner is forbidden.

Except for occasional lapses, the patristic view was upheld through the Middle Ages. There is, however, one point at which a departure from the traditional view did occur; the "Pauline privilege" was interpreted as permitting not only separation but also the remarriage of a divorceé.[14] The theological rationale for this position is that the marriage of a Christian to a nonbeliever differs fundamentally from the marriage of two believers. In the case of the former there is lacking that quality of absolute indissolubility that characterizes the latter.

The qualitative difference between natural and Christian marriage was finally explained by the sacramental conception of the latter.[15] According to this view, developed during the twelfth and thirteenth centuries, marriage is one of the seven sacraments instituted by Christ whereby saving grace is given to believers. By divine action the marriage of believers acquires a metaphysical quality of dissolubility. In Bailey's words,

> Such unions not only exemplified the perpetual marriage of Christ with the Church but also partook of its very character; being likewise effected by grace, they acquired immediately and forever the inviolability of their supernatural antitype. No longer was it held that matrimony *ought not* to be dissolved; it was simply asserted that it *could not* be dissolved.[16]

The Reformation, of course, marked a break with Catholicism, both theologically and ethically. Of central importance for an understanding of Martin Luther's view of divorce and remarriage is his rejection of Church tradition in favor of Scripture as the basis of faith and practice. With Calvin, Luther rejected the medieval notion of marriage as a sacrament. Both reformers conceived of marriage as a calling or vocation and as an ordinance of God that is good and holy, but one that conveys no special grace.

Luther interpreted Jesus' sayings on divorce and remarriage as directives to the individual conscience. Adultery, he believed, automatically severs the bond of marriage, and remarriage is permissible for the innocent party in the case of divorce for infidelity. Luther extended the "Pauline privilege" to include cases of desertion, hindrance in living a godly life, and rejection of reconciliation on the part of an offending spouse.[17]

Following the Reformation, Protestant theological opinion has been divided between the view held by Luther with its restricted permission of divorce and of remarriage and the patristic view that permits divorce for adultery but prohibits remarriage.

An Evangelical Interpretation Of The Biblical Position On Divorce And Marriage

God's Word is the basis of evangelical ethics. In his Word are a number of passages on divorce and remarriage. Because these texts express explicit statements on both issues, they are without question the primary source for the development of an evangelical position. Few will wish to dispute this assertion. But the proper method of interpreting these texts is another matter! Evangelicals today stand in sharp disagreement on hermeneutical questions.

Perhaps the most popular evangelical approach is represented by works like John Murray's *Divorce*. Here the basic biblical texts on divorce and remarriage are ably exposited one after another. The result is a position quite similar to that of the patristic fathers: Divorce is permitted in the instance of adultery but remarriage is forbidden (the patristic position) or strictly limited (Murray).

That this expository approach is inadequate appears from the following considerations:

1. While the biblical passages on divorce and remarriage do present explicit statements on these issues, they are "occasional" addresses. Jesus' words in Matthew 19:3–9 are occasioned by a specific question about divorce from the Pharisees. Paul's words in 1 Corinthians 7:10–15 are a written response to questions on sex and marriage from the Corinthians.[18] Now the understanding of the biblical statements depends in part upon the occasion or setting. Almost without exception the passages on divorce and remarriage are terse commands or exhortations accompanied by little or no explanation. When the occasion of a passage is unclear and no explanation for the command that it contains is given, the interpreter who follows the expository approach strictly is in a quandry. Too often he or she simply takes what is in reality an occasional statement with a particular application and extends it into a universal law.

2. There is solid evidence within the biblical passages on divorce and remarriage of a theology of sexual relationship that is the true basis for particular commands or prohibitions. For example, Jesus in Matthew 19:3–9 refers to God's creation of humanity in sexual duality as the basis of the norm of permanence in marriage. To be sure, these brief didactical references are themselves source material for the biblical theology of sexuality. But as Jesus' quote from Genesis 2:24 indicates, there is an understanding of sexual relationship in the Bible as a whole that provides the backdrop for the interpretation of the "occasional" passages on divorce and remarriage.

What is necessary, therefore, for construction of an evangelical ethic is a theology of sex and marriage based on the whole of biblical revelation. A dialectical relationship exists between the biblical theology and the specific passages on divorce and remarriage: they contribute to the larger whole while at the same time they are interpreted in its light. We now turn to a statement of that biblical theology of sexual relationship.

According to the Bible, God created persons as sexual beings for two grand purposes. First, so that they would experience life in unity with another human being. God's second purpose is for the procreation of humanity. The biblical view of marriage as the union of two persons in the totality of their beings appears first in Genesis 2:24: "For this reason a man will leave his father and mother and be united to his wife, and they will become one flesh." However, it is the New Testament that presents most clearly the concept of marriage as a fully personal community between a man and a woman. While the Scriptures as a whole view marriage as reflecting the union of God and his people, the New Testament writers are more concerned to draw conclusions about marriage from the capacity that the latter has to represent God's relationship with his Church. Paul, for example, writes, "Husbands, love your wives, just as Christ loved the church and gave himself up for her. . . . Each one of you also must love his wife as he loves himself, and the wife must respect her husband" (Eph. 5:25, 33).

To love one's marital partner as Christ loves the Church is to meet the former continually as "Thou." Love like Christ's recognizes the other as an individual or "self" for whom Christ died and for whom God has prepared an eternal destiny.

But the nature of marriage as a fully personal community cannot be understood apart from the sexual union that lies at the heart of it. According to the Bible, sexuality has the capacity of uniting two persons of the opposite sex in a *uniquely* personal manner.

The idea of the "one" flesh relationship that occurs in Genesis 2:24, and which is the subject of discourse by Jesus and Paul, is a fundamental principle in the biblical view of sexual relationship.[19] According to the Bible the act of sexual intercourse establishes an ontological union between a man and a woman. D. S. Bailey notes that although the union in "one flesh" is a physical union, it involves the whole being and affects the personality at the deepest level.[20]

Helmut Thielicke views the male-female duality as constitutive of humaness itself. "What is meant here," notes Thielicke, "is not the coexistence of two sorts of human beings, but rather a polarity which is constitutive of man as such. Therefore, man and woman do not find each other, as it were, *subsequently;* they rather come to each other from each other."[21]

When human sexuality is seen in this way, it is obvious that permanence belongs to the very nature (it is part of the created design) of marriage. The truth of this fact can be seen from two directions. Because each partner has "come to himself or herself from the other," to use Thielicke's words, the preservation of (and even further realization of) the self depends upon the endurance of the marital union. But it may also be said that it is precisely the promise of an enduring relationship that makes possible the kind of self-giving that constitutes the genuine "one-flesh" union. Because God wills that we should experience life in togetherness, he has created persons as male-female. And he has written permanence into the very design of his Creation. Reflecting on the divine action, Jesus responded to the Pharisees,

> Haven't you read . . . that at the beginning the Creator "made them male and female" and said, "For this reason a man will leave his father and mother and be united to his wife, and the two will become one flesh"? So they are no longer two, but one. Therefore what God has joined together, let man not separate (Matt. 19:4–6).

Permanence is required as well for the realization of the second purpose of marriage. For their personal growth and development children need the security that an enduring marriage alone provides.

In summary, God's creation of persons as male-female is for the purpose of unity and procreation; both of these ends require permanence for their realization. Permanence in the marriage relationship is God's will for humanity.

But the Fall has distorted God's Creation. Instead of righteousness and harmony the world is now characterized by sin and brokenness. Like the Creation generally, marriage, after the Fall, is marked by sin—violence, hostility, and unfaithfulness. It is because of sin, Jesus teaches us, that divorce is permitted (Matt. 19:8). As we noted in our analysis of the texts on divorce, neither the Mosaic provision of the "bill of divorce" nor Jesus in his teachings establishes divorce as a law or right. Because divorce is contrary to God's will in the Creation, it cannot be viewed as having any kind of divine sanction. Rather than an act that God requires, divorce is a proceeding that God permits. In the words of Helmut Thielicke, the divorce statute is a "regulation of necessity" that belongs wholly to the fallen world.[22]

We have already seen that Jesus recognized adultery as behavior for which divorce may be the necessary solution. John Murray maintains that the effect of Jesus' teaching in this regard is abrogation of the more permissive Mosaic statute and the establishment of a more strict Kingdom law. But Murray's position runs counter to the whole tenor of biblical theology. Jesus did not come as the new lawgiver. Rather, he sets the divorce statute in the light of God's will as revealed in his creation, and in so doing Jesus showed the provisionality of that statute.

According to the Bible the Christian is to be guided in the conduct of his or her marriage relationship by the will of God manifest in creation and by his or her participation in God's redemption in Christ. By his death and resurrection Jesus has reconciled God with persons and established God's kingdom on earth. Christian marriage, as represented in the New Testament, reflects the realities of the divine action in Christ: it is characterized by faithfulness and love (Eph. 5:22–33) and by peace (1 Cor. 7:10–15).

When the divorce statute is viewed in the full light of Christ and his work, it is clear that the former holds no moral authority over the Christian. The believer is never compelled to seek a divorce, not even when the spouse is guilty of adultery. Should he or she so desire, the Christian may choose to endure the gravest of trials. But it is also true that should the believer divorce an unfaithful spouse, he or she is not thereby "righteous," since there is no law requiring such action.

Reflection on biblical theology makes clear, thus, that the divorce statute is not a divine law but is rather a "regulation of necessity." We must now consider the fact that while Jesus shows the provisional character of the divorce statute he does not abrogate it. In spite of Christ's call for persons to live according to God's design in his creation, and notwithstanding Christ's work of redemption, sin remains in the world; and because of the consequences of sin, God still permits divorce even as he did in the time of Moses.

The more difficult question, as our survey of the history of Christian thought shows, is the legitimate grounds for divorce. This question must be answered in keeping with our discussion above. In reality there are *no* divinely sanctioned grounds for divorce. According to the divine law the Christian should strive to keep his or her marriage together until there is no longer any hope. But Jesus recognizes that adultery may destroy a marital union. Because this is the only cause that Jesus mentions, Murray feels that adultery alone is reason for divorce. But Murray tends to interpret the words of Jesus without regard for their historical setting, and he fails to view them in the light of the whole of the biblical view of sexuality. Because he mentions only one reason does not mean that Jesus accepts no others. His words on divorce are occasional sayings uttered in response to specific questions. They must be understood in that light.

Moreover, Paul may certainly be taken as viewing the desertion of an unbelieving spouse as just grounds for divorce. In our preceding discussion of 1 Corinthians 7:15, we saw that the phrase "is not bound" may be understood as meaning "is released from the bond of marriage."

But Paul's words are also occasional and the thrust of his thought does not in the least suggest that he intends to establish an exclusive list of causes for divorce. To the contrary, Paul in his treatment of Christian morality hardly appeals to the Law at all. In the 1 Corinthians 7:10–15 passage believers are exhorted to be reconciled wherever that is possible. No pattern of conduct ought necessarily lead the Christian to divorce his or her spouse. As long as there is the possibility of reconciliation, God expects us to keep covenant. But when there remains no hope of reconciliation, as when an unbelieving spouse deserts, divorce may be pursued.

That Jesus and Paul cite adultery and desertion of an unbelieving spouse as grounds for divorce indicates that keeping married is not absolutely required. Moreover, consideration of the grounds that are named in Scripture reveals an underlying principle that will provide the individual Christian conscience with more general guidance. We shall consider infidelity and desertion in turn.

Adultery, as a continuing practice, destroys the very foundations of marriage; it shatters the one-flesh union and risks the possibility of progeny outside that parental relationship that God designed for it. A marriage is also destroyed when one partner willingly and permanently deserts the other. While a marriage may certainly endure indefinitely in the face of separation, it does so on the basis of the partner's mutual commitment to reunite. In those cases in which a spouse takes precisely the opposite stand

and commits himself or herself *not* to return, a marriage is destroyed.

Thus, in the instances of adultery and desertion the very meaning of marriage is nullified, and this is clearly the reason that Jesus and Paul permit divorce in such cases. Now, if destruction of the marriage is the reason for the permission to divorce, surely acts other than infidelity and desertion that cause the same result ought also to be recognized as justifiable grounds for ending a marriage. Luther rightly understood the principle underlying the "Pauline privilege" when he extended it to include other offenses. But only such acts that clearly destroy a marriage should be recognized as cause for divorce. Here may be included enslavement and extreme cruelty on the part of one partner by the other. Both acts violate so totally the personhood of the one abused that the marriage itself is impossible of even the shadow of meaning.

It is not possible in the confines of this chapter to consider all those acts for which divorce may be permitted. However, the churches need urgently to clearly define such behaviors that destroy marriage. While the decision to divorce must finally rest with the individual believer, he or she needs in the midst of personal and emotional upheaval objective guidance from the community of faith.

Finally, there remains the question of the remarriage of divorced persons. In the light of Jesus' teachings on divorce the patristic fathers concluded that remarriage is prohibited. Murray reasons that remarriage is permissible only in those cases in which divorce has followed the act of adultery. But Murray adopts here the same legalistic approach that he demonstrates in his discussion of divorce. Jesus is viewed as the divine lawgiver who enacts new legislation, the effect of which is to provide for the dissolution of marriage by justifiable divorce. Because divorce for adultery dissolves the existing marriage, Murray reasons that remarriage is then permissible. Rather than this type of legalistic approach, we have seen that Jesus deals with marriage relationships in terms of creation principles. He says, in effect, that the one-flesh union established by marriage endures (in some sense) in spite of a divorce. This is the only possible conclusion that can be drawn from the statement "[a woman who] divorces her husband and marries another man . . . commits adultery" (Mark 10:12).

But, as we have previously shown, Jesus' words must be understood in the light of their historical context. Among the Pharisees one school of thought held that a man had the right to divorce his wife for the slightest of offenses. Jesus points to the most serious consequence of divorcing one's spouse and marrying another. But that he does not absolutize the one-flesh union is made clear by his words in Matthew 19:9. There he indicates that remarriage after divorce for infidelity does not constitute adultery.

If, as we have argued in this essay, a believer may divorce his or her spouse when the marriage has been destroyed, then remarriage ought to be permitted because the former marriage bond is terminated, even if something of the one-flesh union continues.[23] Divorce for just cause has the consequence of ending a marriage.

Conclusion

Over fifty years ago Emil Brunner decried the fact that the Christian standards of marriage no longer shaped the ideologies of Western societies. The erosion that Brunner lamented has steadily grown worse. In this country today marriage is popularly conceived as a convenient sexual arrangement that may be terminated the moment spouses find themselves "incompatible."

In the face of steady cultural indoctrination the Church must be more diligent than ever in its teaching of biblical principles. Youth must continually be reminded of the distinction between the secular ideology that imprints their minds daily through television, movies, novels, and other popular media and God's will for married life. The biblical call to permanence in marriage can only be embraced by believers. But people of faith need clear, plain talk to guide them along the road to an enduring marriage that is a true reflection of Christ and his Church.

But no matter how clearly we present the biblical principles, or how diligently we teach the Christian view of marriage, many in the Church will fall short of God's best. Experience indicates that though many *know* God's will, they are so weak in their faith that they don't *do* what he wills. Consequently, the typical pastor must counsel people who have divorced without just cause and wish to marry again. In such cases regard for God's call to permanence in marriage makes it appropriate for the pastor to consider with his or her counselee the broken marriage. Is there a possibility of reconciliation even though divorce has occurred? If so, every means ought to be used to effect that end before remarriage takes place. But, in all likelihood, a marriage that has already ended in divorce proceedings is not capable of restoration. Sin has been committed and hard-heartedness has destroyed that which God willed to be permanent. But before remarriage is permitted, the Christian divorced person should be faced with the wrong that occurred in the termination of his or her former marriage. And as Clinton Gardner has observed, remarriage should be permitted for the repentant and only for the repentant.[24]

Finally, the Church must contend with the darkest side of reality as it seeks the realization of permanence in the marriages of all of God's people. The emotionally disturbed and the mentally ill pose problems for which there are no ready answers. To be sure, even where such stark difficulties exist, God's will for permanent marriage should be promoted. Yet, in such dire situations separation and/or divorce may be the only answer. Here and in all circumstances that threaten the health of Christian marriage the Church must avail itself of God's grace in every means available. Sound biblical teaching; lay, pastoral, and expert psychological counseling; and much prayer are especially needed. God is faithful and will give grace to those who call upon him.

Notes

1. All Scripture references are from the New International Version.
2. Melvin L. DeFleur, et. al., *Sociology: Human Society* (Glenview, Ill.: Scott, Foresman and Company, 1981), p. 437.
3. For examples see John Murray, *Divorce* (Phillipsburg, N.J.: Presbyterian and Reformed Publishing Company, 1978), and Larry Richards, *Remarriage: A Healing Gift from God* (Waco, Texas: Word Books, 1981).
4. John Murray, *Divorce,* contains excellent exegetical studies of these passages.
5. *Ibid.,* p. 8.
6. See Murray, *Divorce,* pp. 45–54 and Henlee Barnette, *Introducing Christian Ethics* (Nashville: Broadman Press, 1961), pp. 115–16.
7. Murray, *Divorce,* p. 61.
8. Hans Conzelmann, *First Corinthians* (Philadelphia: Fortress Press, 1975), p. 122.
9. Murray, *Divorce,* p. 72. Murray considers both interpretations in detail.
10. *Ibid.,* p. 75.
11. D. S. Bailey, *Sexual Relation in Christian Thought* (New York: Harper and Row, 1959), p. 88.
12. *Ibid.,* p. 89.
13. *Ibid.,* p. 89. Bailey's quote is from *De nupt et concup.,* i,11 (10).
14. *Ibid.,* p. 111.
15. *Ibid.,* p. 114.
16. *Ibid.,* p. 115.

17. *Ibid.*, p. 176.
18. See 1 Corinthians 7:1.
19. See Mark 10:2–12, 1 Corinthians 6:15–16, and Ephesians 5:22–23.
20. D. S. Bailey, *The Mystery of Love and Marriage* (New York: Harper and Brothers, 1952), p. 44.
21. Helmut Thielicke, *The Ethics of Sex and Marriage,* trans by John Doberstein (New York: Harper and Row, 1964), p. 5.
22. *Ibid.*, p. 109.
23. The intimate sharing of oneself with another in marriage impacts the psyche permanently. If children are involved they constitute, of course, a continuing link between the parents.
24. E. Clinton Gardner, *Biblical Faith and Social Ethics* (New York: Harper and Row, 1960), p. 245.

Howard A. Snyder (Ph.D., Notre Dame), pastor, Irving Park Free Methodist Church, Chicago

The Economy of God and the Ecology of the Church

AT THE END of the American cultural revolution of the sixties, Martin Marty and Dean Peerman published a number of essays in *New Theology No. 8* that reflected on the ferment of those unsettling days. A decade later, two of those essays seem especially noteworthy: "Ecological and Psychedelic Approaches to Theology" by Richard Underwood, and "Starting Points for an Ecological Theology" by Kenneth Alpers.

If psychedelia has now largely evaporated, ecology has not. Even though environmental concerns are presently somewhat eclipsed by the advent of Reaganomics, the ecological time bomb is still ticking. Wastes are still piling up; acid rain still eats away at trees and priceless stone buildings; arable land continues to disappear while population surges. Ecology, like gravity, won't go away, for it is built into the fabric of our created world.

Ecology, however, inevitably raises spiritual and religious values. Underwood rightly points out that "ecology calls for reinterpretation of the man-nature relationship. But ecology in and of itself cannot bring about this reinterpretation."[1] Yet the ecological motif and mind-set should give Christians new insights into the very faith they profess. Here Alpers is on target in suggesting that ecology, as "the study of organisms in their mutual relationships with their environment," provides a suggestive "model for philosophizing and theologizing."[2]

I know from experience that even to bring up the ecological theme in theological discourse is to be accused of faddishness. But I suggest that something of fundamental importance is at stake here. The thesis, in fact, of this essay is that ecology touches on the most fundamental issues of social, political, economic, and spiritual life on this planet, and that it also points to fundamental biblical themes that need to be recovered and articulated today. The task, then, of this essay is to investigate the meaning of ecology and to show that Scripture in fact reveals a divine economy that includes an ecology for both the internal and external life of the Church.

The Bible says that God has "a plan [*oikonomia*] for the fullness of time, to unite all things" in Jesus Christ (Eph. 1:10, RSV). Paul says in Colossians 1:25 that he is "a minister according to the economy [*oikonomia*] of God given to me for you" (author's translation; cf. NIV). It is proper, then, to speak of the economy of God when we speak of God's overall redemptive plan. This was, in fact, how several of the church fathers spoke of God's salvation in the first two centuries of the Christian Era.[3]

These biblical references are more significant than they at first appear, for they are linked to a word picture that is basic to the New Testament doctrine of the Church and, in fact, to the wole biblical picture of the sovereignty and kingdom of God. This picture is the image of the *oikos* ("house," "household," or "family") of God.[4] The kingdom of God may be thought of, and in fact is pictured biblically, as God's rule and proper ordering of his house. Here we recall the many New Testament pictures of the Church as God's household.[5] God's plan or "economy," then, is precisely to bring all things in the created order into harmony under Jesus Christ, beginning with the Church. It is that Christ, head of the Church, should be head of "all things" in the universe. The divine economy will "bring all things in heaven and on earth together under one head, even Christ," as the NIV correctly translates the latter part of Ephesians 1:10.[6]

The important connection to be made here is the link between the biblical economy of God and the contemporary ecological consciousness, and, more generally, the link between economy and ecology. This link is not forced but inherent, for *oikologia,* like *oikonomia,* is also a metaphor based on the idea of "house" or "household" *(oikos).*

Fundamentally, economy may be thought of as the proper arrangement and management of a household, while ecology is the study of the elements that make up such an economy in their interplay with each other. Thus economy and ecology point in the same direction: in our universe, everything is ultimately tied to everything else, and what happens in one part of the system inescapably has consequences throughout the system. It is from this perspective that new insights may be gained for the life and witness of the Church.

Eco-Consciousness and the Church

We are coming to an ecological awareness that is unprecedented in human history. The atomic bomb and the theory of relativity have dramatized how interrelated matter and energy are and the tremendous power packed in the atom. The growing problems of air and water pollution are revealing the intricate balance of our ecosystem and its ultimate vulnerability. The energy crunch is making us aware that earth's bounty is finite and that the key resources fueling our economic growth are rapidly running out. The growing awareness of the economic and ecological implications of the law of entropy is raising the most basic questions about technology and progress. We have begun to think in terms of a small planet, of Mother Earth or Spaceship Earth, of a global village. Computer technology, cancer research, food studies, and other areas of investigation impress on us the balance of systems and forces that make up our habitable globe. We are beginning to understand, for instance, that petro-agriculture is spoiling the land for the future and that a coming virtual epidemic of cancer in which one of every three Americans will contract the disease is due mainly to environmental factors.

We inhabit an intricate, vulnerable biosphere consisting of a few inches of topsoil and a few hundred feet of oxygen. We are becoming ecologically aware, but it may be too late. It is already an open question whether we have time to make the required economic and life-style adjustments for human life to continue past the middle of the next century. Our present economic system is buying disaster for our children and grandchildren, even if we somehow avoid nuclear war in our own generation.

The worldwide ecological crisis is much worse than we had thought and more fundamental than most politicians yet believe. The most critical problems revolve around the rapid depletion of the earth's resources by the industrialized nations, the growing gap between rich and poor, malnutrition and starvation on an unprecedented scale, and the gradual decline of productive arable land due to chemical pollution (including fertilizers and herbicides), overintensive farming, desertification, and urban sprawl. While population continues to climb, the world's long-range ability to grow food is declining. In addition, more than thirty nations face a severe water shortage by the year 2000.[7] And the situation is aggravated as the rich nations gobble up more of the resources of poorer countries in order to fuel an ecologically irresponsible technological materialism and safeguard their extravagant life-styles, raising the specter of nuclear war over oil wells and mineral rights. It is clear that this situation raises basic ethical questions for the Church.[8]

How may the Church legitimately respond to this ecological awareness and make use of ecological categories? There are three possible ways for the Church to view ecology: as a *problem* for the Church's attention, a *paradigm* for her self-understanding, or a *perspective* for the Church's encounter with Scripture.

1. The first approach represents the Church's initial encounter with ecological realities. Ecology and the environment are seen as one more social question that the Church must address. The perspective is that of the Church versus ecology. But this is an inadequate approach, for ecology, by definition, is an all-encompassing perspective and raises questions about the Church's own life and reality.

2. Viewed as a paradigm for the Church's self-understanding, ecology itself becomes the controlling reality. Here the perspective is that the Church must be conformed to the ecological model. The problem with this approach is the problem the Church always faces in using a human system or philosophy. Most ecological thinking thus far is so undeveloped, and as a science is still so dominated by evolutionary presuppositions, that using ecology as the fundamental paradigm for the Church's

self-understanding runs the risk of doing violence to Scripture.[9]

3. The more valid approach, therefore, is to see ecology as a perspective for the Church's encounter with Scripture. Ecology does provide a model. But that model must be controlled, tested, and clarified by the biblical revelation. The question, then, is to what degree an ecological perspective is compatible with Scripture, or to what extent the Bible actually views the Church and the world ecologically. Taking this approach, we come up with some very significant findings.

Ecology and Scripture

Are the biblical and ecological perspectives compatible? Does the Bible present the world to us in a way that is consistent with ecological realities? I suggest that the ecological perspective links up with Scripture at two levels. First, there are some marked parallels between the biblical and ecological perspectives. Second, ecology in fact points to a key theme woven throughout Scripture.

At least five significant parallels may be traced between the biblical and ecological perspectives.

1. *Both ecology and the Bible view the world in a long-range time frame.* Human beings are accustomed to measuring time in terms of a life span, at most. Ours is a short-range view. Most human planning reaches only a few years or decades into the future. But to understand ecological reality, we must speak of hundreds of thousands of years. Ecological problems, for example, may be many generations in building and can seldom be solved in a few years' time.[10]

The biblical perspective is similarly long range. The Bible itself was written over a period of some fifteen hundred years. The Bible traces history back to our first parents—back to creation itself. It makes the historical connections straight through from Adam and Eve to Jesus Christ and on to the final culmination of the kingdom of God. Each human life is seen as important but as fitting into God's long-range purposes in history.

2. *Both ecology and the Bible see the natural world as one interconnected whole.* This is, of course, the point of the ecological perspective. But it is also true of Scripture. Here the doctrine of creation is central. Everything is interrelated because everything comes from the hand of God and finds meaning in God's purposes. God creates matter, and the human form is fashioned from the dust of the earth. Each form of life reproduces "after its kind" and is related to the rest of creation. Even the heavenly bodies come from the hand of God. From this perspective the Bible is profoundly ecological.

Ecology speaks of the web of life—of diversity and mutuality, and of dynamics and change. So does the Bible. Life's interdependent web is pictured historically in many of the narrative sections of Scripture and poetically in Job and many of the Psalms. A large number of the Psalms are really creation hymns, glorying not in an abstract God but in the wisdom, power, and care God displays in the intricate ordering of the natural environment.

3. *Both ecology and the Bible present us with an awareness of limits.*[11] This is one of the hardest facts to face, but it is also one of the most stubborn ecological realities. Above all, our ecosphere is limited in its amounts of matter and energy. Even solar power is limited, both absolutely and in the degree to which it can be captured and used on earth. Resources that appeared limitless to an expanding frontier population now are seen as finite as population bulges into the billions.

But Scripture already provides us with an awareness of limits. At creation God separated the light from the darkness (Gen. 1:4) and established the limits of earth and sea (Gen. 1:9). Creation itself may be seen as a process of separating and setting limits. The psalmist says God "fixed all the bounds of the earth" and "made summer and winter" (Ps. 74:17. See also Deuteronomy 32:8, Proverbs 8:27-29).

Man and woman are limited because of their physical existence, even though created in the image of God. And God marks off moral limits for man and woman, both initially (Gen. 2:15–16), after the Fall (Gen. 3:16–19), and on down through the course of salvation history and the formation of a special people of God. God provides structure and boundaries for the well-being of his creation. So the Apostle Paul says, "From one man [God] made every nation of men, that they should inhabit the whole earth; and he determined the times set for them and the exact places where they should live" (Acts 17:26).[12]

God is forever saying to man and woman, in effect, Here are the limits. Abide by them, according to my purposes, and you will live. Disregard them and you will die. As we view things ecologically, we see that this is true not just in some arbitrary sense, and not just in spiritual things, but physically as well because of the nature of the world God has given us.

4. *Both ecology and the Bible see the natural order as subject to decay.* Plants and animals die, hills erode, and some species become extinct. Ecologically, we face here not just the transitoriness of nature but the fact of entropy, the second law of thermodynamics. Entropy is a measure of disorder in a system. According to the law of entropy, the disorder in our universe is increasing as more and more resources are transformed from usable to unusable form.

Entropy may turn out to be the premiere natural constraint of the new age of ecology, as basic as gravity. Its significance lies in the fact that earth's matter and energy are limited and that no process is one hundred percent efficient. Whenever work of any kind is performed, some matter or energy is used up. In fact, however, matter does not pass out of existence but is transformed from one form to another. While some of the energy derived may be used to perform work, some is irretrievably lost as heat or waste products. For example, when gasoline is burned in an automobile, power is released to drive the machine but most of the energy in the gasoline is lost as heat. Physicists tell us that even the most efficient machine produces some waste, and that the energy lost as waste can never be fully recovered. Thus available energy is always decreasing; waste (as various forms of pollution) is always increasing; and overall the universe is moving from order to disorder as more and more matter and energy are turned into waste products. This process is becoming critical in our age because of the awesome power of technology to speed up the entropy process.[13]

The ecological reality that the natural world is subject to decay is consistent with the biblical revelation. We read that "the creation was subjected to frustration, not by its own choice, but by the will of the one who subjected it, in hope that the creation itself will be liberated from its bondage to decay and brought into the glorious freedom of the children of God" (Rom. 8:20–21). The natural world is not in a perfectly balanced, self-sustaining state. Human sin and rebellion have had their negative impact on the natural order. While it is not clear precisely in what ways sin has affected the world, it does appear that nature is in some fundamental sense disordered because of the Fall. Like human nature itself, the physical world suffers not only from human sin now but from some more basic derangement, some "bondage to decay," because of the Fall. This is reflected in part in the curse pronounced after the Fall (Gen. 3:17–19) and may be in part the result of the catastrophic event of the Flood (Gen. 6:13, 8:21, 9:3). The natural environment was significantly different after the

Flood, as reflected to some degree in Genesis 9 and in the sharp drop in longevity after Noah's time.

It would appear, then, that in the judgments of the Fall and Flood the created order was subjected to decay. The original harmony and balance were broken. Marvelous as it still is, our world is a ruined world. Like man and woman, the earth still shows forth the glory of its maker but in a defaced, partially ruined way.

5. *Both ecology and the Bible show that all behavior has consequences.* Ecologically speaking, we can never say that anything we do simply doesn't matter. The effect of one person's life may be minimal, but it does have environmental impact—physically, socially, economically, and in other ways. Every breath breathed, every dollar spent, and every relationship created modifies the environment. We are tempted to think one person's impact is so small as to be irrelevant, but that is a profoundly anti-ecological attitude. Our new environmental awareness is showing us that when added to the experience of hundreds or millions of others, every person's behavior is ecologically significant *in all its dimensions.*

Ecology also tells us to watch out for long-range consequences. Our behavior touches not only the present world but all future generations on earth. Whether we are speaking biologically (for instance, the creation of families), economically (for instance, the accumulation of wealth), or technologically (for instance, the production of radioactive wastes), our behavior as humans makes waves that ripple ahead into future generations. Thus even from a purely ecological perspective we can say that ethical questions are an inevitable part of life on earth.

In all these respects, the biblical perspective closely parallels ecology. The Bible shows that all behavior has meaning and consequences because of the nature of the physical-spiritual universe in which God has placed us. We are faced again with the perspective, "Do this, and you will live; do that, and you will die." We have tended to think of such consequences as arbitrary fiats of God. God has set the rules and, for his own sovereign and inscrutable reasons, if we break the rules we get punished. But the ecological perspective points to a deeper truth: we suffer the consequences of our actions because of the nature of the physical, spiritual, moral universe God has created—which reflects, of course, the very character of God himself.

The rule is "The soul who sins is the one who will die" (Ezek. 18:4). But this is not an arbitrary rule; it is the nature of the case, part of the spiritual ecology of God's world. In giving the law to his people Israel God said, "I, the Lord your God, am a jealous God, punishing the children for the sin of the fathers to the third and fourth generation of those who hate me, but showing love to thousands who love me and keep my commandments" (Exod. 20:5–6). This is a very interesting passage, viewed ecologically. When God's people sin, they feel the effects down through several generations. But when they love and obey God the blessings also radiate out and into the future. This is not to deny, of course, that God's judgments may be specific and individual, but it is to underscore that the world and God's plan are profoundly ecological. In the biblical perspective, as in ecology, all behavior has consequences, those consequences are often long-range, and ethical questions are inescapable.

In all these ways, then, the ecological and biblical perspectives are similar. From the viewpoint of Christian faith, this is not surprising. If the biblical revelation is reliable, then the closer ecological science comes to the real nature of things the closer it will approach the biblical picture.

Fundamentally, the biblical and ecological pictures both show man and woman living interdependently with the natural environment. Scripture, however, has a fundamental priority over ecology because it reveals what ecology cannot fully understand or explain: the realm of the spirit; the dimension of spiritual reality. According to Scripture, we do not really understand the ecology of the world until we recognize its source, the Lord God, and see that the space-time physical world is interpenetrated and held together by a spiritual world and by spiritual energy which comes from God himself.[14] From this standpoint, we really are not thinking ecologically—even from a scientific point of view—if we do not include the dimension of the spirit.

The Bible gives us a fundamentally accurate, spiritually balanced, and scientifically trustworthy understanding of the essential ecology of human existence. And the modern ecological awareness can provide a key for understanding what is happening to the world today and relating this to the divine economy "for the fullness of time to unite all things" in Jesus Christ.

The Divine Economy

As we have already noted, God's plan is his *oikonomia,* his economy for the fullness of time. The economy of God is the manifestation of the kingdom of God. It is the reconciling and uniting of all things, visible and invisible, under the authority of Jesus Christ.

We have already seen that the biblical revelation is profoundly ecological. But the biblical economy is profoundly economic as well. Economics and ecology trace back to the same basic issues, as we have seen. And it is precisely these issues that Scripture addresses when it speaks of God's purposes and plans.

We have come to understand economics as "the science of how people produce goods and services, how they distribute them among themselves, and how they use them." As with ecology, economy focuses on the interrelationships and interdependence of parts in a whole.

House or household is a key image, then, when we speak of economy and ecology. Household management requires the ordering and arrangement of many resources —food and clothing, space and time, money, people, and social relationships. Each person in the household influences all the others, and each person must be cared for. Both economics (in the modern sense) and the biblical economy are concerned with these matters. Properly understood, the biblical revelation is concerned with all reality, including economic issues, and properly understood, economics is not a matter narrowly of goods and services but also of values and relationships. It is important here to note both these facts: God's economy and kingdom deeply and inevitably involve economic issues, and economics always (and especially today) raises ethical and spiritual issues. Before dealing with the biblical perspective, it will be helpful to note the significance of economic issues and questions today.

THE GREAT ECONOMIC DEBATE

The economic dislocations of the past decade and the advent of Reaganomics in the United States have brought economic questions to center stage as at no time perhaps since the Great Depression. But the popular concern with economics is only symptomatic of a more basic and longer-range debate over the economic options available to us as we move into an age of scarcity.

We are now in a period, argues J. Philip Wogaman, of "a great debate" over economic realities:

> Humankind is engaged now in a great debate of worldwide and historic magnitude on the question of how economic life should be organized. Aspects of the debate are peculiar to each country, but it will ultimately be decided in world, not national terms. The broad outlines of the great economic debate call forth a new global consciousness. It is not likely to be resolved quickly.[15]

Wogaman contends that this historic debate will affect life on earth for many years to come and is inevitably a debate in part over values and ethics. "What is at stake in economic questions," he notes, "is the well-being and community relationships of the whole human family, each of whose members is a person of incalculable worth."[16]

One of the problems of economics as currently understood is that it deals too narrowly with material, quantifiable, and monetary matters. In the process it creates, like technology, its own values and morality in which the highest good is efficiency and profitability. As E. F. Schumacher observes, "The religion of economics has its own code of ethics and the First Commandment is to behave 'economically.' " And "if economic thinking pervades the whole of society, even simple noneconomic values like beauty, health, or cleanliness can survive only if they prove to be 'economic.' "[17]

Such an economic perspective is too narrow, both because it tends to ignore ecological realities and constraints and because it shuts out the realm of the spirit. The inevitable result is suicide—ecologically, spiritually, and thus also economically and physically—for these dimensions cannot be divorced. To think exclusively or even primarily in economic terms is like feeding and clothing a baby but ignoring its emotional and social needs. The result is a cripple, something much less than human.

My point, however, is not just that economics provides too narrow a perspective for dealing with human society, but rather that when limited to the material and the quantifiable, economics betrays the very concept of economy itself. For by definition economy is concerned with *all* elements and factors that affect people and their environment. To put it another way, economics, ecology, and spiritual reality are not three isolated spheres. They are three ways of viewing the one sphere that is our human environment, our *oikos* or house. Economically, we need a new understanding of the importance of the spiritual dimension, just as spiritually we must understand the significance of economic issues. And the ecological perspective is a pressing reminder of the interpenetration of the economic and spiritual spheres.

The Church has a key role to play here—both as a participant in the great economic debate and as a sign and agent for the economy and kingdom of God. In fact, a key part of the Church's kingdom work today should be exploring, advocating, and modeling economic arrangements that are both ecologically and biblically valid.[18] Theologically, this means seeing God's economy through the biblical images of God's house and kingdom.

THE HOUSE OF GOD

Hebrews 3:1–6 exhorts us to "fix [our] thoughts on Jesus," our apostle and high priest, who "was faithful to the one who appointed him, just as Moses was faithful in all God's house." Moses, we read, "was faithful as a servant in all God's house," but "Christ is faithful as a son over God's house." Further, we are told that we, the Church, are God's house (*oikos*). Here is a web of biblical ideas that recur in various ways throughout Scripture and that provides a timely perspective for understanding God's plan in the world.

Hebrews begins with a ringing affirmation of who Jesus is: "The radiance of God's glory and the exact representation of his being"; the one through whom the world was made and is sustained (Heb. 1:2–3). Now we see this same Jesus "crowned with glory and honor because he suffered death" (2:9). Note that the author links this fact with Psalm 8:

> What is man that you are mindful of him, the son of man that you care for him?
> You made him a little lower than the angels; you crowned him with glory and honor and put everything under his feet (Heb. 2:6–8).

This is how man and woman were created—very much like God, and with dominion over God's world and a charge to care for it. God initially left nothing in the created order that was not subject to humankind, the writer says. But as we look around us today, we do not see this. We do not see a fully ordered, balanced, peaceful world. In many ways we see just the opposite. But what else do we see? "We see Jesus, who [also] was made a little lower than the angels, now crowned with glory and honor."

Note the perspective here. Man and woman were created by God in his very image to have fellowship with him and to care for and nurture a beautiful, balanced, dynamic world. They failed. But Jesus has come, very God and very man, to restore the ecological balance of God's order. Through his once-for-all death and resurrection a new, restored order is now at work within the fallen world. And we, the Church, are a part of God's restoring work, for Jesus "is not ashamed to call" us his brothers and sisters (Heb. 2:11). Therefore, as Moses was faithful, and as Jesus was faithful, we are to be faithful servants in God's house.

Biblically, God's economy (*oikonomia*) is to put all things in proper order within his *oikos*. This is the image involved in saying God has an *oikonomia* for the fullness of time to unite and reconcile "all things" in Jesus Christ (Eph. 1:10). It is important, then, that we see just what this "house" of God means and includes.

When we raise this question, we begin to see that the Bible employs the idea of house of God in several senses. These boil down, however, to two fundamental ideas: the church as God's household or family, and the whole created order as, metaphorically, God's house.

First, the Church is the house, household, and family of God. The common designation for "temple" in the Old Testament is, literally, "God's house" (*beth-El*). The Old

Testament speaks much about the tabernacle and temple of God. These were the places where God, symbolically but really, established his presence among his chosen people. But these realities were shadows of things to come. God's will is to dwell in people, not in bricks and mortar, not in crystal and steel. His intention, and the goal of salvation history, is to lead, dwell with, and work through a special people, his servants and stewards. This is what the Church is—the family and household of God.

Where does God dwell today? Not in temples made with hands but in human temples. Not in places but in people. In human hearts certainly, but also, and especially, in a community of people who confess Jesus Christ as Lord and determine to be faithful to him in their life together.

From the perspective of God's economy and ecology, it is significant that nearly all the biblical images of the Church are figures from life. The Church is a living organism. It is a community taking its spiritual life and power from the living presence of the Spirit of Jesus. Combining the images of body of Christ and family or household of God, we get a clear picture of what the Church really is in God's plan. This understanding comes through with particular force in Ephesians 2:19–22 where after describing the Church as Christ's body Paul goes on to say, "You are no longer foreigners and aliens, but fellow citizens with God's people and members of God's household [*oikeioi*], built [*epoikodomethentes*] on the foundation of the apostles and prophets, with Christ Jesus himself as the chief cornerstone. In him the whole building [*oikodome*] is joined together and rises to become a holy temple in the Lord. And in him you too are being built together [*sunoikodomeisthe*] to become a dwelling [*katoiketerion*] in which God lives by his spirit." No fewer than five words in this passage are based on the word *oikos,* which means family or household. This complex of ideas reinforces the biblical picture of the Church as the community of God's people and the agent of God's *oikonomia* and kingdom.

God has a well-ordered plan for how the Church is to live and function. Part of God's economy concerns the way the local congregation is to function—what we might call the ecology of the local church.[19]

Second, *the whole created order is also God's house*. The Church is not the only place God works; rather she is a sign pointing to what God is doing in his larger "house," the created universe. The whole cosmos is, metaphorically, God's *oikos* for which God has an *oikonomia,* a plan for the proper ordering of everything in the world.

God does not dwell in a house made with hands; not even the whole universe can contain him.[20] Yet God inhabits his world![21] As Israel's psalmists often sang, every part of the created order testifies to God's power and goodness and is the sphere of his presence and mighty acts.

In the Old Testament, first the tabernacle and then the temple at Jerusalem became the focal point of God's presence and dwelling. From this point two lines of development can be traced. The one sees God's people, rather than a physical structure, as God's house and temple. This provides the basis for the New Testament understanding of the Church as the household, family, and community of God. The other line of development is equally significant, however, for understanding God's plan. Here the idea of God's house or dwelling is expanded to become a metaphor for the whole created order. The cosmos is the house of God, inhabited and sanctified by his presence.

This development is seen especially in the Book of Psalms. In many of the Psalms, references to God's house or dwelling clearly mean the Jerusalem temple, or Jerusalem itself (for instance, Psalms 5:7, 42:4, 55:14, 116:19). But in some cases the idea is expanded so that the whole earth is pictured as God's house. This is most clear, perhaps, in Psalm 36:5–9.

The Old Testament background enriches the New Testament picture of God's saving work as the manifestation of his kingdom and the proper ordering of all things in God's house under the headship of Jesus Christ. God's salvation centers in the life, death, resurrection, and reign of Jesus, and the New Testament shows how God is working out his economy and Kingdom through Jesus Christ.

The way the New Testament speaks of Christ underscores the double sense of house (both the Church and the cosmos) that we have been describing. In Colossians 1, for instance, Jesus is described as both "the firstborn over all creation" and "the firstborn from among the dead" (Colossians 1:15, 18). In Hebrews, Jesus is both the sustainer and "heir of all things" and the apostle and high priest of the Church (Hebrews 1:2–3, 3:1). Jesus Christ, Lord of the Church, is also Lord of the universe! This is the jolting significance of the original cry of the first Christians, "Jesus is Lord!"

This perspective is reinforced by the way the New Testament speaks of Jesus Christ as "head." Jesus is head not only of the Church but of "all things." "God placed all things under [Jesus'] feet and appointed him to be head over everything for the church, which is his body, the fullness of him who fills everything in every way" (Eph. 1:22–23). In Ephesians 1:10 the verb "to bring together under one head" (*anakephalaiosasthai*) derives from the noun *kephalē*, "head," the word used for Jesus as head of the Church. Jesus Christ is now head of the Church, and God's plan through the Church is to fully reveal Christ's headship over the whole created order.

Thus the double significance of the house or *oikos* of God in Scripture becomes more notable. The whole created order is God's house, his habitation, though now disordered by sin and human unfaithfulness. But God is creating a new humanity, a new family or household, which is the present manifestation of the future reconciliation of "all things." And far from operating in a separate sphere far removed from the world, the Church is God's household right in the middle of the disordered cosmos, existing there both to show what God intends and will do and to be the body of Christ—the presence and agency of Jesus in the world today. For the Lord, the Father of the Christian household, is also the "Father of all" (Eph. 4:6), "the Father from whom his whole family in heaven and on earth derives its name" (Eph. 3:14).

THE SIGNIFICANCE OF GOD'S ECONOMY

In summary, God's economy is his plan to bring balance, harmony, and health, his perfect *shalom,* to his creation. This he accomplishes through Jesus Christ and the Church. The Church is God's *oikos* in a special sense, charged with showing forth and helping to bring about God's peace in the larger *oikos,* the created order. The Church does this in part through understanding the real ecology, in all its dimensions, of the Church and through cooperating with God's design in her life and witness.

In this perspective, God is the divine economist, the creative Lord who from the foundation of the world has established a plan for the fullness of time. And this plan centers in Jesus Christ and the work of the Holy Spirit in and through the Church.

The significance and breadth of God's economy can be gauged by correlating it with three other New Testament words that are also based on the metaphor of *house.* Each Christian is an *oikonomos,* a steward or good manager in God's house. To us is given the task of *oikodomē,* of edifying or building up God's house. And God's plan extends to the whole *oikoumenē,* the entire habitable world. Thus *steward, edification,* and *ecumenical* are all *oikos* words that suggest the dimensions of God's redemptive plan.

STEWARDS AND EARTHKEEPERS

In the light of the contemporary ecological crisis and the divine economy presented in Scripture, we are called to be stewards in God's house and keepers of the earth. We are called to work together with Christ in building and managing his house—both the Church and the world—in a way that is biblically faithful and ecologically responsible. We are given a stewardship (*oikonomia*). We are to be good managers of the resources that God has placed in our hands—resources that are fully adequate to accomplish God's will and plan through the Church.

Stewardship, like so many rich biblical truths, has been robbed of much of its biblical punch by being restricted to questions of the tithe and the use of time. The biblical idea of stewardship is much broader and richer—first, because it ties in with God's overall economy, and second, because it involves the stewardship both of the created order and of God's grace.

It is most urgent that Christians recover a comprehensive biblical understanding of the stewardship God has given us of the created world. This concerns both our lives in the world (how we treat the physical environment, the quantities and kinds of food we consume, our use of land and energy, the kinds of homes and church buildings we erect) and our lives in the Christian community (how well we understand the spiritual ecology of the Church and work harmoniously with God's principles to build a community of the Spirit that shows forth the kingdom of God). We must cooperate with God's ecology for the Church.

So that we may be good stewards of the created order, God has given us his grace. Peter says we should be "good stewards of God's varied grace" (1 Pet. 4:10, RSV). We have been charged with stewardship of the most precious of all resources—the grace of God!

We have been saved by grace through faith, and God has given us gifts by his Spirit. These are our most precious and valuable resources, and we are charged to be good stewards of them. God gives his own life to us. The Body receives its life from the head, Jesus Christ. We are to grow up into his fullness and likeness. We are to have the mind of Christ. Only as this happens will we have the spiritual strength to build the Church as God intends and to witness effectively to and among the principalities and powers of the present age.

The Church has, however, a wider stewardship in God's world as well. The mission of the Church is to glorify God by showing forth his nature and works, the reconciliation and redemption God brings through the death, resurrection, and reign of Jesus Christ. "God . . . reconciled us to himself through Christ and gave us the ministry of reconciliation: that God was reconciling the world to himself in Christ, not counting men's sins against them. And he has committed to us the message of reconciliation. We are therefore Christ's ambassadors, as though God were making his appeal through us" (2 Cor. 5:18–20). God's plan is that "now, through the church, the manifold wisdom of God should be made known to the rulers and authorities in the heavenly realms, according to his eternal purpose which he accomplished in Christ Jesus our Lord" (Eph. 3:10–11).

In other words, the life and work of the Christian community are intimately bound up with God's cosmic-historical plan for the redemption of his world. It most certainly matters *what* the Christian community does and how authentically it demonstrates the mind of Christ and the values of the Kingdom in its daily life. We are saved by grace, not by our works, but "we are God's workmanship, created in Christ Jesus to do good works"—specifically those good works "which God prepared in advance for us to do" (Eph. 2:10).

The Ecology of the Church

Once the inevitable intertwining of social, physical, economic, and spiritual dimensions of reality begins to dawn on us, we are prepared to pursue the ecology of the Church and to guard against unbiblical and unecological divisions between the spiritual and material realms. When we limit our perceptions to spiritual matters only, we are seeing not the Church's real ecology but only some parts of it.

The *real* ecology of the Church encompasses an extremely large number of variables. The Church may, in fact, be the most complex ecosystem in existence, since it includes the total human environment and experience—physical, social, and spiritual. Although these categories are not totally satisfactory or mutually exclusive, we may use them to probe further into the Church's actual ecology.

PHYSICAL ECOLOGY

The Church's physical ecology is made up of the physical bodies of believers and all the material aspects of their lives. It includes the food and clothing Christians use, the products they use or help produce, and the physical energy they consume. It includes their houses and church buildings. Transportation, land use, and the treatment of other life on earth are all part of the actual ecology of the Church. We cannot speak of the real ecology of the Church without taking into account the combined impact Christians have in all these areas. The key question, then, becomes whether the Church's use of money, buildings, food supplies, energy, and other physical resources is in harmony with God's economy or works against it. If Christians claim to be worshiping and serving God in the spiritual realm but committing injustice through extravagant consumption of earth's resources, then they are giving contradictory signals. They are in fact working against God's economy in fundamental ways.[22]

SOCIAL ECOLOGY

The social ecology of the Church concerns the Church as a social organism, a community. It includes the social impact of each believer, but it especially concerns the social reality and impact of Christian families and homes, Christian congregations, and the influence of Christians in their neighborhoods and in the larger human community.

The social ecology of the Church thus includes the total social impact of the Church and of individual Christians, as well as how the Church is shaped by society. Part of this impact involves the moral and ethical values that Christians hold. These values are shown and transmitted by Christians' actual behavior. This is one reason the economic and social behavior of Christians is so important. Whether or not Christians are really cooperating with the economy of God will be revealed in the way they behave in the marketplace.

The real ecology of the Church, then, includes every aspect of the social behavior of Christians. It includes the social and economic impact of the jobs Christians hold, and not just Christians' dependability at work or how they spend their off-the-job hours. And it includes the social impact of how Christians treat the physical world—for instance, whether they care for the earth and work for equitable distribution of food and clothing or are concerned only with their own accumulation and comfort.

SPIRITUAL ECOLOGY

The spiritual ecology of the Church is even more complex than her physical and social ecology and is less available to our understanding and analysis. But Christians insist, on the basis of both Scripture and personal experience, that the spiritual dimension is the most fundamental in the Church's ecology, the reality that gives ultimate meaning to all the rest.

The spiritual ecology of the Church incorporates the moral and spiritual values by which Christians live, but it includes much more. It incorporates the reality of the spirit world, the actual presence of the Spirit of God in the world and the realm of angels, demons, and whatever other unseen principalities and powers the universe contains. It is profoundly unecological to overlook this dimension. Spiritual ecology includes the Church's battle with the kingdom of darkness, "the ruler of the kingdom of the air, the spirit who is now at work in those who are disobedient" (Eph. 2:2).

The spiritual impact of the Church is tied especially to the influence Christians have on one another, the impact of righteous living on society, and the power of prayer. Since prayer is the primary channel of communication between believers and God, it is the key channel through which God's energy is released into the world. Here faith and hope are crucial, for through these, Christians are enabled to work constructively for the manifestation of the kingdom of God in the present order. The key dynamic in the Church's spiritual ecology is faith working by love (Gal. 5:6).

THE CHURCH'S ENVIRONMENTAL IMPACT

Only when we take into account the physical, social, and spiritual ecology of the Church can we begin to gauge the Church's true environmental impact.

We may consider the life of a local congregation in a particular community. What is its impact? Some of the congregation's impact could actually be measured through sociological, economic, or ecological analysis. One could determine, for instance, the combined effect of the energy consumed by Christians or gauge their impact on the community's social fabric. It is true, of course, that much of the Church's impact could not be measured or quantified. But since the social, physical, and economic life of a group of people reflects its spiritual values, some judgment could be made about the total environmental impact of a congregation and concerning its fundamental fidelity or infidelity to the economy of God.

The next questions are, What would be the result of intentional changes in the Church's life? What would be the ecological impact if the congregation decided to align its life more closely with God's economy and kingdom? This is where the life-style changes advocated by a growing number of thoughtful Christians come into focus.

Many Christians ask what difference it makes to live a simpler, more Kingdom-oriented life-style. When we view this question ecologically, we see that it makes all the difference in the world. For the ecological perspective reminds us that every life is linked to every other, that all our behavior has consequences socially, physically, and spiritually, and that our behavior has long-range effects that may continue for generations. In other words, from an ecological standpoint, living for kingdom priorities has far-reaching and highly significant results. Such responsible living in fact helps to manifest the kingdom of God and contributes significantly to the reconciliation of all things in Jesus Christ.

It is not necessary to follow this out in further detail, given the general perspective that has been traced. It will suffice simply to give a few examples.

We may consider the Church's relationship to nature. The Church should be a model of reconciliation between people and nature, thus pointing ahead to the Kingdom. The Church could start, for instance, with ecological responsibility for the land she owns corporately—the millions of acres tied up in church and college campuses and in the Church's sacred cow pastures—church camps—

which not uncommonly run into the hundreds of acres. Just as industrial holdings are managed with no other motive than profit, so church properties are often managed with no other motive than narrowly religious programming. Such property should be used as a model of ecological responsibility. This would mean, at the least, preserving as much as possible of the land in its natural state, protecting resident wildlife, developing as environmentally balanced an ecosystem as is feasible, and using such areas as educational tools to heighten a sense of environmental awareness and ecological stewardship. A similar perspective and concern could be applied also to the land held "privately" by Christians in the form of homes, farms, and vacation or investment property.[23]

In sum, ecological and economic realities in the present time remind the Church of what the Bible itself teaches: the human earthly environment is an interdependent whole, and within that environment (as well as transcending it) the Church is socio-spiritual organism. If we will understand that the world is organized not primarily logically, psychologically, or even sociologically but rather ecologically, we can understand better how to respond faithfully to today's social, economic, and spiritual needs while maintaining fidelity to the biblical revelation.

Notes

1. Richard Underwood, "Ecological and Psychedelic Approaches to Theology," in Martin E. Marty and Dean G. Peerman, eds., *New Theology No. 8* (New York: Macmillan, 1971), p. 153.
2. Kenneth P. Alpers, "Starting Points for an Ecological Theology: A Bibliographic Survey," in Marty and Peerman, *New Theology No. 8,* p. 303.
3. See, for examples, G. L. Prestige, *God in Patristic Thought* (London: SPCK, 1952), pp. 60ff.; John Reumann, "Oikonomia-Terms in Paul in Comparison with Lucan *Heilsgeschichte,*" *New Testament Studies,* 13 (1966–67), p.

150; and, by the same author, "Oikonomia = 'Covenant'—Terms for *Heilsgeschichte* in Early Christian Usage," *Novum Testamentum,* 3 (1959), pp. 282–92, and "*Oikonomia* as 'Ethical Accommodation' in the Fathers, and its Pagan Backgrounds," *Studia Patristica,* 78 (Berlin, 1961), pp. 370–79.

4. Note, for example, 1 Timothy 3:15; Hebrews 3:1–6; 1 Peter 2:5; 1 Peter 4:17.
5. This metaphor underlies much of Ephesians, and especially Ephesians 2:19–22.
6. All Scripture references in this essay, unless otherwise indicated, are from the New International Version.
7. Vithal C. Nadkarni, "The Coming Water Crisis," *World Press Review* (September 1981), p. 55.
8. There is a growing consensus concerning the meaning and gravity of these and related economic-ecological issues among people who are ecologically aware. For good summaries, note, among others, Mark Hatfield, "Finding the Energy to Continue," *Christianity Today* (February 8, 1980), vol. 24, no. 3, pp. 20–21; Jeremy Rifkin with Ted Howard, *The Emerging Order: God in the Age of Scarcity* (New York: Putnam's, 1979); E. F. Schumacher, *Small is Beautiful: Economics as if People Mattered* (New York: Harper, 1973); Ronald J. Sider, *Rich Christians in an Age of Hunger* (Downers Grove, Ill.: Inter-Varsity Press, 1977); Loren Wilkinson, ed., *Earthkeeping: Christian Stewardship of Natural Resources* (Grand Rapids: Wm. B. Eerdmans Publishing Co., 1980); Ron Eldson, *Bent World: A Christian Response to the Environmental Crisis* (Downers Grove, Ill.: Inter-Varsity Press, 1981).
9. This is the fundamental problem with Underwood's otherwise helpful essay, noted previously.
10. Two qualifications are in order here. First, I am speaking of ecological realities, not evolutionary theories. While ecology does necessitate a long-range view, it does not necessarily require assuming time spans of hundreds of millions of years unless one is philosophically locked in to evolutionary hypotheses rather than divine creation. Second, some ecologists also argue for a "catastrophe theory"; that not all

ecological development occurs gradually but may be punctuated by periodic sudden change. Recognizing this does not substantially alter the fact, however, that the ecological time frame is fundamentally a long-range one.

11. Alpers, p. 305.
12. "Inhabit" and "live" in this verse are *oikos* words, forms of the verb *katoikeō*.
13. Cf. Jeremy Rifkin, *Entropy: A New World View* (New York: Viking, 1980), which is to some extent a popularization and extension of ideas that have been around for some time. Rifkin argues that since the law of entropy is grounded in the very nature of our physical existence, it will soon replace the dominant machine-progress view of history that has held sway for the past several hundred years. While some critics think Rifkin has seriously overstated the case of entropy and has applied it more broadly than can legitimately be done, a number of scientists and environmentalists are raising the same question. It is clear, at least, that entropy does seriously affect energy questions on earth. Whether it provides the basis for a world view will continue to be debated.
14. Note especially, for example, John 1:1–3; Colossians 1:16–17; Hebrews 1:3.
15. J. Philip Wogaman, *The Great Economic Debate: An Ethical Analysis* (Philadelphia: The Westminster Press, 1977), p. vii.
16. *Ibid.*, p. ix.
17. Schumacher, p. 45.
18. Wogaman's *The Great Economic Debate* is helpful in this regard. He discusses in turn the economic options of Marxism, *laissez-faire* capitalism, social market capitalism, democratic socialism, and what he calls economic conservationism, applying an ethical analysis to each. Wogaman ends up favoring democratic socialism, arguing that economic conservationism has not yet emerged as a really valid economic option. It is becoming increasingly clear, however, that some form of ecologically responsible economic system is the only valid option for the future. Such a new economic orientation can and will emerge if ecologically minded economists give sufficient attention to its develop-

ment. It is crucial, however, that the perspective of the biblical economy play a key role in this development. For an important contribution in this area, see Herman Daly, ed., *Economics, Ecology, Ethics: Essays toward a Steady-State Economy* (San Francisco: W.H. Freeman and Co., 1980).

19. Viewing the Church as a socio-spiritual and charismatic organism, we may conceive of the ecology of the Church as consisting of the basic components of worship, witness, and community, all of these centering in glorifying God and all dynamically interrelated. While there is not space here to elaborate such an ecological model, I do explore it in some detail in my book *Liberating the Church* (Inter-Varsity Press, 1983).
20. Note Isaiah 66:1–2 and Acts 7:44–50 in this connection.
21. Although not developed here, the motif of the habitation of God is significant throughout the Scripture and dovetails with the perspective outlined here. For a partial development of this theme (with reference to the nature of the church only), see Howard A. Snyder, *The Problem of Wineskins* (Downers Grove, Ill.: Inter-Varsity Press, 1975), pp. 57–68.
22. From the ecological perspective there is no such thing as *adiaphora,* "things indifferent."
23. Christian camps and campuses could learn much from what is being done ecologically at Au Sable Trails Camp and Environmental Center (Route 2, Mancelona, MI 49659).

Barry L. Callen (D. Rel., Chicago Theological Seminary), dean, Anderson College

The Church: Tomorrow's People for Today's World

GOD'S PEOPLE, established in holiness, are responsible for implementing the Christian ethic in practical living. It is in the assembly of the family of God that we find the laboratory of love, allowing for the testing of truth committed to the saints of all ages.

Recently I visited again a local congregation of Christian people who have been worshiping in the same location for many decades. An unusually large percentage of the church's present membership is made up of older people, many of whom carry memories of better times when their church was larger, the tone more "spiritual." The building is quite old, the community economically depressed. Over the objections of some members, the church's pews are new and padded and the carpet is thick, red, and wall to wall. There is a history of deep concern for missions, *foreign* mostly, and of very authoritarian and culturally and doctrinally conservative pastors.

I suppose nearly any sensitive Christian person who looked closely at this or any one of thousands of similar church situations across the land would come to about the same dual conclusion. On the one hand, the Church is a *divine* institution. Our faith, our stewardship, and at least some aspects of our life together as Christians help to make that clear. We believers are not operating merely on our own momentum by means of our own structures and programs. People have been changed and something quite unique has indeed developed among us. It is the Church.

But, on the other hand, while the Church obviously has divine rootage and dimensions, it is just as obviously conditioned, and sometimes seemingly dominated by human factors—too often frailties. Many petty things influence personal relationships. Basic decisions often are made on the basis of very limited information or because of the insistence of a strong personality or just because of who happened to be present and voting that day. Organizational structure in the Church often is dictated by historical precedent and usually is only as relevant to the accomplishment of God's work as the people comprising it are committed to that end. And, for several reasons, the level of understanding and maturity and commitment varies widely among people who call themselves Christians.

What, then, is the Church? The Church is *people,* great people for the most part, limited people to be sure. It is God's people, people just down the street, people who have been privileged to find Christ and one another. The Church is also *organization,* human organization, sometimes relevant and effective in implementing God's work, sometimes obsolete, a poorly conceived structure for projecting the ideals of the faith and helping them to become reality. Always the Church is God's people seeking to be his body in this world. Its members are praying that he might reign in their hearts, speak through their words, act through their structures—in short, be in them and through them for their own sake and for the sake of all humankind.

Because of all of this it is crucial at the very outset to recognize that *three interlocking necessities* must be characteristic of the Church if it is to be worthy of itself and genuinely about God's business. It must have continuity with the past, especially with that decisive period recorded in the New Testament; it must have an openness to adapt and act in the present as God may command; and it must be a pilgrim people willing to face a future that may well render obsolete some patterns of thought and action familiar to the Church in other times and places.

When the Church lacks any of these essential characteristics, there is a serious flaw in its makeup. *Tradition* and *mobility* may seem contradictory to those preoccupied with the past or floating aimlessly into the future, but in the life of the Church they must be seen as complementary. A Church with mobility but ignorant of its tradition has lost its roots and is likely to repeat many of the mistakes of the past. A Church rich in tradition and lacking in mobility becomes a paralyzed and generally useless prisoner of its own past. But the Church that God calls and controls will be vitally in touch with the foundations of its heritage, will be adequately mobile for its present challenges, and will also be lured forward by a vision of the future that ever fulfills the past and gives direction to every new present.

There is a certain mystery about the Church. Theological vision and practical reality join to make necessary an approach to the nature of the Church that involves the paradoxical union between the human and the divine. Because the Church is human, it exists at a given time and place with a given set of persons, all subject to the inevitable conditioning of those people and that moment in history. But because of the Church's divine element it tends to move beyond and rise above the obvious human limitations. Its commonplace features are themselves conditioned by a covenant granted by God and a new creation set in motion by God. The result is a body of frail but faithful people caught between heaven and earth.

In the New Testament this heaven-and-earth body of people is designated in two ways. The people of God are known in *their totality,* the Church, and in *any local congregation* that focuses that totality in a given place, a particular Church. The "local" church is the embodiment of "the Church" in places like Corinth, Thessalonica, and Philippi. There is but one people of God, one Church, although ideally this one Church is to be found in many places at any one time. So, in a real sense, that congregation that I have visited again is called to be nothing less than "the Church" coming into its own in that particular place.

Some real confusion has entered here, since Christians over the centuries have developed organizations that include many congregations and have referred to the organizations as "churches." This terminology is unfortunate, since it employs the word *church* in a way not used in or probably even anticipated by the New Testament. This new usage often takes a Christian's attention and energy away from several crucial facts and central mandates that are more basic than and prior to any contemporary human efforts to structure the life and work of God's people. Although the distinction is subtle and usually inadvertent, it is nonetheless damaging.

The New Testament employs the word *church* often, usually with the words *God* or *Christ* related. The plural of *Church* also occurs frequently, but it is always a *plural of distribution* (i.e., it refers to the several local churches of Corinth, Philippi, Ephesus, and others). It never means denominations, as in a phrase like "World Council of Churches." Actually, Paul recoils at the news that denominations had developed among the Christians in

Corinth: a Paul-party, an Apollos-church, a Peter-denomination, even a Christ-party (1 Cor. 1:12; cf. 3:5). The human factors had surfaced to the point of causing division among Christians and distortion of their understanding of the Church.

The Church is one! It may be in many places, have many members and functions, but it cannot be two or more bodies (cf. Rom. 12:4–8; 1 Cor. 12:12–30). Christians have been called into one body (Col. 3:15) and whether recognized or not, they are intended to be members of Christ's one body (Eph. 5:30) and therefore members one of another (Eph. 4:25). Unfortunately, many Christians think of themselves primarily as members of a "church" (denomination), often, in the process, dulling their own awareness of the larger reality of the body of Christ wherein their true membership lies. By thinking denominationally a person often thinks divisively and pictures his or her role basically as being loyal to a denomination and only vaguely as being a member of the one universal body of Christ, the Church, seeking to transplant *itself* (not a particular denomination) in each locality.

Differing beliefs, styles of worship, and cultural backgrounds do cause Christians to cluster in various ways and function separately from one another. To an extent this is inevitable and possibly even useful. But to the extent that we sanctify certain situations by adjusting the direction of our thought, redefining our words, and reorienting the focus of our Christian lives around incidental circumstances, we have done violence to truth and harm to God's work. As Christians, our new and prime identity is *in Christ* and thereby *among his people*—all of his people!

We cannot avoid and must not do violence to the basic paradox of our Church membership. As Christians we are by virtue of our birthright as converted children of God members of the *whole* Church. In addition, by virtue of personal, family, geographic, and historical circumstances, we go on to find our functional place in the life of the Church by becoming associated with a particular *part* of the Church. We then belong, at one time, to the whole and to part of the whole.

The whole Church without concrete and localized expressions is of itself little more than a dream. But any concrete and local expression of the whole Church that is not defined by and oriented to the whole Church is an alien strain operating in disguise. Our membership as Christians is in the one and only body of believers, the body of Christ. Any secondary membership in some subdivision of the Church's life must be motivated by and function on behalf of the Church itself. If it is otherwise, if some voluntary association of Christians seeks to supplant the Church or to build artificial and unnecessary walls between Christians or if such an association introduces requirements, attitudes, or goals not characteristic of the Church itself, then this association of Christians ceases to be a legitimate part of the whole and becomes a thing of its own, an actual obstacle to the whole.

So the Church includes within itself many people in many settings, clustering together in various ways, yet all one Body. The paradoxes and dangers are always as present as are the truths and opportunities. But in addition to these delicate relationships within the Church itself, the very basic question arises of the appropriate relationship between the worlds in which the Church lives. Since the Church stands between heaven and earth, between the present evil age and the age to come (which is already coming in the Church and its mission), it is critical to understand the in-betweenness of the Church's life.

Although the Church, the body of Christ, has always known that it lives in two worlds, even in two ages simultaneously, it has had constant difficulty keeping a balanced perspective on the two. With dual citizenship come dual responsibilities and a delicate tension that always invites a tipping of the balance. In the attitudes and actions of the Church the supernatural can become so dominant a preoccupation that the Church loses touch with and even interest in the things of this world. Suddenly all is thought to be of God in so immediate a way that the lessons of history, the laws of sociology, and even the knowledge of modern medicine are set aside as irrelevant, human, earthly, somehow the opposites of faith. Practical ministry and timely mission suffer at the hands of spiritual journeys inward and impatient hopes for heaven that short-circuit the here and now.

Too often, on the other hand, the Church becomes overly impressed with the fact that God has set in motion universal laws that now seem to have an almost independent existence. God is remembered primarily as the one who judged all creation to be good, including our own mental processes, our full use and enjoyment of life, and our responsibility to take initiative in structuring and restructuring our own society into useful vehicles for human welfare. We as humans thus become too captivated by ourselves and the tasks that are ours to accomplish. The standards that are to measure success or failure become mostly the fruit of human dreaming and the means for achieving success become mostly the products of human scheming. God is forced to move more in the realm of distant memory and traditional vocabulary and less in the daily consciousness of thinking and acting and humbly obedient disciples. While such self-oriented and socially oriented persons remain within the Church structure and continue to call upon God's name in reference to their own efforts, they do so with decreasing passion and purpose.

Reinhold Niebuhr has reviewed the Church's chronic ineffectiveness in influencing wayward political situations. He has concluded that "among the many possible causes of this failure of Christianity in politics the most basic is the tendency of Christianity to destroy the *dialectic of prophetic religion,* either by sacrificing time and history to eternity or by giving ultimate significance to the relativities of history. Christian orthodoxy chose the first alternative, and Christian liberalism the second.''[1]

There is a rhythm essential to the adequate existence of the Church, a rhythm composed of a careful alternation of point and counterpoint, the natural and supernatural, the past and present, the substance and symbol, the local and universal. To emphasize any at the expense of the others is to break the rhythm and silence the music. Jesus once announced, ''You are Peter, and on this rock I will build my church, and the powers of death shall not prevail against it'' (Matt. 16:18). He intended by such a startling announcement that his Church should live at all times by doing what Peter did. Peter had seen *God himself* behind the figure of the carpenter's son from Nazareth and he had openly confessed his faith in Christ as the Son of God, the Savior of the world, the foundation of a new fellowship of believers, the Church.

God is still alive and always at work, and his Church must see with Peter beyond public opinion and the usual materialistic considerations to the foundational truth of the Christ and his ongoing ministry in the world. Christ's faithful followers, his Body at any point in time, have genuine existence only as they relive that moment at Caesarea Philippi when Jesus was recognized and proclaimed to be the Lord.

The Church is the fellowship of those who have actually become a part of the truth itself. Paul reminded the Corinthian Christians that by typical human standards they had been mostly nobodies (1 Cor. 1:26-29). But he also reminded the same people in the same letter that they were nonetheless the body of Christ (1 Cor. 12:27), the company of committed souls who by the power of God were to continue the ministry of Christ in the world. Even as Jesus was a bridge person, participating in human existence and yet not wholly confined to that level of existence, his disciples would be between heaven and earth, rooted in one, reborn in the other, abiding in one, agents of the other. The inevitable consequence is that the Church is a community of hope, a present reality created by the impact of the future made known in the history of Jesus. It lives between the times and between the worlds.

A most difficult New Testament paradox involves the prepositions *in* and *of*. The Christian community is at the same time *in* this world as a witnessing presence and *of* another world in terms of the source, direction, and power of its own life. The resulting tension centers in trying to define the appropriate border between Church and non-Church—if, indeed, two opposing camps separated by a border is an acceptable way of viewing the matter.

A certain fluidity is introduced when we recall that Jesus tended to view the functions of the faithful in terms of being salt and leaven, caring more for penetration into the bastions of evil than for protection of the sacred places of the religiously devout. He seemed to see the role of God's people less as a privileged group rescued from the world and more as a commissioned group bearing a special responsibility toward all humanity. Accordingly, any people trying to be a remnant, volunteering for the role of misunderstood martyrs, preoccupied with trying to keep themselves pure and undefiled in the midst of a wicked world, may reveal a nobility of intention that is worthy of some respect. But they also reveal a sharp separation from the pattern of risking and loving and persistent penetration that was taught and lived with such abandon by Jesus.

The most pressing question before the Church is, Where shall the witness be made? Not whether—because there is no question that we must. Not when—because we always must. Not even how—because that will come to us in the process of our honest attempts to witness. The prior question is where. Originally the answer came from Jesus as follows: "You shall be my witnesses in Jerusalem and in all Judea and Samaria and to the end of the earth (Acts 1:8); "Go therefore and make disciples of all nations" (Matt. 28:19).

The earliest Christian disciples clearly supposed that they would stay in Jerusalem and in some constructive way associate themselves with the worship routines at the Temple (Acts 5:42). Apparently their original notion of mission was shaped by the assumption that the peoples of the world would finally come to Jerusalem and be blessed by Christ as they came. But with considerable pain they finally realized the folly of this expectation. In fact, the fall of Jerusalem in A.D. 70 clarified beyond all question that the fulfillment of their great evangelistic commission must come in some very different way. The alternative way came to be a philosophy of *diffusion* rather than of *ingathering*. All lands had to be seen as potentially the "holy land." There could and can be no settled and sacred Mecca for Christians, only new frontiers that yet cry out for the word of the gospel. There can be no one cultural pattern or racial stock, no one temple or physical line of blessed descendants from Abraham. There is one gospel, one needy world, one glorious Church.

As the centuries have unfolded, Christians have increasingly come to see the crucial significance of Christ's words to the woman at the well of Samaria: "The hour is coming when neither on this mountain nor in Jerusalem will you worship the Father" (John 4:21). Since that original prophetic statement Christians have struggled to comprehend its full range of implications. Always there has been discovered the tension, persistent in the whole history of Christian ethics and missions, between the tendencies toward penetration of the world in the name of Christ and retreat from the world in the name of local tradition and religious purity.

Purity and penetration—these form a classic pair of

concerns that seem contradictory to each other on the surface, since it is often assumed that being involved with non-religious people and issues inevitably prostitutes one's own religious purity. But it is crucial to see that these must be known as parallel concerns, not contradictory ones.

The Elijah-Elisha paradox is helpful. The mission of Elijah was to maintain the purity of the religion of God's people by fighting all religious adulteration and destroying the encircling idolatry. On the other hand, the mission of Elisha, his successor, was to be a prophet of power in which God was affirmed as active and sovereign in political life, reigning over kings, directing world affairs in very material expressions of his own lordship. The people of God were to be both pure (Elijah) and active on all fronts as agents of their God (Elisha). The mandate was not one or the other, but the paradox and possibilities, even the problem of both affirmed simultaneously.

The first-century church, fired by Christ's example and commission and in the mood of Paul's evangelical zeal, seemed to swing toward a preoccupation with penetration. By contrast, the second-century church had a heightened sense of need and desire for separateness that would protect its fragile life from the world's contamination. Both tendencies are very understandable given the pressure of historical circumstances in each period. Both contained some valid impulses. But a swing too far toward either extreme has a way of destroying the higher truth that can be realized only in the maintenance of the tension itself. And the tension, very simply stated, is that the Church is under divine orders to come out of the world in order that it might be sent back into the world. Christ himself both calls and sends. The Church comes to know two lives, one in the rewards of contemplation and renewal and the other in the exertions of inspired action in the world.

The work of the Church proceeds ideally by a delicate and dyanmic uniting of individual piety and group action, of a journey inward to the foundations of spiritual life and a journey outward to the concrete policies and procedures that introduce redemptive changes into the prevailing patterns of the world. In the dramatic life of Dietrich Bonhoeffer, for instance, we see courageous action directed at the verbal poison and social madness that came to grip a whole people. But we also read a very significant portion of a letter that Bonhoeffer wrote to his brother, Karl Friedrich, in 1935: "The restoration of the Church must surely come from a new kind of monasticism, which will have only one thing in common with the old, a life lived without compromise according to the Sermon on the Mount in the following of Jesus."[2] Here was and should still be a Christian monasticism on mission in the world!

Being divine agents in the world is difficult and invites misunderstanding and even persecution. Reverend John O. Eby wrote to *Newsweek* magazine to report what he saw as a most awkward irony in two articles that that magazine had printed in an earlier issue. He reported, "I am an American Baptist minister and the irony is one that all of us pastors face. Article one is about Pope Pius XII, who is being accused of 'playing politics' because he was silent in the face of injustice. Article two was about the 'social activism' of the ministers in the '60s who are being criticized for 'playing politics' because they spoke out against injustice. Is it any wonder that so many ministers are bald?"[3]

Benjamin E. Mays, a noted Black Christian who rose from bitter memories of slavery in South Carolina to being a mentor of Martin Luther King and a valued advisor to American presidents, has raised in his autobiography difficult questions that the Church must not ignore. He reports that for years he struggled to know how to live in a racially segregated society without accepting that which was "ugly and mean, stupid and cruel" as normal or inevitable. Then comes his major and not so surprising admission: "Segregation in the House of God has been a great strain on my religion."[4]

Mays was caught between the ideals of his faith and the realities of his world. He knew a "church" that concentrated on self-culture in spiritual matters and settled for indifference in other matters. Those Christians apparently longed for purity. They left out penetration. Their protected purity was no longer pure, for it was detached from a vital piece of its own essence, *mission*.

The basic question comes down to defining the task of the Church. And the answer turns out to be plural rather than singular. The Church is to be purist and penetrationist, Elijah and Elisha. In his opening remarks as chairperson of the World Congress on Evangelism (Berlin, 1966), Carl F. H. Henry emphasized to participating Christian delegates from more than one hundred countries that *justice* and *justification* are concerns of equal importance to God. "The God of the Bible is the God of justice and justification. The Christian evangelist has a message doubly relevant to the modern scene; he knows that *justice* is due to all because a just God created mankind in his holy image, and he knows that all men need *justification* because the Holy Creator sees us as rebellious sinners."[5] Jesus never prayed that his disciples should be removed from the world. His concern was that the evil of the world should be removed from their hearts so that *as they were in the world* they would be able to present a genuine alternative to its misery and lostness.

This place—the world—presents a real dilemma for Christians. We are taught to shun it when it comes at us and gets in us as "worldliness." We are commanded to love it and seek its transformation, since "God so loved the world" (John 3:16). We are sometimes paralyzed by the paradox.

Christians typically have seen personal surrender to the grace of God as the appropriate means of resolving humanity's inner problem of selfish attachment to "the world." But recently many have been struck by a related truth that involves a more positive and aggressive approach. This thrust in doctrine emphasizes public mssion as the consequence of private renewal. Once our inner world is transformed, are we not under a commission to take responsibility for shaping the life of the world outside of ourselves? Modern humanity holds the scales of nuclear life or death for the planet in its very unsteady hands. God has made us responsible for our share in human history.

In past centuries, persons viewed themselves as persons-the-subjects. They belonged and obeyed. They tended to visualize themselves as passive respondents to the forces of life, obedient citizens of the powers that be. Sometimes these dictating forces were identified with the uncontrollable furies and bountiful harvests of nature. At other times people thought the political powers in control or the existing religious and cultural traditions should remain unquestioned. But such passiveness is ceasing to be the way of modern humanity's history in general or of the Christian's self-understanding in particular.

Today we tend increasingly to see ourselves as *persons-the-makers*. We boast of having come of age, since our technical capacity has bolstered our ability and will to stand up to life and answer back. If rain is needed, make it! If the planet is severely overcrowded, surely ways can be found to control births and even transport us to other worlds. If a given society's institutions seem inadequate to meet felt needs, the institutions can and should be changed. If the life-style of parents seems unsatisfactory, decide upon and "do your own thing." For good or for ill, we moderns are beginning to claim a larger share of responsibility for our own history.

God is not separate from all of this determination and potential. As did the biblical writers, we also must see human history as the arena of God's action. In this very world God has revealed himself and his purposes. The exodus from Egypt, for instance, was not understood by the Hebrews as merely a successful labor revolt that gave them the freedom to mold their own future. No! It was God at work on the historical scene, enabling them to shape the future according to his promise.

Might we conclude that such a significant process of modern history as our sometimes frantic quest for freedom and dignity is inside God's present arena of concern and activity? If God is not the fostering agent, is he not at least deeply concerned and involved? To believe in the living God is necessarily to believe that he is somehow at work in the world where persons live and love, suffer and die, where their bodies are mangled by the machines of war and their spirits are crushed by chronic poverty, where they hunger for bread and justice and love, where they dig ditches in the dust and reach for the sky in faith.

Persons in all parts of our world are on the move, God is far from dead, and his disciples are commissioned to relate themselves responsibly to the present fulfillment of divine goals. The time has surely come for the Christian community to stop thinking of human history simply as the vague framework within which a few fortunate people participate in the drama of redemption. It is also our time and place of mission!

God's love has never been restricted to some select little company of pampered disciples who find it necessary to languish for the moment in the unpleasant surroundings of this world. Christians are indeed pilgrims whose final home is beyond this present world. But we pilgrims have a mission *in this world,* a mission that drives us deep into its very life.

The time has arrived for Christians themselves to come of age by taking responsibility under God for this world! New Testament religion is very personal, but it is hardly private. It involves a Church and a world. In John Wesley's very blunt words: " 'Holy solitaries' is a phrase no more consistent with the gospel than 'holy adulterers.' The gospel of Christ knows no religion, but social; no holiness, but social holiness. *Faith working by love* is the length and breadth and depth and height of Christian perfection."[6]

We Christians do not find ourselves in the exclusive and comfortable domain of an *either-or* option. We must have the vision and courage to live in some *both-and* realms. Though we may find peace with God one at a time, we as the Church must engage this world *together*. Singly we may be Christians, but only together do we become the Church that can be God's effective instrument in the world.

Jesus is Lord! But Lord of what? I have struggled with the contention that the Church somehow misapplies the lordship of Christ when using it as a stimulus for involvement in economic and political problems. Some of the most devoted Christians I know are influenced by thinking such as the following: Christ forbids the Church to enter into the sphere of Caesar. If the Church really takes the lordship of Christ seriously, then she must listen to him as he defines the separate jurisdictions of state and Church, as he declares that his kingdom is not of this world, as he maintains that he is not a divider of wealth, as he limits the Church to spiritual weapons.

I appreciate this concern for the purity and the privileged position of the gospel. Certain ambiguity and risk are indeed involved in trying to bring to reality a world-changing message in a world unready to hear and unwilling to be changed. Trying to achieve justice in the public sphere will undoubtedly necessitate the strategic use of political power and will involve difficult decisions with unclear "moral" implications. But the alternative to meaningful engagement with crucial public issues is unthinkable.

The "whole counsel of God" is not recognized until we

have affirmed the lordship of Christ over the larger worlds of learning and culture and government. The Christian community is obliged to press the divine claim upon the nations of the earth, including all the power structures that persons have devised to order their lives together. Jesus Christ still forgives sinners one by one and allots them individually a place in his kingdom; but this marvelous process of rebirth is the *beginning* of the story and *not the end*. The gospel that we celebrate is not an individual gospel any more than it is a social gospel. It is a gospel that admits to no limits. It is a message of life for the total person, including every aspect of that person's world.

The New Testament book of Revelation perfectly combines the apocalyptic and prophetic traditions found sporadically throughout biblical materials. What is joined is a sober realism about the roots of power and the fruits of idolatry and a stern call, not for Christians to be passive, but for them to be keenly aware and ethically responsible. Human history is indeed the arena of evil, the place of persecution. But it is also the arena in which God has worked out human salvation and in which his people are called to live redemptive lives.

This dual role of personal evangelism and social transformation raises urgent questions of motive and method. The Church, for instance, must not seek converts merely as an effort to enlarge and maintain its own institutions. It must not play subtle statistical games with human souls. Nor must it relate to society's problems with an eye toward gaining political control for itself so that it can impose its will on all people. It must not become too fond of the use of power, nor must it totally shun the use of power out of fear of becoming too fond of it. It must never be deluded into thinking that morals can be legislated, nor must it allow itself to forget that enlightened legislation can nonetheless be an instrument by which a society may educate and discipline itself for good. In short, the Church always finds itself walking a fine line that necessitates delicate distinctions and a willingness to act upon them despite the nagging presence of ambiguity.

A major thread that runs through the many writings of Reinhold Niebuhr is his continuing struggle with the relationship between the *ideal* and the *real*. He recognizes that the central problem of political philosophy is the relationship of our imaginary communities to the communities in which we actually live. Because of this persistent struggle there is a continuing tension between Christian ideals for society and a political cynicism that comes from involvement in what society actually is. As a Christian, Niebuhr's conclusion, of course, was neither to give up the ideals nor to yield finally to the paralysis of cynicism. It was both to hold on to the ideals and to recognize the realities for what they are. Along the continuum between these, Christians must discover constructive ways of dealing effectively with the realities out of the vision of their ideals.

As E. Clinton Gardner put it, "Love makes use of the structures of justice, not as eternal norms to which life must perennially conform but rather as *ad hoc* efforts to strike a balance between the final moral possibilities of life and the immediate and given realities."[7] For the Christian, then, it must be assumed that the distance between what appears possible at any given time and the perfect divine will for that time is covered by grace. But never must such gracious coverage of the gap between the ideal and the real be used as an escape from engagement in the continuing struggle for the ideal. It is an *in-between* situation, a difficult place wherein we must live courageously for Christ.

For the Church to be so involved, it must make some assumption about another classic point of tension, the appropriate relationship between the Church and the civil government or state. Unfortunately many evangelical Christians have done little thinking at this point—and often even less meaningful acting. As Senator Mark Hatfield once said in reference to the United States,

> We have taken the Constitutional doctrine of separation of Church and State, and converted it into a practice of separating the world of faith from the world of politics. The result is clear: our political system is threatened by a vacuum of moral values and the evangelical church is threatened by a vacuum of social relevance.[8]

It is the God-Caesar paradox. Christians have a dual allegiance and this awkwardness is further complicated because of the difficulty of keeping the appropriate tension between the two responsibilities. Often the fault is on the side of rendering unto Caesar those things which are God's. One helpful way of maintaining the necessary corrective is to keep Romans 13 and Revelation 13 in active dialogue. Romans 13 suggests to some that the Bible teaches total and unquestioning allegiance to the state. But its teaching must always be seen in the light of another biblical teaching, Revelation 13, which pictures the state as a "beast" and an enemy of the Church, or Revelation 18, which prophesies the downfall of any nation that becomes a modern Babylon, corrupted by its own wealth, injustice, and idolatry.

The immediate teaching of 1 Peter 2:18 is "Fear God, honor the king, be subject to your masters, suffer for goodness' sake and God will bless you." But the larger context of the Bible and human experience tempers the apparent rigidity of this one verse. While it is usually best to be obedient to human governments, Jochebed disobeyed civil authorities by preserving her son, Moses; Rahab betrayed her own government by assisting the spies from Canaan; Daniel disobeyed the king's decrees; Jeremiah preached boldly against disastrous government policies. All of them were blessed by God for their varying degrees of outright civil disobedience. Peter did write, "Be subject for the Lord's sake to every human institution" (1 Pet. 2:13). But after one of his arrests by authorities for his own civil disobedience, he also said, "We must obey God rather than men" (Act 5:29).

As Christians grow up into the stature of Christ, rejoice in their membership in the fellowship of Christ's continuing Body, the Church, and participate in a mission to spread the Good News, to be catalysts for the conversion of lost men and women, and to be change agents in wayward societies, a pervasive tension is always felt. It all goes on halfway between heaven and earth. The whole life of the believer is lived under the constant tension between the now and the hereafter, between the part and the whole, between momentary defeat and eventual triumph. As the ancient prophets Micah and Isaiah lived lives of faith in their troubled times, they exhibited, in the words of John Bright, "an apparently inconsistent juxtaposition of uncompromising doom and unequivocal assurance."[9]

For Christians, the clearest focusing of this paradox is seen in the life of Jesus. He taught that the kingdom of God was being realized in that ongoing present, particularly in conjunction with his own ministry, and that this kingdom also strained and yet strains forward to a final consummation beyond human history. We can only understand the mission of Jesus when we keep in view these two poles between which lies everything that he ever said or did. The one pole is the conviction that the kingdom of God is future, distinctly removed from the evils of this world. The other pole is the consciousness that this kingdom is already in the process of coming to realization in the very midst of this world. At least its partial breaking in upon this present order is no longer to be held off entirely. The Church is here!

And just how should the Church, an emissary from elsewhere, today's sign of tomorrow's triumph, conduct herself as she lives between heaven and earth, between here and hereafter? With some degree of indifference as people did at Laodicea (Rev. 3:14–22)? Nervously as at Thessalonica (2 Thess. 2:1–2)? Curiously as did many who kept pestering Jesus for signs? Or, with Paul, will the Church be "looking for the blessed hope and appearing" while realizing the concurrent necessity of "living soberly and righteously in this present world"? Too often the Church seems near death from an overdose of expectancy. It gets paralyzed by paradise, somewhat like a woman in waiting who has grown so large that she can barely manage to clothe herself let alone be of much use to others.

Jesus found a "church" establishment led by persons who went through all of the right religious motions while they themselves were dangerously close to blindness and death on the inside. Likewise, we find the Church all too often perishing in the rigidity of some noble liturgy, usually at the hands of leaders who manage to encase in the corridors of a churchly museum some ancient spiritual traditions that once throbbed with life. This is hardly the style of a pilgrim people carrying in their hardened and humbled and trembling hands the divine seeds of the future! Eternal life, the bloodstream of the Church, means being really alive. It is contagious. It constantly finds ways of removing chains, altering circumstances, even opening tombs, always changing the present by the power of God's future.

Jesus once said, "On this rock I will build my church, and the power of death shall not prevail against it" (Matt. 16:18). It is undoubtedly true that most Christians understand that this saying pictures the Church as successfully on the defensive, a divine fortress that will never collapse in the face of any assaulting foe. But, as appealing and comforting and even true as such an image may be, it is not the most helpful image. It is too static, too defensive a posture. Christ thought of his disciples as on mission. They were on the offensive. The gates of death, not the gates of the Church, were being stormed. And the good news was that those gates of death cannot always be impervious to the onslaughts of love. No gate need remain shut permanently if the redemptive fellowship of Christ's new people is sufficiently faithful to its marching orders!

One good definition of the Church can be constructed from unusual uses of the verb *to be*. The Church is that body of believers who are dedicated to being a body of *Kingdom people*, an advancing actualization of the *is-ness* of the *shall be*. The kingdom of God is *already* and is *not yet*. It is that in which we now live and for which we yet wait. It is our task and our hope. It is an accomplishment and a gift. We work. We wait. We live between the times as we find ourselves caught up in a tension between the age to come and the present evil age.

At one time, the reality of the future penetrated the present. About 587 B.C. Jeremiah was under palace arrest in Jerusalem while the Babylonian warriors were clamoring outside the walls (Jer. 32). The city was doomed. The land was already overrun. And what was Jeremiah doing? Buying a piece of property as though a real estate transaction was sensible in the midst of his country's total collapse! It was a prophetic action in that Jeremiah was able to see the triumph of tomorrow. Thus, in him, tomorrow already was present.

What good did Jesus really do with his loving and integrity and faithfulness and sacrificial death? Being mocked on a criminal's cross seemed even more useless and tragic than Jeremiah's land purchase. The answer is that there was no obvious good—unless in Jesus tomorrow had happened. Unless in Jesus, God's own future had broken into human life with an Easter power that eventually will be all in all.

The resulting challenge to the Church in all times is perfectly clear. The Church is to buy options on God's future! The Church must not sit and merely wait. It must not be overwhelmed by the forces of evil, retreating into a protective shell. It must rather be God's colony in humanity's world, agents of love and justice and peace that carry the marks of God's future.

Look around you. In your own life of commitment to God and humanity, as a member of his Church, this should be the day that tomorrow happens again—through you! And the Church should be nothing short of that fellowship of *tomorrow's people* who are sharing with Christ the urgent task of rearranging the realities of today's world.

Notes

1. Reinhold Niebuhr, *An Interpretation of Christian Ethics* (London: SCM Press, 1948), p. 151.
2. As quoted by Mary Bosanquet, *The Life and Death of Dietrich Bonhoeffer* (New York: Harper & Row, 1968), p. 150.
3. *Newsweek* (May 7, 1973), p. 12.
4. Benjamin E. Mays, *Born to Rebel* (New York: Charles Scribner's Sons, 1971), pp. 113, 243.
5. Carl F. H. Henry and W. Stanley Mooneyham, eds., *One Race, One Gospel, One Task* (Minneapolis: World Wide Publications, 1967), p. 16.
6. *The Works of the Rev. John Wesley* (London: John Mason, 1856), vol. XIV, p. 305.
7. E. Clinton Gardner, *Biblical Faith and Social Ethics* (New York: Harper & Row, 1960), p. 268.
8. As quoted in Clouse, Linder, and Pierard, *The Cross & The Flag* (Carol Stream, Ill.: Creation House, 1972), p. 10.
9. John Bright, *A History of Israel* (Philadelphia: The Westminster Press, 1959), p. 278.

Leon O. Hynson (Ph.D., University of Iowa), professor of church history and historical theology, Asbury Theological Seminary

The Ordered State and Christian Responsibility

IN THE WESLEYAN HERITAGE,[1] the approach to the state has been characterized by a consistent conservatism in the tradition of the English Protestant Reformation.[2] Founded primarily upon an exegesis of Romans 13:1–7 that was congenial to kings and governments but frequently disadvantageous to the citizen, this conservative stance has given to the state a quasi-divine (or sacred) status quite contrary to the way in which the New Testament views it. Important as the state is in the divine order, is there scriptural undergirding for this traditional obeisance?

Many questions are raised by an intensive examination of the New Testament evidence. How are we to interpret Jesus' counsel to "render unto Caesar the things which are

Caesar's; and unto God the things that are God's'' (Matt. 22:15–22)? Is this a norm for Christian conduct? Quite clearly it was one of Jesus' skillful rejoinders to an attempted entrapment. With that context in mind, are we to build a doctrine of the Christian's responsibility to the state upon it?[3] When the collectors of the temple tax sought to ascertain Jesus' loyalty to Jewish law, he counseled payment not on the ground of the legitimacy of the tax, but on the pragmatic basis of avoiding offense (Matt. 17:24–27).[4]

We should notice the general attitude in the Gospels toward the tax collector. In the example of Matthew (Levi), Zacchaeus, the parable of the Pharisee and the tax collector, one looks in vain for any affirmation of their work. Zacchaeus is motivated by Jesus' ministry to restore fourfold that which he has taken unjustly, and to give half of his possessions to charity (Luke 19:1–10). Hearing the murmurings of disapproval that he was the guest of a sinner, Jesus spoke the word of forgiveness for Zacchaeus. He came to save those who were obviously, and confessedly, lost. What was the nature of Zacchaeus' sin? That he was a tax collector? It is likely that he had used his position to oppress taxpayers and that seems to be the essence of his sinfulness.

In the instance of Levi (Luke 5:2–32) may be noted the association of tax-gatherers *and* sinners and Jesus' comment that he had come to save those who were obviously sinners. In Jesus' teaching about church discipline (Matt. 18:15–17), he declares that refusal to submit to the discipline of the Church requires that the sinner be treated as a ''pagan or a tax-gatherer'' would be treated, a rather blanket critique of the tax collector.

Finally, in the parable of the Pharisee and the tax collector, Jesus makes the point again that the penitent sinner is the one whom God forgives. Why does Jesus frequently refer to the tax collector as a prime example of sinfulness?

Is it the acknowledged greed of the official? His collaboration with the hated conqueror Rome? The evidence suggests that these were central considerations. Nevertheless, it is rather striking that Jesus chose such persons as his examples of depravity if he was especially concerned to affirm the obligations of citizens to render unto Caesar the things that are Caesar's. Have we imposed upon Jesus of Nazareth a political quietism for which there is no good evidence?

The teaching of Paul in Romans 13 provides the most detailed treatment in the New Testament on the responsibilities of the Christian to the state. Defining Paul's intention in the passage has exercised some of the best minds in the Christian tradition. In general, Reformed theology has espoused the position that the state is given for the correction of sinful persons in society. It has not excluded the ruler from necessary correction, arguing that revolution is justified when the monarch fails to carry out the purposes for which government exists. Anabaptists tend toward a total separation of the Church and state with each shaped by its own standards for different persons (i.e., the one for Christians and the other for sinners). The Church, through its exercise of discipline, regulates the lives of believers while the state employs the sword to punish and correct sinful persons.

The Wesleyan position, while more oriented toward political quietism, is less servile and unquestioning than often assumed. Wesley was both a loyal citizen and a critic of the state, recognizing and rejoicing in the Glorious Revolution of 1688–89, the Dutch revolution against Spanish Catholicism, and even initially the American Revolution. His support was based upon both religious and pragmatic bases. The Glorious Revolution inaugurated an era of civil and religious liberty unparalleled in English history. The revolt against the Duke of Alva and Spanish domination was proper for the Netherlanders. The American Revolution seemed to be an expression of resistance to injustice but Wesley's changed perceptions led him to view it as an essential undermining of English liberty in the cause of republicanism and radicalism.

The Wesleyan interpretation of Romans 13:1–7 has generally been more conservative than Wesley's approach.[5] Wesley's own position may be identified as hierarchialism. Asserting the primary of divine government, he asserts that the state is ordered under God (i.e., it has its fixed role and responsibility under [or, responsible to] God). As part of the earthly order given by God, it participates in all of the contingencies and dependencies characteristic of that order. It possesses no sacred qualifications, nor does it participate in the divinity of the Creator. By way of analogy to the creation of man—male and female—the state in some measure images God. Nevertheless it is dependent, limited, impermanent. From time to time human government has been accorded divinity or a near approximation.[6]

The state in its function to maintain order possesses the right to punish evildoers. It may also reward those who keep the law. It is the "creature" of God for guaranteeing safety *and* peace. The evildoer receives condemnation, not the righteous person who does good. For Paul the one who "resists" (v. 2) is not the one who does the good but evil. Paul says nothing about those who do good and therein resist the ruler who is doing evil. When Paul says "rulers are not a terror to good works," he is not describing the ruler who persecutes the saints and sets in motion a series of evil and even demonic laws. Why does Paul not recognize the problem of a perverse government, like Nero's, that distorts the purposes of government?

Surely Paul is setting forth in Romans 13 the picture of the divine intent in establishing the state. He does not describe the state as it was in A.D. 64 but the state as God intended it for the "last days," that entire era of Christian history to be consummated in the "day" (vv. 12–13).[7] If we were to ask Paul about the relationship of the Church (and Christian) to the state in that larger area of the relation of believers to one another, he would insist that the Christians settle their own problems without recourse to the infidels or the unjust (1 Cor. 6:1–9).[8]

Government in the Corinthian characterization—"the ungodly," "the unbelievers" (NIV)—is sharply contrasted to the benign description of rulers in Romans 13. What is the explanation for this difference? In the former is a strong negative; the latter is positive. Romans 13 describes government functioning at its proper level within its sphere of competency. It is in essence a characterization of the state performing at its God-ordered level. Written to the Roman Christians, the definition of the state may well be the Apostle's clear picture of what the state ought to be. Assuming that Rome could hardly know what God's plan for the state is, the Pauline interpretation could assist the Christians in Rome (even in Caesar's household?) in understanding and communicating the proper role of the state. If interpreters look into the Romans 13 characterization of the state, rather than deriving a picture of servile adherence to it, they may see the contrast between the state under Nero—corrupt, treacherous, and unjust—and the state ordered under God—rewarding the good, punishing evildoers, respecting the rights of conscience or recognizing the priority of the divine claim over the will of the state.

Several scholars, notably John Yoder and Martin Hengel,[9] have asserted that Paul's argument in Romans was intended to support a stable context for the proclamation of the gospel. Wesley interpreted the passage as in part "a public apology for the Christian religion."[10]

When the state is recognized as an "order" under God, given by God for justice, peace, and order, then the appeal to subordination or subjection makes sense. Christian subjection to the state is a concomitant of subjection to masters, to parents, to pastors, to husbands or wives, and vice versa. Paul's counsel to wives to be subject to their husbands (Eph. 5:22) is set in the larger context of the mutual subjection of believers (Eph. 5:21), and their submission to the Lord Christ.

This understanding of the state's role and the subjection of citizens is clearly supported by the context of the Romans 13 passage. The context—Romans 12:17–21 and 13:8–10—describes the rule or law of love that is to govern all of the Christian's relations, including the state. A study of the teaching of Paul in Romans 12 and 13 demonstrates the significance of the rule of love, the rights and limits of the state, and the priority of the divine will over subordinate orders.

These chapters are crucial in their qualification of the relationship between faith and politics (*ecclesia* and *polis*). Romans 12 and 13:8–14 are seen as the larger context for understanding Paul's intentions in 13:1–7.[11] Four principles are enunciated that, while offering no support whatever to anarchy, do place the state in a relationship of subservience before, and responsibility to, God.

The first principle declares that Jesus Christ, who transforms and renews, is to be the norm for living. The world's standards are not the criteria by which Christians shape their values. Our loyalties to this age are assumed with full awareness of their secondary significance. Paul charges, "Do not conform yourselves to the standards of this world" (Rom. 12:2, TEV). This principle prevents the Christian from a misconception of the worth of anything temporal, including the state. Because everything human is bound and shaped by time, human acknowledgement of, and subjection to the state are mandated. This subjection is qualified by the principle that life is to be lived on the basis of norms set by the transformed life that Christ exemplifies. If subjection to the state is taught (and it is), subjection to Christ is declared in the strongest possible sense. Our bodies or selves are to be presented to God as a "living sacrifice, holy and acceptable to God, which is your spiritual worship" (12:1). In contrast to this total commitment to God, service to the state is minimized. *Minimized,* but not demeaned! It is the will of God that we accept the state as the present order for human and social justice. To infer from this that obedience to the state possesses soteriological significance is to miss Paul's point. The state has nothing to contribute to final salvation. However, disobedience to the state on the ground of conscience, which is certainly inferred in 13:5, is the one legitimate reason for disobedience. Limited as that is, this inference represents a broad qualification of the authority of the state, one that the state in practice would have difficulty recognizing.

Principle two represents a very important norm for Christian attitude and action. In sum it is the claim that all of our responses and relations are to be governed by love (Rom. 12:9–21; 13:8–10). Couched in this challenge to love, the Pauline affirmation of the state is not merely a pragmatic political argument, or a statement that exalts the state to quasi-deity. Paul emphasizes the quality of Christian love ("Let love be genuine" 12:9), and the consistency of love (offered faithfully to friend or enemy, the mighty or the small, the saint or the sinner). The counsel "Do not be overcome by evil, but overcome evil with good" (12:21) summarizes the charge to faithful love.

Romans 13:8–10 addresses the second table of the Decalogue dealing with the rights and needs of the neighbor.[12] Love is the essence of the commandments, for one "does no wrong" (13:10) in a loving relationship to the neighbor. *Christian* love is the central ethical norm that includes justice, mercy, and forgiveness. Within the governing influence of love, one cannot accept injustice toward the neighbor, whether injustice flows from self (when love becomes sentimentalized or trivialized), from others, or from institutionalized sources such as the state.

Love will also shape our relation to the state, supporting its exercise of justice; presenting an ideal by which to judge its application of law (so that it cannot act unjustly without being aware of its failures); and insisting on a continual correction of its thirst for *more* authority over the citizens. The state governs by justice, not love, but the Christian citizen lives in a loving relationship with the state, a relationship defined as subjection. Subjection is submission to the state that acts justly. It is not possible to stand in the relation of love to a state that contravenes the integrity of love (or a critical element in love, which is justice).

The third Pauline principle cautions Christians to be unsurprised at persecution and opposition (12:14–17). That will be the customary response of the evil world. While it is never right or just, oppression because of the faith we hold is a reality of life for the Church. According to Paul, oppression must never mold us after its pattern but should become the occasion for modeling patience, blessing, humility, submission, and charity. When we respond to intolerance, persecution, and vengefulness in like manner, our life-style is being determined by the world around us, not Christ within us. As the Church lives out the disciplines of Christ, it will experience the responses of the age that Jesus faced in his era. A radical discontinuity with the spirit of evil can only produce conflict. Indeed, this universal antagonism should be interpreted as the macrocosm of the doctrine of original sin. The microcosm is the inclination to self-sufficiency and pride in everyone who lives.

E. Stanley Jones has written about the early Christian response to persecution and suffering: "I will match my power to suffer against your ability to inflict suffering. I will wear you down by my spirit, by soul force against physical force, by going the second mile, by turning the other cheek."[13] Finally, this "strange" behavior brought oppression to an end in Rome. When the fear of death has ceased to be a threat, the enemy has no power over the believer.

Principle four emphasizes the temporary character of every human structure (Rom. 13:11–14). The state is an "order" or program of the Creator for the extent of human history. The state is necessary but penultimate.[14] We live in the "last days," the time of the end. Since the Church was born at Pentecost, it has been called to view life in the context of eschaton. The state possesses from God a definite order (or place) in time. It is preliminary, not ultimate. The Church in glory—the Church triumphant—will be freed from the tension of the "two kingdoms." Presently Christians will take very seriously their responsibility to both, but ultimately only to the glorified Church of God.

These four principles offer guidance for the Christian in responding to the claims of the state. That these insights surround Paul's interpretation of the functions and responsibilities of the state should not be viewed as coincidental. They provide the backdrop for understanding the believer's relation to the state.

The content of Romans 13:1–7 is illuminated by the context. Yoder has written,

> The entire text thus sees Christian nonconformity and suffering, love as driven and drawn by a sense of God's triumphant movement from the merciful part into a triumphant future. Any interpretation of 13:1–7 that would make it the expression of a static or conservative undergirding of the present social system would therefore represent a refusal to take seriously the context.[15]

What is the Pauline position in these verses? How consistent with this stance is the position of Wesley and his heirs? Paul's concerns may be expressed in five primary statements.

First, the passage insists that the state exists by the divine purpose and permission (13:1). Paul's purpose is not to engage in political theories concerning forms and origins of government, whether democratic or monarchical. He stresses the theonomous ground of authority, exalting God as the ultimate power. In other terms, he asserts a hierarchy of powers—God over all and the powers of the state given their place under God. Paul does not say that the actual existence of a particular form of government is either *de jure* or *de facto* evidence of divine establishment. *Government* exists because God has willed it for the best interest of human society. That is the extent of the divine mandate. *Particular* kinds of government exist by divine permission and patience, but this must not be taken to suggest *divine approbation*. There is considerable indication that the German Third Reich was posed by its apologists as a messianic order.[16] Here was the state as an idolatrous substitute for the one God.

Further, Paul's position opposes anarchy where any social regulation is resisted. It contradicts a relative political ethics where a political system is approved *simply* on the basis of power politics or by a majority. One can say simply because the real issue here isn't the type of government, but the relation of human government to divine rule. The state is derived and contingent, never autonomous.

Second, the state is ordered under God. To use the word *ordained* of the Authorized Version is inadequate, since it connotes something sacred, or sanctified by God. The more appropriate words are *appointed, assigned* or *arranged*. John Wesley used the terms "subordinate to," or "orderly disposed under God," concluding that Paul taught obedience to the state, since its officers are "deputies or vicegerents" of God.[17] While his renderings for the word *ordered* are sound, his conclusions in the notes are inadequate, reflecting a conservative position that would favor the *status quo*.[18] Yoder explains Romans 13:1

by asserting that God "orders them [the powers], brings them into line, [and] by his permissive government he lines them up with his purpose."[19] Paul teaches that there is a divine scheme or order in human affairs. God has made provision through the state for orderly life. The state that *he* has ordered is *that state* that exercises justice and righteous law. This is the implication of Paul's comments in 13:3–4.

The Apostle also provides a corrective to any tendency to idolize the state. H. Emil Brunner asserts, "No form of State glorification, no defense or justification of the State is asserted here, but solely reverence before God."[20] Against Brunner, there is little question that Paul is offering support to the state as possessing right to exist, Brunner's primary claim is correct. The state is a minor light that pales before the light of God. It has no claim to autonomy.

This position recognizes the biblical hierarchy of powers: God over all and the state (as well as the Church and the family) under God. It is the basis for appeals to conscience. If God orders human powers, they are dependent and subservient. God alone is without contingency. His authority is ultimate; all other powers are penultimate, temporary, derived. Paul never confuses human law with divine law. Therefore, we must permit no interpretations of the "judgment" of Romans 13:2 that would apotheosize the state. That is nothing more or less than idolatry. To argue that the "judgment" of 13:2 means divine or eternal judgment is to exalt the state to deity.

Third, Romans 13:1–7 calls Christians to submit to the governing authorities. Submission means voluntary respect or adherence. The state possesses a legitimate place in the divine arrangement for human society. One error of much history has been a self-serving interpretation of Paul by the Caesars, the führers, or the kings whose theologians developed a hierarchalism that proposed an equal responsibility of citizens to Christ and Caesar. A second error is the model of a hierarchy of derived powers in which the state is placed *above* the Church, or the Church *above* the state. Instead, a horizontal model must be employed that emphasizes the legitimate functions of each "order" (family, church, state), with proper regard for the rights accorded to each, where the focus is on authority, not force.[21] The rightful powers of the state (e.g., taxation) cannot be qualified by Church or family. However, when the state taxes the Church in those areas where the Church is carrying on its spiritual and educational functions,[22] then the state has exceeded its authority and has resorted to force. The state (or any other sphere) may abuse its authority in a specific area. When the Church, as in the Middle Ages, interdicted kings and nations to prevent kings from lawful exercise of political right, then the Church has employed power in contradiction of its authority. When the Jesuit interfered in the affairs of state, employing subterfuge to influence kings, this was the Church functioning *over* the state, or trespassing on the state's ground. Each sphere, however, must assist the other toward a correct use of its power.

Fourth, Paul's view of the state in Romans 13 is affirmative in that he emphasizes the positive function of the state—the state's responsibility to execute justice. He does not deal with the opposite problem of an unjust or demonized state. Revelation 13 makes a powerful biblical presentation of the enemy state, which has set itself in stark antithesis to the Church of Jesus Christ.[23] Paul, in 1 Corinthians 6:1–10, does echo in milder form the Johannine condemnation of the state.[24] Cullmann claims that the Corinthians passage demonstrates a limited recognition of the rights of the state. "Everywhere the Christian can dispense with the State without threatening its existence, he should do so."[25] The Christian must avoid those perfectionist illusions that suggest the state either is unnecessary (anarchism) or that it is the bearer of the divine image. The latter illusion leads to an uncritical acceptance of derived government. One historical model for this is acceptance of the Third Reich by many German Christians.

Fifth, Paul's appeal to conscience (13:5) is a two-edged sword. When the Christian acts in accordance with a (biblically informed) conscience, the possibility of obedience to the just state and disobedience to the unjust state are clear alternatives. Paul explicitly teaches the responsibility of submission and implicitly the limits of obedience. Our relationship to the state is sharply qualified by our relation to Christ. Within that Christocentric commitment are the appeal to love and to conscience, and the awareness that the world is passing away. Paul neither gives the state a blank check for requiring Christian obedience, nor does he release Christians from responsible adherence to the state. The qualifications possess immense import. In other terms, Paul can never be misconstrued to give *equal* place in the Christian's life-style for Christ and Caesar.

One concluding point should be raised. Whenever the Christian lives within the Pauline framework of affirmation and qualification, the state cannot *rightfully* or *justly* punish that person. If and when the state responds with punishment (and it is assumed that it will), the state is acting in the arrogance of power. It is acting against justice. To the degree it does so it is becoming immoral, moving away from what it was meant to be—an instrument for restraining evil and wrong—and moving toward the crescendo of evil imaged by the beast of Revelation 13. Thus the state acts outside its legitimate, (i.e., divinely intended) sphere of authorization. This is where the tension results in suffering for the conscientious believer. *In this context,* suffering should be viewed not as the consequence of wrongdoing by the believer, but by the state.

The implications of this line of argument are serious, suggesting much diversity in the response of citizens to the state. Is the state sturdy enough to sustain that diversity? History teaches us to be less than hopeful on that point. In an attempt to achieve some progress toward balance between the divinely authorized orders—family, church, state—some clear distinctions are sought. This essay quests for understanding through the concept of "sphere law" or sphere authority.[26]

Distinguishing The Orders Of Creation

In traditional Lutheran ethics much attention has been placed on the orders of creation: Church, state, and family. The problem that Luther faced was how to relate the orders to each other without disturbing the divine order. If the state is ordered (or arranged under) God, so also is the Church and the family. What differentiates the "orders"? The same person who is a constituent part of a family is also by choice a member of the Church, and first by birthright, second, by choice, a citizen of the state. Every person has the freedom not to be identified with a particular family, church, or state, although one may not forfeit descent from a particular lineage or change the fact of being born in a certain political state. The orders are intertwined, then, in the persons who belong to family, church, or state.

In the inaugural creative order, the family was largely self-contained, encompassing family, church (the father was priest), and state. Medieval Christianity gave us the ascendant church, able to rule both family and state by its sanctions (such as excommunication and interdiction). The modern state has outstripped and surpassed the influence of family and church and through its frequently self-given authority, acts for the church and the family in many functions that exceed its legitimate sphere of authority. Rousas Rushdoony has stated,

> The modern state . . . claims to be the total order and the

> sovereign order. . . . The modern state therefore as sovereign claims prior jurisdiction in every sphere of life. It claims the right to legislate (for the sovereign is the source of law) for every realm, and its right of legislation, however, generously or cautiously applied, is a total right. The state as sovereign is simply the state as god.[27]

The state as "god"! This is nothing less than an institutional assertion of divine prerogative, a forthright violation of the first table of the Decalogue. On the level of the earthly city (the *polis*), it is the assumption of the powers of the heavenly kingdom. It is original sin in maximum social expression.

A recurrent interpretation of Romans 13:1–7 engenders both an idolatry of the state and provides a virtual blank check to the state to work its will. As John Bennett makes clear, this passage and 1 Peter 2 "have been the proof texts of all rulers who sought obedience from their subjects. They have been greatly misused in the interests of tyranny in every century of Christian history."[28]

Of course there is another danger, equally perilous, and in an era of social and political terrorism it displays the potential for undermining civilization. That is the problem of anarchy that offers no solutions and destroys any form of order, even the circumscribed order of totalitarianism. That political state that fosters anarchy in the interest of defeating an opponent-state will inevitably face the cancerous intrusion of terrorism in its own life system. The language of Romans 13 and 1 Peter 2 respectively is consistent in its rejection of both the deified state with its consequent idolatry, *and* the elimination of political order with its corollary of terror.

Now to return to our problem. How do we develop a theory of sphere-authority that, recognizing the lordship of Christ over all spheres, asserts the legitimacy of family, Church, and state under God? It may be appropriate to say the "orders" are separate ("neither derived from or valued lower than any other''), and equal (each sphere or order having its God-given laws and moral criteria). Here it is not permissible to confuse the realms as though the state might be the community of love, and the Church the wielder of the sword.[29]

However, the orders must not be interpreted as essentially antithetical, if they are seen as divinely mandated. While any talk of essence is nonsense to the pragmatist, the theological notion is important, stressing the possibility of good in the orders, even while acknowledging the potential for evil. That the state, for example, is (in essence) demonic is asserted by some, but is here affirmed as from God. That the state *becomes* evil, or is demonized, in the exercise of its authority is evident. Thus we interpret the ''beast'' of Revelation 13.

The Orders: A Revolving Relationship

What model best interprets the separate but equal character and expression of the orders? How may we demonstrate their necessary interaction without permitting the intrusion of one into the legitimate sphere of the other? May we stress the value that biblical faith places on state or Church without permitting our evaluation to lead toward deification?

The traditional relation in Church and state has been the hierarchical or vertical model. In medieval Christianity may be seen the ascendancy of Church over state. The model employed was that of Pope Gregory VII (d. 1085), who believed that the Roman church, symbolized by the sun, was regnant over the state, which was symbolized by the moon. The model is one of derivation from greater to lesser. Having no light of its own, the state shone in glory because of the greater glory of the Church.

Earlier, the Roman state under Nero, Decius, or Diocletian had viewed the Church as a festering atheism within the Roman Empire. Denoted atheists because of their rejection of Roman gods, the early Christians were charged with proposing an alternative power that threatened to destroy the established political order. There was no conception of Church *and* state, but only that of the deified state with its sacred Caesar and its panoply of gods that were central to the Roman apparatus of state. The Church had no recognized existence.

When Licinius and Constantine in A.D. 313 began the process of legitimizing the Church, the Church was drawn into the state's structure. In a real sense, that process that culminated in the exaltation of Christianity by Theodosius (A.D. 381) meant that a new faith replaced the old in the state structure. It is a classic illustration of the identification of Caesar and Christ. Caesar becomes the dominant figure. In the Constantinian order the Church exists but its position does not approximate equality in its own sphere (sphere authority). It is tolerated, approved, or legitimized by a superior. Where the Church is tolerated, that is, receives legitimacy from the state, its status is not separate and equal under God, but is inferior, depending on the generosity of the state. P. T. Forsyth has demonstrated this with great clarity. What Dooyweerd designates as "sphere sovereignty," Forsyth describes as the "corporate personality" of Church or state:

> If the Church has not a corporate personality then its rights within the State are conferred instead of recognized. They are *conferred* by the State . . . instead of being *recognized* by the State as a gift and moral prerogative from God. And that vassalage is a situation which no Church could accept and remain a Church of grace, of the Holy Ghost and the new creation.[30]

Rejecting the individualist view of the Church as a gathered convenanting group that meets for mutual edification, Forsyth insists that this offers nothing for the state to recognize. Where individual religious autonomy prevails, the Church lacks the intrinsic corporate personality —the koinonia—that the state may and must recognize. The Act of Toleration (1689) in England was an expression of concession by the state. It was toleration by a higher authority and placed the dissenting churches, as it had earlier placed the established church, in debt to the state for their existence. In fact, the state in its sphere authority may and must recognize the Church. The state does not grant a right to exist out of its restricted authority.

Forsyth's theology of Church and state was developed in a nation where the Church was still the established church and in a restricted yet significant sense monolithic. How may the concept of sphere authority be developed in the United States with its increasing religious pluralism?

Much has been said about the interaction of the orders of creation and their relative privileges and responsibilities. However, as the Lutheran experiment demonstrates in sixteenth-century Europe, providing checks and balances among the several orders is complex. The general conclusion of scholars is that Luther's concept of "two kingdoms" or "two realms" failed to provide the "relative autonomy of the 'orders' (free from Church-rule yet bound to God-rule)" that Luther's teaching suggested.[31] William Lazareth indicates that Luther's ethics teaches a sharp distinction between the two kingdoms while stressing their right "to coexist in harmonious interaction and coordination as complementary expressions of the triune God's creative and redemptive activity among men."[32] The kingdom (or reign) of God is ruled by gospel and the kingdom of the world by law. Since every Christian lives in both kingdoms simultaneously,[33] the lines between Church and state must not be drawn too sharply.[34] The Christian requires both the gospel and the Law to fulfill the divine intent for humankind.

we must be cautious lest we presume a simple solution to a problem that has lasted for centuries. In America, for example, Jefferson's "wall of separation" dictum has been developed to the greater benefit of the state than the Church. In an increasingly secular world, that will be the normal course of events. Is this a desirable pattern? Not if the divine order calls for sphere authority, as I believe Paul should be interpreted. What, then, shall be the contours and guidelines for the concept of sphere authority?

There is first a rejection of hierarchical models and language, except when referring to the sovereignty of God from whom all creation flows. The orders or spheres shape and are shaped by the same human beings (i.e., those in the Church are at the same time citizens and members of families. In that complex relation the rightful exercise of each sphere of authority must be permitted and worked out. Several propositions seem appropriate to state both the interaction of the spheres and the limitations on each sphere, as seen in the following.

PROPOSITIONS

1. Family, Church, and state[35] are ordered under God. An absolute hierarchical relationship prevails—God *over* all human authority.

2. Neither family, Church, nor state are subordinate to one another. A relative horizontal standing describes the orders of human authority. If all of these are under God they are directly answerable to him. God's authority is preeminent. All authorities are responsible to him for every action. Sphere authorities are responsible to one another eminently. Where the authority of the family is at issue, the Church and state must yield.

3. Neither family, Church, nor state may fill or assume the order assigned by God to the other. Although none is subordinate to the other, each is responsive/responsible to

the authority of the other. When one order fails in the exercise of its proper authority, it is not the place of the other to assume the sphere authority that has been abrogated. For example, if the state is demonized (i.e., becomes the "beast" in the abuse of its authority) it is not the place of the Church to seize the state's authority. Rather it shall challenge, censure, and correct the state.

4. There will be inevitable overlapping and interaction because the "orders" impact upon the same persons in society. Education, for example, is one of the most common points of interpenetration and tension. The family possesses the essential responsibility for the education of the child.[36] That was the original pattern in the Judaeo-Christian tradition. (See Deuteronomy 6:4–25 for a biblical precedent.) The Church is concerned for education so that the child (and the adult) may receive, understand, and communicate the values of faith and spirituality. The state insists on education to prepare the person for the duties of citizenship. Nevertheless, the family holds a place of authority above that of the Church or the state; that is, it is the authority sphere responsible for education. The family may decide for public, ecclesiastical, or private (family directed) education, but the primary right is the family's.

In developing the lines of sphere authority, these positions are indicated.

1. The family is *under* God.
2. The Church is *under* God.
3. The state is *under* God.
4. God is over all; each authority sphere is under him and on a level with one another.

Further, three assertions are made:

1. The family is not the state or the Church;
2. The Church is not the family or the state;
3. The state is not the family or the Church.

As spelled out in the concept of a revolving relationship, family, Church, and state stand in a dynamic relation to one another, *around* and *under* the center, Jesus Christ the Lord. This is illustrated by the following schema. Indicated in the interlocking spheres that receive consistency and meaning through the divine center are the separate spheres and their inevitable interaction in human experience. The overlapping section of the spheres demonstrates, for example, that education, while primary to the family, is the concern of all. Indicated also in the circles are the areas of competency and responsibility that pertain to the authority sphere. The list is not intended to be exhaustive.

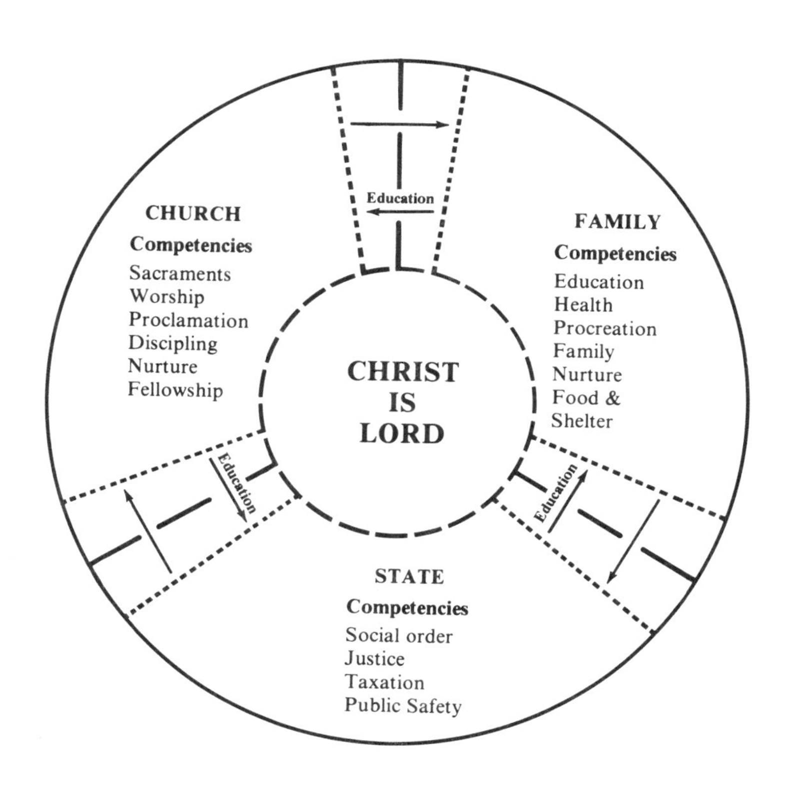

Key

1. The inner circle portrays the center (i.e., the central authority, Christ).
2. The bold, broken lines between the spheres point out the *separate* sphere authority.
3. The dash lines parallel to the bold lines illustrate the overlapping and interaction of the spheres in real life or in human experience. The arrows illustrate the interaction of the spheres in many areas of life; in the illustration above, in education. Cooperation is necessary, but when one sphere seeks to assume the competencies of the others it violates the principle of competency and the divine order or arrangement. I have throughout followed Luther in speaking of three "orders" or spheres.[37] Others suggest four or five orders of creation.

In summary, neither family, Church, nor state may fill the order assigned by God to the other. Neither stands in a relation of superiority (or inferiority) to the other. Each is chosen or mandated to achieve a limited and specific purpose or task that only it can fulfill. Although clearly assigned by God, none participates in his divinity. When any sphere strives to assume an authority withheld from it, it participates in the arrogance and self-assertiveness that violates the divine intent. On the institutional level it participates in pride. After the analogy of the Fall, it wrenches itself out of its subordinated relation to God. Hence it distorts its relation to the other authority spheres.

The Wesleyan Synthesis

In light of the arguments developed through this essay, Wesley's own contribution, in the historical context of eighteenth-century England, is now addressed. The ecclesiastical context was the Church of England, reformed by the events of the sixteenth century, but still profoundly Catholic, and still the established church. The state was a regulatory presence in the affairs of the

Church. The political context was an era of change, surely signaled by the Act of Toleration, the departure of James II, and the ascendancy of William and Mary. In the shifting politics of the century of Wesley, order was severely tested by revolution. The crescendo was reached in the American Revolution and the severance of the Colonies from the British Empire.

The economic context of the Wesleyan movement was characterized by population growth, a huge expansion in the nation's budget and indebtedness, the dawning of the Industrial Revolution, enlargement of land holdings to the detriment of small farmers or persons living on farmland, and the shift of populations to an urban setting. Socially there emerged an increased sense of displacement, weakening of social morale, and deterioration of morality, as Hogarth made so poignantly clear in his artistic works such as "Gin Lane."

In this setting Wesley labored to address the issues that impinge upon Church and state interaction.[38]

ORDER

The Church of England in Wesley's era was the inheritor of a powerful Reformation concern for order. *The Book of Homilies* (1547) included a sermon on obedience, stressing the divinely designed order in heaven and on earth. The homilist applauded the divine arrangement and asserted "that in all things is to be lauded and praised the goodly order of God, without the which no house, no city, no commonwealth, can continue and endure, or last."[39]

That English concern for orderly procedure was evident in the Glorious Revolution (a "bloodless revolution"), and its Act of Toleration. This heritage certainly filtered down into Wesley's consciousness[40] and shaped his response to the American Revolution, which was at the same time an English revolution. Possessing strong feelings of attachment to individual liberties and rights, Wesley came to believe that the Revolution was disastrous to social order and to the hardwon benefits of the Glorious Revolution (1688–89). His exegesis of Romans 13:1–7 also stresses this theme of ordered human society and state authority derived from God's authority. The tract *The Origin of Power*[41] espouses the same concept. One of Wesley's great fears was the potential anarchy that results from unchastened rebellion. Government cannot exist on a sound footing where its citizens venture upon the treacherous swamp of political and social radicalism.

In political terms Wesley's Tory background is a significant force in his concern for order. Toryism, however, was only one part of his political mosaic.

LIBERTY

If Wesley was commited to order, it was to a particular *kind of order wherein civil and religious liberties are guaranteed.* Wesley was sure that the state is called to ensure religious as well as civil liberty. In his essays on liberty[42] he complained that the English state prior to the Revolution of 1688 had violated religious conscience repeatedly, in harsh and inhumane ways. He excoriated the kings, including James I and Mary, for their violation of religious rights when nonconformists chose not to conform conscience to expediency. Thousands of persons, including Wesley's paternal grandfather, were "at one stroke, turned out of house and home, and reduced to little less than beggary, . . . because they could not assent and consent to that manner of worship which their worthy governors prescribed!"[43]

This theme is sounded repetitively in Wesley's tracts, letters, and sermons. He admired the monarchy as he found it in his century and believed it to be the most adequate governmental bastion for the preservation of human rights. Wesley does not become so starry-eyed about government that he can ever forget that it exists under God to assure the rights of life, liberty, and property, to offer defense against nations whose ideologies propose antitheses to these rights, and to provide for public safety and the public interest.[44]

Wesley's preoccupation with liberty reflects the Whig perception of politics with its orientation to individual values. In his ecclesiology, it represents the Puritan and pietist zeal for religious diversity.

THE ESTABLISHED CHURCH

Wesley was a member of the Church of England all his life. Even though he took several steps that constituted a *de facto* separation, he fought any attempts to effect a legal departure. His mature ecclesiology gave significant recognition to the religious liberties of dissenting Protestants,[45] but he was always loyal to his church.

Acknowledging the principle of religious diversity,[46] Wesley sustained his love and hope for his church and nation. He took the position that an established church was a "political institution," not a biblically founded "ecclesia":

> Q.7. What instance or ground is there in the New Testament for a national church?
>
> A. We know none at all. We apprehend it to be mere political institution.[47]

When questioned about the validity of spiritual governance by unbelievers, the Methodists recognized that "he may be a governor in outward things by a power derived from the King."[48]

Finally, the Methodists took the stance of obedience to church governors "whenever we can, consistently with our duty to God. Whenever we cannot, we will quietly obey God rather than men."[49]

No doubt remains that Wesley sharply qualified obedience to the established church, insisting that in all indifferent things (adiaphora) obedience is owed to church governors, but that matters of conscience require a prior responsibility—to God alone.[50]

In describing the historical relationships of Church and state, Wesley seems more negative than positive despite his lifelong involvement in the Church. He regarded the shift from persecution to conformity under Constantine a reflection of an era of spiritual decline and decay. In several important sermons Wesley spelled out his belief that the gold of the Church under persecution was to become dross when the Church lived under the benign state. His sermon "The Mystery of Iniquity" states,

> Persecution never did, nor could, give any lasting wound to genuine Christianity. But the greatest it ever received, the grand blow which was struck at the very root of that humble, gentle, patient love, . . . was struck in the fourth century by Constantine the Great when he called himself a Christian, and poured in a flood of riches, honours, and power, upon the Christians; more especially upon the Clergy. . . . Then, not the golden but the iron age of the Church commenced.

From this critique Wesley moved to the conclusion that iniquity so abounded in the world that "the whole world never did, nor can to this day, show a Christian country or city."[51]

THE "ESTABLISHED" STATE

Wesley's concept of the state represents an essential conservatism. Although he never buys into the Reformed conviction that citizens have a right to revolution against bad government (i.e., government that does not exist for the governed), his position may be designated a "modified conservatism." In several instances, particularly the Glorious Revolution, and even initially the American Revolution, Wesley expresses support for the establishment of a new government that guarantees the religious and civil rights of the people.

The characterization of "established" state has reference to Wesley's claim that a particular government, such as the monarchy in England, is rooted in an original consent drawn by persons who lived long before. He distinguished persons under the state of nature and under the rule of the established state. In the original state of nature a contrast is drawn that thereafter binds the citizen and his or her descendants, by passive consent, to laws passed even when they were passed before his or her birth.[52]

When does the state of nature exist? Persons possessed the right to self-government, Wesley asserted,

> before any civil societies were formed. But when was that time, when no civil societies were formed? I doubt hardly since the flood; and, wherever such societies exist, no man is independent. Whoever is born in any civilized country, is, so long as he continues therein, whether he chooses it or no, subject to the laws . . . of that country.[53]

That position leads to the "established" state, a conservation of state authority. This is the heart of Wesley's political conservatism, which is reinforced by his parallel theological arguments against revolutions that are destructive rather than supportive of human values.[54] Wesley's position amplifies the implicit argument against anarchy in Romans 13. The citizen does not support revolution except on the most serious level of conscientious concern. Certainly revolutions like the French or Russian would be seen as the sacrifice of the basic human values that states are to ensure.

Wesley takes the position that the state exists under the divine mandate. Using a theological claim, Wesley insists that authority originates in God. On the distributive level, government may be monarchical, republican, or oligarchical, but its origin is in none of these.[55]

Is it possible for the state to become demonic by an abuse of its authority and competency? Wesley's definition of power seems to challenge the characterization of the state as demonic in essence. The authority of government rests upon God's ultimate authority. Wesley argued that, while in created humanity the political image means the possibility of government, in the rebellion of the first man this government capacity has weakened and became limited. God only entrusts fallen humankind with "an exceeding small share of knowledge" lest men and women should again seek to be as God. Humans cannot govern adequately, being limited by loss of righteousness and poverty and understanding. Still, it is God's will that government exist among persons; thus, God ordains the magistracy. Evidently not all people are fit to be governors, but God does will that some serve.

John Deschner has argued in his *Wesley's Christology* that Wesley may in Ephesians 6:12 have seen political power originating in demonic power. He cites Wesley, who quoted Ephesians 6:12, "They are . . . *governors of the world!* So that there may be more ground than we are apt to imagine for that strange expression of Satan in Matthew 4:8, 9." Deschner insists that this claim is not found systematically in Wesley's description of the state. Wesley's *Notes Upon the New Testament* leaves this in question, with Ephesians 6:12 and John 17:15 giving intimations of such a view. Notice Wesley's comment on Revelation 11:15, "The kingdom of the world is become the kingdom of our Lord."

> This province has been in the enemy's hands; it now returns to the rightful master. . . . In reality, all things (and so the kingdom of the world) are God's in all ages: yet Satan and the present world, . . . are risen against the Lord . . . God now puts an end to this monstrous rebellion.

However, no suggestions like these are found in

Matthew 4:8,9; Luke 4:6; Romans 13:1–6; Titus 3:1; and 1 Peter 2:13,14.[56] Thus, while the *Notes* are uncertain on this theme, the approach systematically developed in the political tracts does not permit the view that the state is demonic in character. Wesley's interpretation of Revelation 11:15 does permit the conclusion that the state may become demonic in its exercise of authority.

What is the Christian's responsibility to the state? Surely persons who share immediately with all creation in its benefits and its travail should participate where possible in the life of the state. From what source shall the redemptive dimension be drawn except from those who are participants in the redemptive community.

In an important letter to a Methodist preacher, Walter Churchy, Wesley wrote in 1777:

> Loyalty is with me an essential branch of religion and which I am sorry any Methodist should forget. There is the closest connexion, therefore, between my religious and my political conduct.[57]

It is perfectly clear, however, that when the laws of the state, specifically the Erastian state in Wesley's England with its close Church-state ties, conflicted with the divine calling to proclaim Christ, Wesley was prepared to resist and violate those laws. Far from passively accepting punishment, Wesley wrote classic appeals to bishops, officers of state, members of Parliament, government officials, and even the king, to seek relief and religious freedom.

REFORM

In final summation of Wesley's assessment of the question of Church and state in his nation, we are drawn to his goal—reformation. The dictum that impelled Wesley and his Methodists—and which should drive Christians today—is the classic statement of the Methodist *raison d'etre:*

What may we reasonably believe to be God's design in raising up the Preachers called Methodist?
Not to form any new sect; but to reform the nation, particularly the church, and to spread scriptural holiness over the land.[58]

Notes

1. By "Wesleyan heritage" I am referring to the Methodist family of churches and institutions primarily in England and North America.
2. See *Certain Sermons and Homilies* (London: The Prayer Book and Homily Society, 1852), pp. 95–107, 517–64, for two sermons on obedience written during the English Reformation. See my discussion of these in "Church and State in the Thought and Life of John Wesley," unpublished Ph.D. dissertation, University of Iowa, 1971.
3. Martin Hengel, in *Was Jesus a Revolutionist*? (Philadelphia: Fortress Press, 1971), pp. 33–34, addresses the issue of revolution and the perversion, by twentieth-century connoisseurs of revolution, of the New Testament presentation of Jesus. Jesus cannot be stretched or distorted into a first-century exponent of the violent overthrow of the state. Hengel writes,

   > Nor can one adduce the incident of the tribute money at Mark 12:12–17 to prove that Jesus held a conservative attitude of faithfulness to the state. When Jesus demands and receives the tribute coin, the Roman silver denarius, from his opponents—which no real Zealot would touch because it bore the image of Caesar—he only desires to call the attention of his opponents to the consequence which comes from their use of Caesar's money. If they use that "which belongs to Caesar, bearing his picture and inscription," then Caesar can also demand it back in the form of tribute. This whole complex of "what belongs to Caesar" is, however, unessential in view of the nearness of God. Instead of "and to God, what belongs to God," it should really be translated adversatively, "*but* to God what belongs to God." That is all that really matters, the other is an adiaphoran, the end of which is at hand and which is senseless to take too seriously, either positively or negatively. World power is neither justified nor condemned; it is deprived of

its power, however, through the word "but," which points to God's side.

Hengel quotes E. Bloch approvingly: "The world of Caesar is, moreover, as unimportant and, in spite of its glamor, as unessential as a one-night stopover in an inn, when early the next morning preparations are made for traveling on again." It should be made clear that this is no denigration of the necessity of the state on the temporal level. That would be utopian or perfectionist on the one side or anarchist on the other. Rather this represents a comparison of the temporal state with the eschatological, eternal reign of Christ. See note 7.

Dale Brown in "When Taxes are Due" *Christian Century* (August 26—September 2, 1981), pp. 837–838, comments that most interpreters see Jesus avoiding a simple yes or no to avoid being identified either with the Herodians or the Pharisees, tax supporters or despisers, respectively. "Certainly, when Caesar fulfills his proper functions," writes Brown, "there may be times when taxes are due." Brown knows that the decision at this point is a crisis of conscience. In such a situation one may ask, Who is better able—the Church or the state—to judge the rightness of the claim? No simple answer is worthy, for clearly there are times when the Church may be as self-serving as the state. Nevertheless, the difference between the Church and the state is important. Recognizing that churchmen/women carry out state functions, their ability to apply Christian principles to state questions is severely limited, *especially* in a pluralistic society. Setting the issue of the rightness of state action along the plumbline of Christian principle is surely possible and *relatively* simple for the Church in its exercise of the ethics of conscience. For a churchperson who is secretary of state, for example, the use of that plumbline is circumscribed, if not out of the question. The conclusion, then, is that the Church's judgment on matters of conscience, while subject to human finitude, is not restricted by the institutional encumbrances that are germane to state authority, especially in the state's necessary exercise of force.

4. The temple tax amounting to a half-shekel was collected annually from Jewish males aged twenty or more. Its history goes back as far as the postexilic period, to the time of Nehemiah.
5. We recall exceptions to this in the abolitionism of Orange Scott, Jesse T. Peck, Gilbert Haven, and others who appealed to natural law, and who, in their arguments, called upon Wesley's own concessions to civil disobedience. See Wesley's "Thoughts upon Slavery" *Works,* XI, pp. 70–74.
6. The expectation of Decius, Caesar (A.D. 249–251), that the people accord him the honor due to a god; the unquestioning subservience expected by certain French and English monarchs; and, the so-called imperial presidencies in American history are examples.
7. Oscar Cullman's classic interpretation of the Romans 13 passage emphasizes the decisive eschatological element present, described by Paul in 13:11–14. Paul's call for adherence to the state is made in the awareness of its temporality and the permanence of Christ's kingdom of love. (See *The State in the New Testament* [New York: Scribner's, 1956], pp. 50–70 [Chap. 3—"Paul and the State"].)
8. See Cullman, pp. 60–64, for discussion of 1 Corinthians 6:1–10.
9. Yoder mades this point in *The Christian Witness to the State* (Newton, Kans.: Faith and Life Press, 1964), p. 13.
   Hengel, in *Victory over Violence: Jesus and the Revolutionist* (Philadelphia: Fortress Press, 1973), p. 62, writes, "Despite all the persecution and defamation to which he was exposed (2 Corinthians 11:23ff.), Paul was able to affirm the *Pax Romana* because it provided a kind of 'liberated zone' for the missionary proclamation of the gospel."
10. Wesley, *Notes* (London: The Epworth Press, 1966, rpt), (Romans 13:1), p. 571.
11. This position is in agreement with John Yoder's position in his *The Politics of Jesus; vicit agnus noster* (Grand Rapids: Wm. B. Eerdmans Publishing Co., 1972), pp. 179ff., which argues that Romans 12 and 13 form one literary unit.
12. Why does Paul speak only concerning the second table of the Ten Commandments, or the relation to the neighbor?

One suggestion is that Paul is here addressing horizontal, human, and personal, rather than divine relationships. This removes Paul's whole discussion of the state from the soteriological dimension. Disobedience to the state entails only temporal, not eternal, punishment. It is conceivable that disobedience to the state by a citizen *could be* a subliminal rejection of divine authority. Disobedience, therefore, should be based on conscience. Outside of matters of conscience, the expectations of the state may be considered adiaphora that the citizens should respect and obey. Of course, conscience has a final appeal (i.e., Holy Writ).

13. Quoted by M. S. Augsburger, "Facing the Problem," in *Perfect Love and War,* Paul Hostetter, ed. (Nappanee, Ind.: Evangel Press, 1974), p. 14.
14. Cullman, pp. 58–60, emphasizes that our subjection grows out of our hope. Paul writes, "Rejoice in your hope, be patient in tribulation, be constant in prayer" (Rom. 12:12).
15. Yoder, *The Politics of Jesus,* p. 198.
16. For example, see "The Platform of the German Christians" (Deutsche christen) 1932, in Clyde A. Manschreck, ed., *A History of Christianity* (Englewood Cliffs, N.J.: Prentice Hall, Inc., 1964), pp. 529–30; Yoder, *The Politics of Jesus,* p. 200.
17. Wesley, *Notes* (Rom. 13:1), p. 572.
18. His larger view, detailed later in this essay, is less supportive of static government.
19. Yoder, *The Politics of Jesus,* p. 203. The word Paul uses for subjection in 13:1 is *hupotasso. Tasso* means to order or arrange with reference to a specific place, position or relation to another. *Hupotasso* means to subordinate, or to order under another. In Romans 13:1 the state is arranged or ordered *under* God.
20. Quoted by James Leo Garrett in "The Dialectic of Romans 13:1–7 and Revelation 13," *Journal of Church and State* (Autumn 1976), pp. 433–42.
21. It is of utmost importance to keep this discussion in the context of the relationship, on the horizontal level, of the several powers. The state does not possess authority *over* the Church. Neither does the Church possess authority over the

state. Each possesses authority in specific areas and each must proffer the other those rights, carefully avoiding any trespassing. Of course there will be human problems that simultaneously entail the authority of each "order." My argument is that cooperation, not force, must be the pattern of procedure. The state must employ force in carrying out its normal authority. But where the rightful authority of the other sphere is concerned force is inappropriate.

22. When the Church is acting purely as a profit-making organization, it should be taxed. Its business is not purchasing huge commercial interests (e.g., newspapers that tout its views), but the development of matters germane to spirituality, worship, and Christian education.
23. Garrett, pp. 433–442, speaks of "The Dialectic of Romans 13:1–7 and Revelation 13." The argument of Romans 13 is "the truth of what the State is meant to be," while Revelation 13 describes the state demonized as the beast of anti-Christ.
24. Cullman, pp. 72–73, argues correctly that in Revelation 13, the state "demands what is God's, . . . frees itself from the "order," and becomes a satanic power."

> In Romans 13 Paul says of the powers *(exousiai)* that they stand within God's order and that we must therefore obey them. Here [Revelation 13] they have emancipated themselves; or rather they believe they have done so.

25. Cullman, pp. 60–61.
26. In *The Christian Idea of the State* (Nutley, N.J.: The Craig Press, 1968), pp. 27ff., Herman Dooyweerd develops the concept of "sphere sovereignty." Rousas Rushdoony criticizes the phrase (p. ix) because "sovereignty" possesses a theological connotation. He suggests "sphere laws." I prefer "sphere authority" to these, understanding "sphere" to mean either family, Church, or state.
27. *Ibid.,* pp. x-xi. Rushdoony develops the argument further:

> This again is an ancient pagan political concept. The divinity of the social order appears in various forms in pagan states. . . . The political order is the definitive and defining order of man. The modern state . . . is making clear its claim, to sovereignty and total jurisdiction, its claim to total law. The modern state

therefore seeks total control: its goal is to replace the predestination of men, to substitute for God's eternal decree the state's temporal decree.

28. John C. Bennett, *Christians and the State* (New York: Scribner's Sons, 1958), p. 158. Martin Hengel, *Victory over Violence,* pp. 62–63, states,

    Despite all the persecution and defamation to which he was exposed (2 Corinthians 11:23ff.), Paul was able to affirm the *Pax Romana* because it provided a kind of "liberated zone" for the missionary proclamation of the gospel. He shared this relatively positive attitude toward the Roman state with the majority of Diaspora Judaism, of which he was himself a product. It is against this background that we must read Romans 13:1–7; under no circumstances should this passage be misunderstood as an eternally valid prescription for an attitude of reverence toward the state. Probably Paul formulated this excursus with one eye on the special situation of the Christian community of Rome, only a few years after Claudius's banishment of the Christians (Suetonius *Claudius* XXV. 3). This much-misunderstood and much-abused text is corrected by Acts 5:29 as well as by Revelation 13 with its vision of the demonic power of the totalitarian state. One must also not overlook the setting of Romans 13:1–7; it is set within a framework expounding the law of love (12:17–21 and 13:8–10), in which for Paul—as for Jesus—the law is summed up, transforming itself radically into promise, that is, gospel. Christian love, *agape,* defines the limit of the power exercised by the state and society; through love the believer gains the liberty to "use good to defeat evil" (Romans 12:21). As 1 Peter, the Pastorals, and later the apologists show, early Christianity firmly maintained this attitude, informed by *agape,* toward the world in which it found itself, despite the persecutions on the part of the Roman state beginning with Nero and Domitian.

29. Dooyweerd, p. 20.
30. P. T. Forsyth, *Theology in Church and State* (London: Hodder and Stoughton, 1915), p. 160. Forsyth writes,

    The concession theory of corporate life . . . reduces even toleration to a form of Establishment. It *is* concession and not recognition. . . . If the Churches are but religious associations they exist by sufferance, by a right whose source is in the State. And the State which confers that right has the right to withdraw

> it. . . . The State is not the source of all right in other societies (Church, family, etc.) to exist. . . . It can but practically recognize and respect the real right, which descends straight out of heaven from God, and which belongs to a personality, collective or simple.

Forsyth (pp. 164–65) concludes that toleration is not the prerogative of the state.

> No church's right is at any time in possession of the State, and how can it be received from it. . . . If the State confer anything on a Church it establishes it in so far. If it confer liberty it establishes that liberty. And that is not religous liberty. Religious liberty . . . belongs to the Church . . . in such a way that if the State does not recognize it . . . the State is in collision with the Kingdom of God. . . . All that the State can do is to recognize the innate right of the Churches and get out of the way, owning that this is a region where it can confer nothing, . . . and which it cannot enter, except at the invitation of the Church itself to settle questions (like those of property).

It should be pointed out that Wesley interpreted religious and civil liberty in a theological framework. They originate in God. In Forsyth's terms, then, the state or the Church can only *recognize* them.

31. Cf. William Lazareth's "Orders" and "Two Realms" in *Dictionary of Christian Ethics,* John Macquarrie, ed. (Philadelphia: The Westminster Press, 1967), pp. 238–39, 348–49.
32. *Ibid.,* p. 349.
33. Luther's theology of the simultaneous character of sinfulness and righteousness (*simul justus et peccator*) in the life of the Christian suggests a precise involvement in both kingdoms.
34. I do not intend to equate *Church* with *kingdom of God* or *state* with *kingdom of the world. Church* and *state* are more narrow terms. Nevertheless, the two-realms doctrine seems to permit a practical identification of kingdoms with orders, leading to subservience of Church to state in the sinful world of human relations.
35. This sequence is used in the essay as the probable sequence in which the "orders" were given by divine arrangement.

36. In 1925, the Supreme Court (*Pierce v. Society of Sisters*, 268 U.S. 510), overturned a State of Oregon law requiring every child between eight and sixteen to attend a public school during the period that the public school operated. The Society of Sisters opposed this law and the court sustained them. Mr. Justice McReynolds delivered the unanimous opinion of the Court:

    > We think it entirely plain that the Act of 1922 unreasonably interferes with the liberty of parents and guardians to direct the upbringing and education of children under their control. . . . The child is not the mere creature of the state; those who nurture him and direct his destiny have the right . . . to recognize and prepare him for additional obligations.

    Dietrich Bonhoeffer writes, "Marriage and labour, . . . possess their own origin in God, an origin which is not established by government, but which requires to be acknowledged by government. Through marriage bodily life is propogated and men are brought into being for the glorification and service of Jesus Christ. . . . The parents are for the child the deputies of God, both as its begetters and as its educators" (*Ethics* [New York: The Macmillan Company, 1955], pp. 344–45).
37. See Lazareth, p. 238.
38. Here I will offer a summary of the key concepts involved in Wesley's idea of the ways in which the Church (or, Christians) and the state are related or are separated—concepts that illumine the basic problems inherent in Church-state relationships. For the larger discussion see my "Church and State in the Thought and Life of John Wesley."
39. *Certain Sermons*, pp. 95–96. G. R. Elton, *England under the Tudors* (London: Methuen and Co., 1955), pp. 395–96, shows that the sixteenth century was passionately committed to order and that every means of propaganda was used to preach order, obedience, and passivity. The Church was called to bear much of this apologetic burden.
40. See my "John Wesley and Political Reality" *Methodist History* (October 1973), pp. 37–42.
41. See *Works* XI, pp. 46–53. Written c. 1772.
42. "Thoughts Upon Liberty" (1772), and "Some Observations on Liberty" (1776), in *Works*, XI, pp. 34–45, 90–118.

43. *Ibid.,* p. 39.
44. See Wesley's "Thoughts on the Present Scarcity of Provisions," *Ibid.,* pp. 53–58, which stresses in part the need for the state to consider public welfare. See my "Christian Love: The Key to Wesley's Ethics," *Methodist History* (October 1975), pp. 44–55; "Evangelism and Social Ethics in Wesley's Theology," *A.M.E. Zion Quarterly Review* (July 1981), pp. 2–18.
45. See my "War, the State, and the Christian Citizen in Wesley's Thought" *Religion in Life* (Summer 1976), pp. 204–219.
46. He rigorously restricted the extension of religious liberty to Roman Catholics on the ground that Catholics would exercise their liberties to subvert the English government and to tout their views. He assumed that the dictum "No faith can be kept with heretics" would regulate the actions of Catholic citizens. See my "Church and State in the Thought of John Wesley," pp. 267ff.
47. See Albert C. Outler, ed., *John Wesley* (New York: Oxford University Press, 1964), p. 173. This was the position of The Fourth Annual Conference in its June 17, 1747, session.
48. *Ibid.,* pp.153-54.The Second Annual Conference, August 1, 1745.
49. *Ibid.,* pp. 172-73.
50. "In every individual point of an indifferent [i.e., *adiaphoron*] nature, we do and will by the grace of God, obey the Governors of the Church. But the testifying the gospel of the grace of God is not a point of an indifferent nature." *Works,* VIII, pp. 34–35.
51. *Ibid.,* VI, pp. 261-63.
52. *Works,* XI, p. 83.
53. *Ibid.,* p. 96.
54. See my "Human Liberty as Divine Right" in the *Journal of Church and State,* 25:1 (Winter 1983), pp. 57–85 for analysis of Wesley's support of that monarchy that ensures human rights.
55. See "The Origin of Power," *Works* XI, pp. 46–53. Most analyses of Wesley's politics do not distinguish between the theological argument with its concern for origin, and the

political argument that emphasizes diversity of government forms. John Locke's position stated the origins of civil contract. Wesley pushes origins of power back to God, but does admit that present human authority may be traced back to human consent *under God*.

56. See *Notes,* p. 991 (Rev. 11:15); p. 26 (Matt. 4:8–9); p. 215 (Luke 4:6); pp. 571–73 (Rom. 13:1–7); p. 802 (Titus 3:1); and pp. 878–79 (1 Pet. 2:13–14).
57. Wesley, *Letters,* VI, p. 267.
58. *Works,* VIII, p. 299 (1745).

R. Duane Thompson (Ph.D., Boston University), professor of philosophy, Marion College

A Christian View of the Arts

THIS ESSAY PRESENTS an analysis of the role of the arts for the Christian. Art is a humanly created object whose primary purpose is to produce an intrinsically satisfying experience. The arts traditionally have included literature (poetry and prose), music, architecture, sculpture, painting, theater, and dance. Conflict between arts and crafts goes back many centuries and has tended in Western culture to produce a "high art" perspective that gives little place to the crafts. With current emphasis upon the pragmatic, the crafts are being lifted into prominence alongside *les beaux arts* (the traditional fine arts).

Aesthetic is a broader term than art in the sense that it specifies the nature of the experience in relation to the arts as well as to a host of other things such as "elegant" mathematical proofs and natural objects (sunsets, mountain ranges, dizzying heights, beautiful human forms, and so on). The intrinsically satisfying experience to which these objects give rise may be called aesthetic, and the philosophical analyses of such experiences and their objects are called "aesthetics."

These definitions are adequate for the discussion before us, and it is not necessary to examine all of the possible and actual definitions that could be cited. Numerous general textbooks will provide all of this type of example that anyone may wish.[1]

There are several religious and moral objections to art. Such objections have ranged all the way from the very foolish to the most highly sophisticated. Since St. Augustine is one of the key opponents of the arts, and since he has the advantage of having lived at the right point in history, and because his theological impact has been so profound, it will be helpful to examine briefly some of his attitudes toward the arts.[2]

For Augustine, art is a detractor from the true condition of human beings. Audiences (readers) often shed tears over poetry but not over their lost condition. Evil is made sweet by artistic productions. Art is a purveyor of pleasing untruth. Moreover, art gives a false justification for human sinfulness. Augustine accepts Plato's objection that art transfers human sins to the gods, but he takes the further step of insisting that art gives divine sanction to human sin. Furthermore, he condemns pagan literature for its faulty education of youth.

Augustine condemns drama and acting outright. He totally rejects the Aristotelian conception of catharsis by which the individual is relieved and purged of some of the immature or corrupting emotions and attitudes. In tragedy there is a masochistic self-enjoyment in the suffering of others. Consequently, the essence of the impact of theater is that it engenders sympathy with evil. If one really wishes to understand suffering and real tragedy, one must contemplate and understand the divine drama of human sin and God's endeavor to save humankind. Though Augustine permits a limited acceptance of church and moral art, he is continually insistent that art, as everything else, must not usurp the place of God in the affections; art must be "used" and only God can be "enjoyed." Even something as pure as church music can entice the worshiper to "stick" at some level below that of sincerely resting in God alone. In fact, the primary nature of sin is idolatry, or committing oneself to anything, however good, other than the true worship of God.

Augustine's influence can be seen in the negative view of art that has characterized much of Christian history. A contemporary Catholic, Jacques Maritain, enumerates three major religious and moral concerns with art: (1) in art there is the connivance (dalliance) with evil; (2) the world of the aesthete is sensuous; (3) the production of evil requires experience of it. Maritain analyzes these objections and expresses his own highly positive attitude toward art as he has in several earlier works.[3]

DeWitt H. Parker, in a more general manner, provides a three-fold enumeration of people who question the value of art for life: "To the puritan, art is immoral; to the philistine, it is useless; to the proletarian, it is a cruel waste."[4]

Let us now examine a bit more carefully four of the most important moral and religious arguments against art: (1) the puritan objection, (2) the proletarian objection, (3) the objection that art is too material and sensuous in nature to be worthy of attention from genuinely spiritual persons, and (4) the position that art contains only fantasy and illusion while Christians are concerned with reality.

Puritanism is a term used to identify various views and usually it appears with invidious meanings. It is here used simply to mean that since many works of art contain in them moral evil, sympathy for evil is therein awakened.

Plato serves as one of the earliest and most powerful exponents of moral regulations of art. The heart of the intelligent puritan objection to art in general is expressed in Plato's arguments: the artist must make contact, and the person who portrays evil must not only understand evil but must feel for it and feel it. This is to say that in order to grasp aesthetically one must understand appreciatively. But appreciative understanding in art may cultivate appreciation beyond art (i.e., the person may become infected with evil, and his or her being may develop a habitual involvement in the evil). His or her aesthetic appreciation may result in moral (immoral) action.

Plato has very little sympathy for passive acceptance of objectionable materials—for the dramatizing of one's emotions unless they are perfectly commendable ones. The question thus arises, Is evil portrayed artistically still evil? Plato's response is *yes*. In art evil is in a form that I may feel I need not fear; it is allegedly innocuous; thus I can meditate and feed upon it. Such an attitude is dangerous.

The second major objection to art is that art is a luxury, a cruel waste. Many people have the bitter experience of want, and one has only to compare the laborer's wages with wealth that is tied up in objects of art, art museums, and symphony halls, architectural edifices, and theaters. Parker calls this the proletarian objection, and it is one that could be related to a Marxist or proletarian revolutionary approach. However, there is an element in this objection that is deeply Christian, for the early Christians did not believe in "conspicuous consumption" but rather shared their holdings in a primitive communalism. More recently Christians are raising the issue as to how followers of Christ can be honest with themselves, compassionate toward those in dire poverty, and innocent before God if they do not share their good fortune with the less fortunate.[5]

A third major objection to art is that the world of the aesthete is sensuous, and to be absorbed in the material is to lose the reality and value of the spiritual. Art is situated in lower-level reality, and reflection, meditation, prayer, and similar activities are much higher in the divine hierarchy. Berndtson very aptly says, "Art . . . has an emphasis on sensation that has no parallel elsewhere."[6] At this point he contrasts art with mathematics, the sciences, practical action, ethics, and religion, for "art steeps itself in the senses as though sensation were life, or the gateway to life: one of which it is."[7] While Berndtson does not hereby condemn art, his statement represents a strong religious argument against art.

The final objection is that art deals with a world of fantasy and illusion while Christ presents reality in its fullest sense. Malcolm Muggeridge, who has served in numerous capacities in television, speaks in a highly negative vein:

> The prevailing impression I have come to have of the contemporary scene is of an ever-widening chasm between the fantasy in terms of which the media induce us to live, and the reality of our existence as made in the image of God, as sojourners in time whose true habitat is eternity. The fantasy is all-encompassing; awareness of reality requires the seeing eye which comes to those born again in Christ. It is like coming to after an anaesthetic; the mists lift, consciousness returns, everything in the world is more beautiful than ever it was, because related to a reality beyond the world—every thought clearer, love deeper, joy more abounding, hope more certain. Who could hesitate confronted with this choice between an old fantasy and a newly discovered reality?[8]

While Muggeridge's negative attitude toward television is not shared by all Christians, there is a growing expression of outrage and disgust. Most of the concern does not arise from the illusory character of television but rather from its depiction of evil that drags down the viewer. Muggeridge's point is that something extremely unreal infects all participants in the media.

Muggeridge presented an incisive critique of television in the opening of his lectures on the relationship of Christ and the media. He noted,

> It is a truism to say that the media in general, and TV in particular, and BBC television especially, are incomparably the greatest single influence in our society today, exerted at all social, economic and cultural levels. This influence, I should add, is, in my opinion, largely exerted irresponsibly, arbitrarily, and without reference to any moral or intellectual, still less spiritual, guidelines whatsoever. Furthermore, if it is the case, as I believe, that what we still call Western civilization is fast disintegrating, then the media are playing a major role in the process by carrying out, albeit for the most part unconsciously, a mighty brainwashing operation, whereby all traditional standards and values are being denigrated to the point of disappearing, leaving a moral vacuum in which the very concepts of Good and Evil have ceased to have any validity. Like a building site, which has been cleared, but with nothing erected on it; just a great, empty space, where rubbish is thrown, where children play and quarrel and fight, and lay-abouts sleep, and the rain collects in puddles. Future historians will surely see us as having created in the media a Frankenstein monster which no one knows how to control or direct, and marvel that we should have so meekly subjected ourselves to its destructive and often malign influence.[9]

What an indictment of the media! Muggeridge's style is so great and his understanding of the media so significant that his attack brings home directly the serious moral weakness in the mass media.

While television and the film are doubtlessly capable of artistic attainment, the sheer amount of production and the variety of audiences toward which the productions are directed, along with the primary focus of much of the purpose of these activities (namely to achieve a profit), means that there are monumental hurdles to be overcome before artistic excellence can be achieved. Often the purpose is primarily entertainment and audiences feel excited or at least very interested but certainly not very fulfilled. The effect of an evening's "brute curiosity of an *animal's* stare,"[10] to use the language of Jacques Maritain, is often just the occupation of time, the feeling of limited insight, and the communication of little that is helpful. Of course, many sermons have come up with the same result, and often without entertainment! With all of the faults of religion and religionists, we dare not be too hasty in throwing stones and pronouncing anathemas.

One who spends his or her time analyzing such experiences will note the general vacuum in contemporary culture that television and the film may reveal as well as help produce. Gilkey says,

> Perhaps the best examples of this vacuum, this apex of technological efficiency combined with this abyss of pointlessness are, first, the elegant, accurate, true-toned and true-colored TV, able to produce in our living rooms the most totally perfect and satisfactory picture—and yet what it produces in our living room hour by hour is, on the whole, true-toned multicolored garbage.[11]

Occasionally both of these forms produce something genuinely profound and unusually perceptive. The general Christian may not have time or energy to wade through all of the debris and garbage in order to get to the insight, but some Christians will discover insights in knowing both TV and the film and will enable us to communicate with our age by such knowledge. It is doubtful if we shall be able to understand our times if we fail to have a true grasp of the significance of the mass media any more than we can understand our times if we fail to understand science, its modes of thought, and its technological achievements. Even Muggeridge tips us to this insight with his statement

"The media in general, and TV in particular . . . are incomparably the greatest single influence in our society today, exerted at all social, economic and cultural levels."[12]

Rather than responding to all of the foregoing objections in a direct fashion, the next phase of this study will be to describe the nature of art. Once this has been shown there will be certain indirect and direct implications for the preceding objections. Let us now turn to some of the elements contributed to life by art.

The imaginative element is critical to all artistic creation and recreation. The artist must imaginatively assemble ordinarily unrelated experiences or objects. He or she must help us to look the second time, to explore beneath the surface of ordinary experience. Imagination penetrates ordinariness and things taken for granted. It carries us to the boundaries of what we normally see and inspires us to move beyond the circumscribed commonplace.[13]

Consequently, art is much like religion, especially in its prophetic function. Without the prophetic element, religion declines into mere politics, social action, superficial propriety, and massive ordinariness. However, religion's imaginative spark produces one of the greatest challenges to humankind, both individually and in community.

Creativity must be included along with imagination. Imagination is more than fantasizing; it entails production, events, and emerging new realities.

Something is communicated in aesthetic experience. Does the artist always produce his intention in the work and does the appreciator always understand what that intention is? The answers to both questions are *no*. It is even possible that the artist is not fully aware of what he or she intended, at least not if what appears in one medium is made to appear in another form. For example, what a poet says in his or her poetry cannot be said without residue in prose or music. The dance is not identical with the critic's analysis, the choreographer's comments, or illustrations placed in a booklet. Nevertheless, what the artist says in his or her particular manner communicates a unique form of meaning and experience to the appreciator.[14]

When communication occurs, insight is achieved. A sense of freshness appears in a "flash of insight." This certainly does not need to be something new to history or a particular culture; it is sufficient that something different or novel appears to the individual. Often two rather different items are juxtaposed and the mind grasps relationships of a new order. It is important not to suggest trappings of "mystical transport," although the high excitement that arises when one sees something new may well be misinterpreted.

Heightened sensitivity to and sympathy for other persons is often engendered by art. At times religionists may tend to be harsh and intolerant. When religion sees itself in the role of final arbiter of the truth, it can become very difficult to live with. A more caring attitude may be developed in some persons through the influence of art.

Religion is often peculiarly capable of forgetting that there are different perspectives or dimensions experienced and held by other persons. Religion may tend toward an oversimplification of the human situation. It may even commit the fallacy of a single cause—religious in general, divine, a particular denomination, or some such understanding of the foundations of human existence. In response to these possible shortcomings of religion, art may very well provide fresh perspectives and make us all aware of the genuine complexity of the human situation.

Art uncovers actions and events totally foreign to the world of the aesthetic perceiver. For example, the worlds of espionage and foreign intrigue, politics, banking, entrepreneurial activities, celebrity experiences, high society, and multitudes of other activities and experiences are outside the immediate experience of most readers of this essay. Nevertheless, through artistic elaboration in novels, short stories, plays, and films these perspectives come to life in an extremetly challenging and rewarding fashion. One is thus introduced to a multiplicity of experiences in a period of time that is very brief, in a manner that is open to careful examination before one would need to confront such issues in a real-life situation.

In a work of art in which integrity, truth, and greatness are present, more than superficial actions and events are revealed. The underlying emotions, motivations, and reflections of the key people are laid bare. Thus principles underlying real lives are explored. Such fundamental insight may be part of Aristotle's classical comment that "poetry is something more philosophic and of graver import than history."[15] Facts, dates, and events of history need to be grounded in interpretation in order to become enriching to one's personal understanding. Aesthetic experience provides just such an elaboration.

It is important to examine the role of beauty in the arts. Some works of art seem to be dominated by ugliness. It would take us too far afield to explore beauty in its depths, so I shall be content to suggest two things: it is not necessary to insist in an absolute manner that all art objects are beautiful, and one can define beauty in such a manner as to show it generally present in any truly great work of art.

Religion also desperately needs beauty. If God is regarded as the locus of beauty, the source of beautiful things, and the source of human creativity, then religion cannot afford to reject beauty, for in so far as religion does so it will be rejecting that characteristic and function of God. While very ordinary and occasionally ugly surroundings and activities are related to the worship of some, in the main, great and beautiful architectural designs have been produced as the expression of love for God and as the most appropriate milieu in which to worship. Beauty, of course, is not predicable only of vastness or of ornate style. Some small and rather plain chapels are profoundly beautiful. Moreover, often religious rituals are beautiful in a very simple or quite unelaborated mode. Finally, morality and beauty must go together to keep beauty from the mud and morality from forming uncouth and barren alliances.

The real purpose of art is not to promote a specific theological perspective or moral point of view. It is to achieve an intrinsically satisfying experience. This is much of art's claim to a significant degree of independence. When a product of artistic creation is examined and the desire for revision predominates, the nature of the experience is not primarily aesthetic but rather practical (i.e. action rather than aesthetic contemplation). It is not necessary for action to be absent, but practical urgencies must be held in check so that the experience can continue in the aesthetic mode until a sense of fulfillment is achieved.

At this point it may be helpful to distinguish entertainment from aesthetic experience, for the nature of the aesthetic and art will be better understood as the contrast is made. Rader, an outstanding contemporary philosopher with a major portion of his work in aesthetics, gets to the heart of the matter:

> The basic criterion of art is the richness and the fineness of the value-appreciation that it yields. I am using the word "appreciation" not in the superficial sense of amusement or entertainment, but in the deeper sense, so eloquently stated by Dewey, of a memorable and satisfying experience.[16]

Steinkraus contrasts art with the circus:

> A whole circus is a composite of what art is not and thereby gives us a clue to what good art is. Regardless of the fun it provides for all ages, a circus is contrived, aims for effects, seeks to thrill, to satisfy the curious, to sell tickets, to be gaudy, to sparkle, glisten, amuse, titillate the senses and excite.[17]

Berndtson puts it this way: "Entertainment is pleasure of a relatively passive kind and of little scope."[18] In entertainment "there is emphasis on novelty and exaggeration and on forms that do not tax attention."[19]

It may not be surprising to find religion attacking amusement or entertainment because of its superficiality, for religion's seriousness may find the element of play highly unacceptable. And since all play is questionable to a certain turn of mind, religious or otherwise, the total rejection of play does not feel the need to distinguish between a superficial play with its accompanying entertainment and a more profound play in which deep experiences find incalculable personal fulfillment.

Now the element of intrinsicality, an intrinsically satisfying experience, gives rise to the problem of art for art's sake. Art *in itself* may have elements of the illusory, play, and the superficial, but when taken in the context of human nature's needs, activities, and values, it performs a critical function. From the biblical perspective, a totally serious turn of mind, or a work ethic without relief is unacceptable. God requires the Sabbath. The human person cannot bear up under total seriousness, although some can bear it more than others. Nevertheless, God has provided a Sabbath for all, and all need such rest. For some, aesthetic experience brings a comparable rest.[20]

One weeping on a screen is open to very easy caricature. This occurs most likely when one is only glancing at a particular segment apart from its context, or when one is asking questions such as, Is this really true? In other words there is a failure to understand the point of it all. However, similar examples could be pointed out in sermons in which strong emotions are expressed. If the listener is not fully aware of what is happening, distaste can easily arise. But the main point of all this is that genuine artistic productions reveal dimensions of life, not just dimensions of a play world, although life is revealed in a playful manner.

The world of art can be taken seriously (though not literally) with great justification, but the world of art *in itself* is not a real world. But what world *in itself* is a real world? Is morality? or religion? or banking? or politics? *The only real world is the whole world;* and any way of looking at the real world that professes absolute and isolated reality is extraordinarily naive (at best) or wicked (at its worst). The real world requires the confluence of all vectors of experience, activity, and life. No facet is absolute and final in an isolated and self-contained mode of being. Every facet must dialogue with every other facet in the real world.

Consequently, the contrast is between a reduced understanding of life and world and an interrelated understanding of the same. To reject or even reduce art (e.g., to only Christian artists and their forms of expression) is to reject something of what it means to be human, or it is to reduce human nature. One might say that to the extent that we reject art, just to that extent we reduce our own humanity and that of others. As a result, we damage the *imago dei* and the God in whose image we exist. Thus, a truncated view of art leads to a truncated view of humanity, which leads to a truncated view of religion, which leads to a truncated view of the world, and which finally leads to a truncated view of God.

If one were very narrow minded, one might be tempted to insist that people who do not enjoy the richness of art also negate their own spiritual insights. It would probably be more charitable and more realistic to say that the vastness of the world and God can only be partially grasped by even the most brilliant and well-informed human mind. Thus, when we discover the fallibility of human beings in art, we should be led to acknowledge general human fallibility. In such a spirit of humility we shall all be more inclined to repent of our narrow grasp of the extraordinary vision that God has and forgive one another for all of our inabilities to enjoy to the full what God has provided for us. But there are some who still do enjoy art, and it would be unfortunate for those who enjoy something else to deny these persons the extraordinary delight and fulfillment that they discover in the arts.

A slightly different way of approaching this issue may be discovered by analyzing the biblical principle of seeing the Old Testament in the greater and higher light of the New Testament. Theologians do not say that the New Testament can give no insights beyond that of the Old Testament, for we are enriched by the addition of the New Testament. One way of saying it is that the Old Testament is the New Testament concealed and the New Testament is the Old Testament revealed. Thus the higher is pointed toward and anticipated by the lower; and the lower is fulfilled by the higher. If the higher did not appear the lower would be impoverished; and the lower is enriched by the higher.

This approach is very theologically acceptable to biblical scholars. It is expressed well by Charles Taylor in a totally different context as he examines the Hegelian methodology of hierarchy:

> This notion of a hierarchy of forms is the negation of reductivist explanation, which looks forward to being able to account for the higher functions of organisms with the same explanatory concepts and principles by which one accounts for the lower ones, and indeed, would extend this homogeneity of explanation downwards to the inanimate.
>
> If anything a theory like Hegel's is the exact inverse of a reductivist theory. For to the extent that one level illuminates others, it is the higher which casts light on the lower, being a fuller realization of what the lower is aiming at. But we cannot take this too far, for the lower cannot be accounted for by the principles of the higher which are richer and more complex. They are related to the higher by impoverishment. Hence they are different kinds of entity, and not just applications of the same basic principles, as on the reductive hypothesis.[21]

Using the preceding methodological precedure, it is now possible to say that with respect to life and interpretations of it, the richer is the whole, which throws light upon the interpretation of any facet of the whole. A human being has numerous facets, all of which contribute to human existence. The elimination of any one of these aspects is an impoverishment or reduction of human nature.

Now any religionist who condemns art, politics, sexuality, economics, or any other phase of what it means to be human is interpreting the whole in an impoverished manner. The truly rich interpretation requires one to explore both religion and art from the perspective of the whole.

Excluding everything except God from one's consciousness is a mode of concentration that has certain kinds of benefits; the distractions of human existence are so plentiful that some focusing is essential to any single consciousness, and without focusing, total disjointedness would occur. But to insist upon a certain limited conception of God and to fail to have a great enough God to have created the world of which we are a part is to engage in concentration upon a fantasy, not reality.

All forms of cultural development have given great assistance to religion. Philosophy was especially employed in the Middle Ages as the *ancilla theologiae* (the handmaid of theology). Science has enabled determined students of the Bible to dig more deeply into the text through all kinds of strategies of analysis with the technological instrumentation that can penetrate the unsolved mysteries of language and culture.

No study is more akin to religion than is art itself. The Bible is literature. The language of the Bible is more like poetry than like science. This is not to claim that the Bible is not accurate in science or history.

Religious experience, with its ritual, its frequently vague pronouncements (note the often misinterpreted statements of the oracles), its richness due to multiple interpretations,[22] its ecstasies, is much more like aesthetic experience in these respects than political, scientific, or business experiences.

There are significant moral concerns that can be brought to bear upon art and aesthetic experience. When a work cannot support the aesthetic attitude (i.e. when there is a breakdown of "physical distance" [Bullough]), then the work itself is reduced as a work of art. As a result it becomes pornography, propaganda, or possibly a type of moralism.

Aesthetic excesses may create immaturity, the end of growth, or emotional and mental fatigue. Excesses may result in superficiality, becoming a pale copy rather than a genuine aesthetic expression, prettiness rather than beauty. Fantasy certainly is possible at this point. The aesthetic may result in the substitution of vicarious aesthetic experience for reality and tangible action. Thus it may serve as an escape mechanism. However, none of these moral concerns is an argument against art or the aesthetic.

From my perspective it is no argument against the aesthetic to say that it is tied to the sensuous or the material. Since God created the whole world, matter is no less holy than spirit. There may be interesting problems arising as a result of the nature of the universe (whatever it means to say that something is material); but none of these interesting concerns should eliminate art from the life of a spiritual person. Berndtson may help us to see why religion condemns art, for if art is as steeped in the senses as he suggests, then when "religion frequently regards the world of sense as an appearance, or a transition to a better estate in the next life, or a place of trial,"[23] the opposition is diametric and irreconcilable. But here is where religion must see the importance of the delicate balance that holds all of the facets of existence in a fragile tension.

Nor is the argument against luxury and art in the presence of human need fully adequate. Jesus accepted expressions of love, even though poverty in his time would have dictated selling the ointment and giving the proceeds to the poor.

The key moral and religious issue is what to do with works of art that are aesthetically good and morally bad. Wolterstorff's perceptive analysis of much of the Christian interpretation of evil in art is helpful:

> Sadly but pervasively characteristic of Christians in the last century or two is extraordinary tunnel vision. Always it is the profane and the sexual that draw the fire of their attack—and then not only the illicitly and perversely sexual, but sometimes just any explicit acknowledgement of the sexual. Going unnoticed is the cultivation of greed, of militarism and nationalism, of sexism, of racism, of capitalism. Always it's the "dirty movies" and the "filthy books" that catch the bullets. Those "clean" hymns of praise to nation, to unbridled competition, to humanity walk the field unharmed. What a distorted understanding of the moral life such an outlook reflects! Not, of course, that the libertarian individualists in our society are any better. First racism, then militarism, then sexism, catch all their attention; a novel cultivating racism draws from the liberal a scorn no less withering than that drawn from the Christian by a "dirty" film. But the cultivation of unbridled lust finds him indifferent if not approving.[24]

I fully concur with Wolterstorff's breadth of concerns and with his analysis of the situation. His approach is really Christian, as well as undeniably aesthetic. He understands the need for a Christian approach to the arts, but he is more than a casual observer or an outsider to aesthetic appreciation. He is profoundly and genuinely interested in the arts.

The question must be asked, Are we as Christians interested in cultivating an aesthetic consciousness or are we not? And can we pay the price for such a consciousness without destroying or polluting our own moral sensibilities? Or do we really only want to promote, or propagandize for a point of view? Granted that the point of view that we wish to promote is Christian and granted that we wish to promote it from a wide number of angles, is it necessary to insist that every artistic product promote the Christian message if it is to have any adequacy? How would we respond to a charge of ulterior motives?

There is no desire to encourage the excesses of art for art's sake in some manner that accepts anything, however degraded or immoral, in order to lift up art. The *quest* for *insight* is *not absolute,* and some levels of pollution may be just too great, even though the insight gained by wading through it would be enormous. Some condemn religion, morality, political realities, and anything else that would insist upon a large view of the persons with all facets of human experience having their day in court. This study is aware of the dangers and suggests that the risks are worth taking. We are not interested in knowledge for its own sake or expression for its own sake in any absolute sense; but even as we are interested in people for their own sakes, apart from any dictatorial insistence upon a theological perspective, we may have some sense of interest in knowledge, art, and intrinsically valuable experience genuinely and as Christians. A program of evangelism may fall short because of our efforts to overwhelm people rather than to suffer with them in their free and sincere efforts to achieve their own well being. The value of evangelism falls short when we are only wanting to count scalps or pelts.

If religion loses its sense of tension with the other facets of life, if religion comes down too hard with its superiority over other elements of life, and/or if religion fails to recognize that life requires a *delicate balancing* of all its facets, then it needs the severe critique of all other facets of the world that God has created. Art may be just the most potent and incisive critique of such religiosity both historically and at present.

In sum, art is a most important dimension in human experience and existence. In this sense it is not optional but integral. It provides so many supportive elements for religion; nevertheless, it must be given a genuine freedom or independence in order to function in the real world. Art does have features that, excessively developed, may be subject to criticism, but there is nothing that is not open to excesses and weaknesses, certainly not religion or morality. And the intrinsic value of the aesthetic experience enables laborers in the real world to find exhilaration, joy, and rest. It does not produce salvation but its fruits are not necessarily alien to it.

Notes

1. Cf. the following texts for a variety of examples of treatment of the basic themes: Arthur Berndtson, *Art, Expression, and Beauty* (New York: Holt, Rinehart and Winston, Inc., 1969); James L. Jarrett, *The Quest for Beauty* (New York: Prentice-Hall, Inc., 1957); DeWitt H. Parker, *The Principles of Aesthetics,* 2nd ed. (New York: Appleton-Century-Crofts, Inc., 1946); Melvin Rader and Bertram Jessup, *Art and Human Values* (Englewood Cliffs, N.J.: Prentice-Hall, Inc., 1976); and Warren E. Steinkraus, *Philosophy of Art* (Beverly Hills: Benziger Bruce & Glencoe, Inc., 1974).
2. St. Augustine, *The Confessions.*
3. Jacques Maritain, *The Responsibility of the Artist* (New York: Charles Scribner's Sons, 1960), passim.
4. Parker, *Principles,* p. 271.
5. Cf. Ronald J. Sider, *Rich Christians in an Age of Hunger: A Biblical Study* (Downers Grove, Ill: Inter-Varsity Press, 1977) and Robert E. Webber, *The Moral Majority: Right or Wrong?* (Westchester, Ill.: Cornerstone Books, 1981).
6. Berndtson, *Art,* p. 13.
7. *Ibid.,* pp. 13-14.
8. Malcolm Muggeridge, *Christ and the Media* (Grand Rapids:

William B. Eerdmans Publishing Company, 1977), p. 30.
9. *Ibid.,* p. 23.
10. Jacques Maritain, *Creative Intuition in Art and Poetry,* the A.W. Mellon Lectures in the Fine Arts Bollingen Series, 35:1 (New York: Pantheon, 1953), p. 190.
11. Langdon Gilkey, "Can Art Fill the Vacuum?" *Criterion* 20, no. 3 (Autumn 1981), p. 8.
12. Muggeridge, *Christ,* p. 30.
13. Cf. Peter Berger, *Invitation to Sociology: A Humanistic Perspective* (Garden City, N.Y.: Doubleday and Co., Inc., 1963), pp. 20–24, 29–35.
14. Cf. Susanne K. Langer, *Philosophy in a New Key: A Study in the Symbolism of Reason, Rite, and Art* (New York: The New American Library of World Literature, Inc., 1948 [1942]).
15. Aristotle, *Poetics,* 1451b.
16. Melvin M. Rader, *A Modern Book of Esthetics,* 4th ed. (New York: Holt, Rinehart and Winston, 1973), p. 18.
17. Steinkraus, *Philosophy,* p. 93.
18. Berndtson, *Art,* p. 253.
19. *Ibid.,* p. 254.
20. Cf. Charles L. Allen, *The Ten Commandments: An Interpretation* (Westwood, N.J.: Fleming H. Revell Company, 1965 [1953]), pp. 24–28.
21. Charles Taylor, *Hegel* (Cambridge: Cambridge University Press, 1975), p. 84 footnote.
22. Cf. John Dominic Crossan, *Cliffs of Fall: Paradox and Polyvalence in the Parables of Jesus* (New York: The Seabury Press, 1980).
23. Berndtson, *Art,* p. 13.
24. Nicholas Wolterstorff, *Art in Action: Toward a Christian Aesthetic* (Grand Rapids: William B. Eerdmans Publishing Company, 1980), p. 173.